The Creative Power of Anthroposophical Christology

Rudolf Steiner working on the figure of Christ,
the Representative of Humanity, January 1919

The Creative Power of Anthroposophical Christology

Sergei O. Prokofieff

Peter Selg

2012

SteinerBooks

SteinerBooks
610 Main Street, Great Barrington, MA 01230
www.steinerbooks.org

Translated by Willoughby Ann Walshe.

1. *The Christology of the Book* AN OUTLINE OF OCCULT SCIENCE was originally published in German as *Die Christologie des Buches "Die Geheimwissenschaft im Umriss." Vorträge zur anthroposophischen Christologie Band 3* by Verlag des Ita Wegman Instituts, Arlesheim, Switzerland, on the 100th anniversary of the publishing of Rudolf Steiner's *An Outline of Occult Science* 2010.

2. *The First Goetheanum and Its Christological Foundations* was originally published in German as *Das erste Goetheanum und seine christologischen Grundlagen. Vorträge zur anthroposophischen Christologie Band 2* by Verlag des Ita Wegman Instituts, Arlesheim, Switzerland 2009.

3. *Christ's Reappearance in the Etheric in Relation to the Fifth Gospel* was originally published in German as *Die Wiederkunft des Christus im Ätherischen. Zum Fünften Evangelium. Vorträge zur anthroposophischen Christologie Band 1* by Verlag des Ita Wegman Instituts, Arlesheim, Switzerland 2009.

4. *The Christmas Conference and the Founding of the New Mysteries* was originally published in German as *Die Weihnachtstagung und die Begründung der neuen Mysterien. Vorträge zur anthroposophischen Christologie Band 4* by Verlag des Ita Wegman Instituts, Arlesheim, Switzerland 2010.

Library of Congress Cataloging-in-Publication Data is available.

ISBN 978-0-88010-733-4

Contents

Preface to the American Edition

This book comprises four smaller booklets that have been published recently in German by the Ita Wegman Institute Publishing Co., Arlesheim, Switzerland, founded and directed by Dr. Peter Selg.

This publication is based on a number of conferences conducted at the Goetheanum to deepen various aspects of anthroposophical Christology, at which Peter Selg and I presented lectures. Some of those talks are made available in this book to English-speaking readers.

Originally, four conferences were involved. They each took place around the time of Ascension, and focused on the internal development of the central anthroposophical impulse with its Christological foundation. The first conference (held in 2007) explored the subject of Rudolf Steiner's book *The Philosophy of Spiritual Activity*, in which the scientific basis for the anthroposophical research method was introduced. The second conference (2008) was devoted to Rudolf Steiner's book *An Outline of Occult Science*, of which he said it represents a summary of Anthroposophy as a whole. One can say that the results of what had already been examined methodically in the first book flowed fully into this second book; as living fruit, it now presented the practical application of the method to a wider audience.

The third conference (2009) studied primarily how the same impulse now found its artistic implementation and refinement, in the basic idea for the shapes and colors of the First Goetheanum as a complete work of art. In this building, the contents of *An Outline of Occult Science* were visible as though in a mighty imagination. Finally, the fourth session (2010) analyzed the social renewal of this central anthroposophical impulse. This was first done through the founding of the General Anthroposophical Society at the Christmas Conference 1923–1924. At that meeting, Rudolf Steiner created the suprasensory foundation for this human community; and he presented it to the members as the spiritual foundation, and also as the source of all new social forming forces. This foundation opened the doors of the new Christian mysteries to members of this society.

After the completion of these four events, anthroposophical friends in Holland decided to repeat the sequence of these meetings in their country. It would be fitting if this spark of enthusiasm for the topic would be taken up in other countries as well. The contents of this book might provide encouragement and help.

In the written form of the conference lectures a problem was discovered: the contents from both our presentations on the first theme had already appeared in written form. Peter Selg had written "Rudolf Steiner's Inner Condition at the Time of *The Philosophy of Freedom:* A Study" (available in German; not yet available in English) and I had written *Anthroposophy and the Philosophy of Freedom: Anthroposophy and Its Method of Cognition. The Christological and Cosmic-Human Dimension of The Philosophy of Freedom* (London 2009). For this reason we decided to include instead in this publication two other lectures by us, because they fit in well with the characteristic Christological subject as the basic orientation of this series. These are the lectures on the Fifth Gospel that we held during the Easter Conference of 2009 at the Goetheanum.

Thus, the eight lectures contained in this book form a unity covering a far-reaching topic that has its origin in Rudolf Steiner's Christology.

SERGEI O. PROKOFIEFF

Goetheanum, Dornach, Easter 2011

1.
The Christology of the Book *An Outline of Occult Science*

Preface by Sergei O. Prokofieff

PETER SELG

The Earth as Centerpoint of the Cosmos

Developmental History and Christological Context of the Book *An Outline of Occult Science*

Epilogue: Christian Morgenstern

SERGEI O. PROKOFIEFF

An Outline of Occult Science and the Mystery of Golgotha

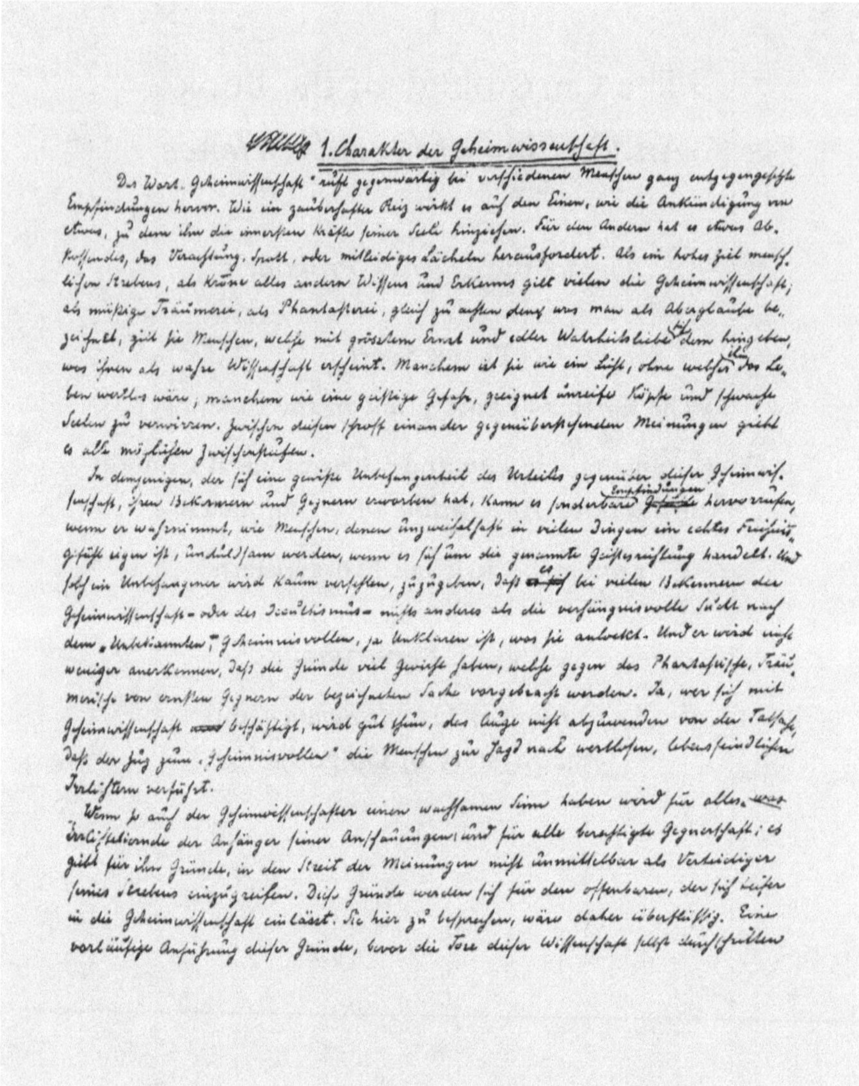

1. Charakter der Geheimwissenschaft.

Das Wort „Geheimwissenschaft" ruft gegenwärtig bei verschiedenen Menschen ganz entgegengesetzte Empfindungen hervor. Wie ein zauberhafter Reiz wirkt es auf den Einen, wie die Ankündigung von etwas, zu dem ihn die innersten Kräfte seiner Seele hinziehen. Für den Andern hat es etwas Abstossendes, das Verachtung, Spott, oder mitleidiges Lächeln herausfordert. Als ein hohes Ziel menschlichen Strebens, als Krone alles andern Wissens und Erkennens gilt vielen die Geheimwissenschaft; als müssige Träumerei, als Phantasterei, gleich zu achten dem, was man als Aberglaube bezeichnet, gilt sie Menschen, welche mit grösstem Ernst und edler Wahrheitsliebe sich dem hingeben, was ihnen als wahre Wissenschaft erscheint. Manchem ist sie wie ein Licht, ohne welches ihm das Leben wertlos wäre; manchem wie eine geistige Gefahr, geeignet unreife Köpfe und schwache Seelen zu verwirren. Zwischen diesen schroff einander gegenüberstehenden Meinungen giebt es alle möglichen Zwischenstufen.

Dem denjenigen, der sich eine gewisse Unbefangenheit des Urteiles gegenüber dieser Geheimwissenschaft, ihren Bekennern und Gegnern erworben hat, kann es sonderbare Empfindungen hervorrufen, wenn er wahrnimmt, wie Menschen, denen unzweifelhaft in vielen Dingen ein echtes Freiheitsgefühl eigen ist, unduldsam werden, wenn es sich um die genannte Geistesrichtung handelt. Und solch ein Unbefangener wird kaum verfehlen, zuzugeben, dass es bei vielen Bekennern der Geheimwissenschaft – oder des Occultismus – nichts anderes als die verhängnisvolle Sucht nach dem „Unbekannten", Geheimnisvollen, ja Unklaren ist, was sie anlockt. Und er wird nicht weniger anerkennen, dass die Gründe viel Gewicht haben, welche gegen das Phantastische, Träumerische von ernsten Gegnern der bezeichneten Sache vorgebracht werden. Ja, wer sich mit Geheimwissenschaft beschäftigt, wird gut thun, das Auge nicht abzuwenden von der Tatsache, dass der Zug zum „Geheimnisvollen" die Menschen zur Jagd nach wertlosen, lebensfeindlichen Irrlichtern verführt.

Wenn so auch der Geheimwissenschafter einen wachsamen Sinn haben wird für alles Irrlichtelierende der Anhänger seiner Anschauungen und für alle berechtigte Gegnerschaft: es giebt für ihn Gründe, in den Streit der Meinungen nicht unmittelbar als Verteidiger seines Strebens einzugreifen. Diese Gründe werden sich für den offenbaren, der sich tiefer in die Geheimwissenschaft einlässt. Sie hier zu besprechen, wäre daher überflüssig. Eine vorläufige Anführung dieser Gründe, bevor die Tore dieser Wissenschaft selbst aufschließen

Rudolf Steiner: Manuscript page from *An Outline of Occult Science*

Preface

In the last preface of the book *An Outline of Occult Science* (written only two and a half months before his death), Rudolf Steiner wrote that this book contains "the outline of Anthroposophy in its entirety." This statement indicates that the book deals with a complete sketch of Anthroposophy. In the years following the first publication, Steiner developed and deepened this outline, in numerous lectures and publications.

As Rudolf Steiner always emphasized, the new Christ-knowledge forms the central theme of Anthroposophy. It also forms the nucleus of *An Outline of Occult Science.* As he was writing this book, he said in a lecture: "For the anthroposophical world viewpoint—in its entire tableau of reincarnation, nature of man, consideration of the cosmos, and so on—the Christ being is in the center. [...] It is a panorama with a main figure, and everything else refers to it."[1]

The year in which Rudolf Steiner wrote this book (1910) is inseparably connected with the most important event of our time. In this year Steiner, as a Christian initiate, could already perceive the approaching etheric appearance of Christ in the suprasensible world. Consequently, Rudolf Steiner's spiritual observation of this mighty occurrence is like a backdrop for his entire work in *An Outline of Occult Science.*

As Rudolf Steiner published this book at the beginning of 1910, he began at the same time to announce the appearance of Christ in the etheric—for the first time in Stockholm on January 12, 1910. Thus, the distribution of the book and the new announcement about Christ went hand in hand throughout Europe.

Sergei O. Prokofieff
Goetheanum, Dornach
January, 2010

The Earth as Centerpoint of the Cosmos

The Developmental History and Christological Context of *An Outline of Occult Science*

Peter Selg

Die

Geheimwissenschaft

im Umriss.

Von

Dr. Rudolf Steiner.

Leipzig
Verlag von Max Altmann
1910

Title page of the first edition 1910

A FEW MONTHS before his death, even on his sickbed in the studio of the Dornach woodworkers' shop, Rudolf Steiner was still working on a new edition of his book *An Outline of Occult Science*. Typeset proofs came frequently from the printing office of the publishing company Der Kommende Tag in Stuttgart. The woman who worked there concluded her letter of November 18, 1924, with good wishes for him: "I will try to carry your lectures in my heart so the burden you bear for all of us will be alleviated a little."[2]

Rudolf Steiner's final preface, dated January 10, 1925, was written on slips of notepaper, which were received by his estate. He read through the earlier prefaces in the previous editions (from 1909, 1913, and 1920) once again; very possibly he reread the whole book. It was part of his life and work history, on which he reflected at the end of his biography. He noted for himself:

> 15 years ago: experienced imaginatively 1902 – 1904
> Since then more concrete and factual = The images
> could have been less thoughtful!
> Leap from thinking to imagining!
>
> Nothing borrowed from ancient texts
> complete in itself
> the formulation of how one speaks who owes
> his education to natural science and philosophy
> and who speaks in their style—also one learns to
> think mathematically through mathematics!
>
> Imagining: a person has a "perception," which
> makes it possible to look at things from an outside
> viewpoint. He transplants himself to a place from
> which the whole universe can observe itself![3]

Finally Rudolf Steiner composed an extensive, new, and last preface for *Occult Science*. In it he commented on many things—including his "frame of mind" at the time he wrote the manuscript in 1909, and the place of the book in his collected works:

> Originally my plan was to include its essential content as a last chapter in the book *Theosophy*, which had appeared long before. This was not possible. At the time *Theosophy* was released, this content did not take shape in me in the way *Theosophy* had. Before my soul was an imagination of an individual person's spiritual being, which I could describe; but the cosmic connections to be presented in *Occult Science* were not there. Some details were available, but not the whole picture.[4]

> According to my frame of mind at the time, the contents of the book had to be given in thoughts for representing spiritual concepts; thoughts that are suitably advanced formations of the ideas used in natural science. A person will note in the "preliminary remarks to the first edition" printed here, how I felt strongly responsible to natural science, in everything I wrote at that time about spiritual knowledge. But in such thoughts alone, a person cannot represent what is revealed to spiritual vision as the suprasensible world. For this revelation cannot be grasped by mere thought content.[5]

According to Rudolf Steiner, the task consists in bringing visions into thought form "without losing their imaginative character within this form." He wrote further in January 1925:

> All that stood before my soul as I worked on *Occult Science*... In 1909 I felt that with these prerequisites I could produce a book that: first, brought the content of my spiritual vision to a certain, sufficient degree poured

> into thought-form; and second, could be understood by every thinking person who places *no obstacles* in the way of understanding.[6]

Publication at this time (1909–10) seemed to him a "risk," because of the paradigms and prejudices of natural science that had been disseminated, and their presence in public opinion. Nevertheless, he decided to go ahead with the publication:

> Before my soul was the fact that now, at this time, when the consciousness of humanity has withdrawn farthest from the spiritual world, information out of this supra-sensible region corresponds to the most pressing necessity.
>
> I assumed there are people who, more or less, feel the remoteness from all spirituality to be such a difficult obstacle in life, that they welcome messages from the spiritual world with inner longing.[7]

Rudolf Steiner's book finally found broad distribution—despite a form of presentation that was not easy to understand, but which he had consciously chosen:

> I have striven quite consciously not to give a "popular" presentation, but one that makes it necessary for readers to enter into the content with the right effort of thought. I have formed my books in such a way that reading them is already the beginning of spiritual training. The calm, sensible thinking that is required by this reading will strengthen the soul forces, and make them capable of drawing near to the spiritual world.[8]

Shortly before his death Rudolf Steiner knew that his anthroposophical spiritual science was still highly controversial to the public. In his last preface to the book he once again defended it, its content, and the form of its appearance: "*My discoveries of the spiritual, of which I am fully conscious, are results of my own vision.*"[9] An Outline of Occult Science was one of the many books that Rudolf Steiner published over four decades, beginning with his *Fundamentals of a Theory of Knowledge of Goethe's World Conception* (1886). Not only that; *Occult Science* also formed the focal point of all this work, and was at the center of all discussions. "*The book contains the outline of Anthroposophy as an entirety. Therefore, it will be met primarily with misunderstandings and objections.*"[10] Rudolf Steiner considered the spiritual-scientific contents of his research to be permanent. In the end, he wrote about *Occult Science*:

> Since the time in which the imaginations described by the book first flowed together into a complete picture in my soul, showing man's visionary research into the historical origin of humanity, into the cosmos, and so forth, I have always come to new individual results with full details. Nevertheless, what I first presented in *Occult Science* as an outline 15 years ago has changed in no way. All that I have been able to say since then appears, when it is introduced at the right place in the book, as a further explanation of the outline at that time.[11]

*

Rudolf Steiner emphasized in the preface to the last edition that in 1909, he felt writing *Occult Science* had become possible because of many years of preparation ("In 1909 I felt that I could achieve a book with these prerequisites"). By the end of 1909, he had written down the manuscript, which then went into print.

It had been a special year in the Anthroposophical Movement, especially with regard to Christology. In January 1909, Rudolf Steiner spoke for the first time in Berlin about the double figure of evil; that is, about the polarity of Lucifer and Ahriman—a central theme of Anthroposophy, having fundamental significance for world development and world understanding. In the great lecture cycles of the following months, he unfolded the "principle of spiritual economy" in the development of Christianity, and talked about the stages of Christ's emergence on earth in the course of evolution. Specifically, his Easter lectures in Cologne and the following fundamental cosmological course in Düsseldorf, "Spiritual Hierarchies and Their Reflection in the Physical World," deal with Christology. In May 1910, Rudolf Steiner spoke with this orientation in Kristiania (Oslo), Norway, about "Theosophy Based on the Apocalypse." In June, he lectured in Budapest about "Theosophy and Occultism of the Rosicrucians"; then just as convincingly in June/July in Kassel about "The Gospel of St. John in Relation to the Three Other Gospels—Especially to the Gospel of St. Luke." In August there was "The East in the Light of the West—The Children of Lucifer and the Brothers of Christ," in Munich. In September, he spoke in Basel about "The Gospel of St. Luke," and in October in Berlin about "Anthroposophy."

Writing *Occult Science* probably followed in the last three months of the year, after the return from Barr on Odilienberg, the mountain vacation site of writer and Theosophist Edouard Schuré, whom Rudolf Steiner visited with Marie von Sivers every year in late fall, in connection with lecture tours. Around October 10, Rudolf Steiner was again in Berlin at Motzstrasse 17; on October 12, he wrote there the preface to the book edition (of his essays, that had been originally published as articles) of *Knowledge of the Higher Worlds and Its Attainment*. Where and how Rudolf Steiner found the time before the end of the year for the handwritten draft of the comprehensive *Occult Science* manuscript is not known; he must have written most of it during the night, because his lecture activity continued unceasingly. During the weeks in question, he spoke both privately and publicly in Berlin (in the Architects' House on Wilhelmstrasse);

conducted the general assembly of the Theosophical Society's German Section; and worked on the production of a Christmas play. Between October and December, he undertook five more lecture tours alone—in Switzerland as well as to Bratislava, Düsseldorf, Hamburg, Munich, and Prague. Yet the manuscript pages kept going to the printer, and always ended with the sentence: "Continuation of Dr. Rudolf Steiner's manuscript *Occult Science*, follows directly after what is found in print."[12] Rudolf Steiner wrote a lot; he wrote neatly, extremely fast, and practically without mistakes. Possibly he wrote from pre-existing manuscripts; that is not certain, however.

The table of contents drafted in October 1909 maintained its validity until the end; it seems that as Rudolf Steiner applied pen to paper, the original detailed concept of the whole still determined the final version. From the beginning, the table of contents comprised seven chapters, with cosmology placed in the middle as "World Evolution and the Human Being," which Rudolf Steiner later called the "essential content" of another book, *Supersensible Facts of Earth Evolution.*[13]

1. The Character of Spiritual Science
2. The Essential Nature of Humanity
3. Sleep and Death
4. World Evolution and the Human Being
5. Knowledge of Higher Worlds (About Initiation)
6. The Future of the World and the Human Being (Present and Future of the World and Humankind's Evolution
7. Spiritual Scientific Details (Facts from the Area of Spiritual Science)

By arranging the chapters in this way, he intended that "clarity about the present-day human being"[14] would be established.

*

At the end of 1909, Rudolf Steiner was probably happy that the time had come to write the book, after he had prepared for many years. Since 1903, he had been writing and giving lectures on the origin and nature of the cosmos. He had also communicated much in private classes in the early years of the Anthroposophical Society, as well as in attachments to letters to Marie von Sivers.[15] He had announced that a treatise on cosmology would be the second part of his book *Theosophy, Introduction to the Sensible World Determination and Human Knowledge*, which appeared in June 1904. "[...] A second volume of my *Theosophy*, which will appear soon, will deal with cosmology," he stated on June 9, 1904, in the Berlin branch.[16] A few weeks later, in July 1904, Rudolf Steiner began with essays, "From the Akasha Chronicle," in the magazine *Lucifer-Gnosis*, which he published. In August 1904, he informed his esoteric student Amalie Wagner he would write his third *Theosophy* book next, "very soon."[17] In December of the same year, he negotiated with his Leipzig publisher, Max Altmann, concerning a draft of a lecture on *Secret Doctrine*.[18] Writing this work, however, was delayed however for five years.

Rudolf Steiner's essays "From the Akasha Chronicle," which appeared in July 1904, did not bear an author's name at first; rather, they were simply designated "reports." They dealt with the history of humanity, and the earth's origin, and were not in chronological order, but were written starting from the present-day earth condition, proceeding back in time. On February 13, 1905, Edouard Schuré wrote to ask Marie von Sivers whether the published remarks about the "Lemurian epoch" were taken from the *Secret Doctrine* by Helena Petrovna Blavatsky, which Schuré assumed ("it seemed to me to be the case"). At the same time, he emphasized his esteem for Rudolf Steiner's form of presentation ("In any case the matter has gained clarity by going through Rudolf Steiner's pen").[19] Marie von Sivers took time in answering. Four months later, on June 16, 1905, Schuré read in her letter the clear words, "For what he reports to us from the Akashic Record, Dr. Steiner does not need to lean on the *Secret Doctrine.* The living source that streams through him is much richer than all that he has presented so far. ... He wants to help us come to clarity about what is handed down through *Secret Doctrine*, and continue it, expand it."[20] Marie von Sivers energetically accredited Rudolf Steiner's original research in the Akashic Record to the spiritual world memory[21] which enabled him to rearrange, correct, and expand the traditional occult knowledge about humanity and Earth evolution, which had been propagated by Blavatsky and others. Marie von Sivers knew Rudolf Steiner had entered the Theosophical Society consciously in 1902, (three years before her correspondence with Schuré). His decision had been based on his understanding of the spiritual origin and background of the movement. He had dealt, to a certain extent, with Theosophical literature, and taken up the spiritual threads; also he approached the comprehensive prerequisites of Theosophical listeners and readers when possible, without completely adapting to the customs of the Theosophical Society. His own spiritual research was original and specific. It was not based on existing literature, even when Steiner took the literature into consideration, and occasionally referred to it in his accounts.

A few months before, he had written in a letter to Marie von Sivers: "You write to me so nicely about the lectures of the past weeks. It is clear that in lectures I must free myself from dividing things into seven parts, as was customary in the beginning, especially in Sinnett's *Esoteric Buddhism.* The three-part division in my *Theosophy* is the only possibility for really penetrating into things. Constant segmenting into seven parts while ignoring the three divisions, only leads to confusion. Oriental mystics as well as Westerners have criticized Sinnett's schematization from the beginning; nothing very practical comes out of this partitioning into seven elements. ... In the beginning a person could not have established a connection with the Theosophical Society, if he had not joined in the perpetual multiplication with seven. But gradually this mechanical multiplication must be replaced with the living spiritual reality."[22]

Writing *An Outline of Occult Science* was in this regard important and necessary, as an independent contribution to the questions about the origin of the world and humanity, which were much discussed, both inside and outside the Theosophical Movement. Rudolf Steiner wanted to publish the book right after it was conceived and mentioned in 1904, and he approved of the publisher's announcement in 1905. In *Reports From the Theosophical Movement* under the heading "New Theosophical Literature," it was announced: "Soon there will appear *Occult Science*, by Dr. Rudolf Steiner. (Leipzig, M. Altmann)."[23] A corresponding follow-up release appeared in March 1906, two months before Rudolf Steiner's extensive cosmogony lecture cycle in Paris, in which Edouard Schuré, as well as the Dutch mathematician and astronomer Elisabeth Vreede, participated.[24]

One year later, in August 1907, *Reports* and *Lucifer-Gnosis* announced the new edition of the out-of-print *Theosophy* along with additional sentences written by Rudolf Steiner: "Also the continuation of this book will soon appear under the title *Occult Science*. Only the author's absolutely necessary non-stop lecture activity has delayed the appearance of this book for so long. Now, it should under all circumstances, be presented to the public."[25] However, despite this promise, Rudolf Steiner's potential readers had to wait even longer. They discovered further announcements in February and December 1908, as well as in March 1909. In the second edition of *Theosophy* of 1908, there was also a notice about the forthcoming book. Rudolf Steiner continued the essays, "From the Akasha Chronicle," until May 1909. Nothing further was published, despite the announcement in the last contribution: "In the following articles a few things will be said about the future of the earth and humanity."[26] Instead, the already published "Akasha" essays appeared—along with the subsequent essay "Stages of Higher Knowledge"—in 1908, as special edition. Then the year 1909 came; and at its end, Steiner finally wrote the long-intended book. In the *Reports* of January 1910, for the first time, *An Outline of Occult Science* was advertised as published ("soft cover DM 5.00; hard cover DM 6.00").

*

Writing the book took seven years; a long time, in a sense. Rudolf Steiner's cognitive work on cosmological questions, however, went back much further. He did not say when he first occupied himself with cosmological and cosmognomical contents. In his autobiography *The Course of My Life*, he described only his intensive dealing with the Copernican world system in early youth. He wrote, among other things, about the priest of his home town Neudörfl, where he lived after his seventh year: "I am also very thankful to this priest for my later spiritual orientation, which is especially due to a strong impression that imparted. He once came into the school, gathered together in the little teacher's room the 'riper' students, among whom he included me; unfolded a drawing he had made, and used it to explain the Copernican world system to us. He spoke very vividly about the earth's movement around the sun; the turning of the earth on its axis; the slanting position of the earth's axis; about summer and winter; as well as zones of the earth. I was quite taken with the matter; I drew its likeness for days, received from the priest special instruction about sun and moon eclipses; and then, as well as later, directed all my curiosity to this object."[27] Also in the following years of his youth, Rudolf Steiner occupied himself a great deal with contemporary theories of physics; and the path of natural scientific materialism for knowing and explaining the world, its being, and its origin.

Then, at the end of his youth, at the beginning of the new epoch of Michael, he met the Rosicrucian figure Felix Koguzki,[28] an apparently insignificant medicinal herb gatherer. In Koguzki, however, lived "tremendous occult depths." Koguzki was "*fully initiated* in the secrets of the effectiveness of *all* plants and their connection with the cosmos and human nature," Rudolf Steiner stressed in 1907 in a letter to Edouard Schuré.[29] As Rudolf Steiner stated in his early theosophical lectures right after the turn of the century, esoteric Rosicrucian schools knew not only the trinitarian nature of the creative godhead, but also the seven planetary stages of earth development from old Saturn to future Vulcan.[30] They possessed cosmological "beginning truths"[31] and on their training path received knowledge about the microcosm and macrocosm. Much of the content in *Occult Science* may already have become clear to Rudolf Steiner through his encounter with Felix Koguzki, as well as through meetings with his second occult "master," to whom Felix led him. This second person carried out with him studies "resulting in ideas through which the seeds of *Occult Science* could be sought. "The man who developed from the boy, later wrote about these things," Rudolf Steiner said in an autobiographical lecture in 1913.[32]

Rudolf Steiner's inner esoteric cognitive path was further enhanced by study of contemporary natural science. He scrutinized Ernst Haeckel's materialistic understanding of evolution, among other things. Rudolf Steiner (who was personally invited to Haeckel's 60th birthday in Jena 1894) proceeded on both paths—the path of scientific study, and the inner path of esoteric cognitive study.

Still in his Vienna period, he came into close connection with the occultist Friedrich Eckstein, who had conducted day-long conversations with Blavatsky in Ostende, and who was considered an expert on the old occult wisdom. Rudolf Steiner had come to know him in the 1880s through Sinnett's book *Esoteric Buddhism*, which was translated into German in 1884. Rudolf Steiner did not like the book,[33] even though it contained "... an overview of world phenomenology and the great course of cosmic events, including questions connected to the nature of humanity, as well as relations in life that go beyond birth and death."[34] As Rudolf Steiner said in a lecture on December 12, 1912, in Berlin, he thought the *form* of Sinnett's presentation was especially problematic, particularly in regard to the author's position on contemporary natural science, and his cognitive method of approach to it. "What was reported in this book could have an amazing effect initially. Whoever turns his gaze to spiritual things could declare himself to a certain extent in agreement with most of what is in Sinnett's *Esoteric Buddhism*. Much does not contradict what a person could think; even when one stands firmly on natural scientific ground. But one thing contradicted the natural scientific training at that time. Although the book could be perceived as an interesting period piece, it is impossible to be fully in agreement with it: the way of presentation; the connections of things; and the way in which these things are elicited from their sources, for example, are not justified by strict natural scientific education and reality. Even if a natural scientifically trained person were in agreement with individual results and information in this book, he would feel repelled by the entire formulation."[35]

The difficulties Rudolf Steiner had from the beginning with Sinnett's presentation, accompanied him on his path in the Theosophical Society. He was prepared in 1902 to become its general secretary: "I did not become a member until I knew the spiritual forces which I have to serve, are present in the Theosophical Society."[36] The theosophical public, Rudolf Steiner wrote later, was the only one at the turn of the century "that completely entered into spiritual knowledge"..."I never could have worked in the way of these theosophists. But I perceived a spiritual center living in them, where a person could make a dignified start, if he was sincerely earnest about spreading spiritual knowledge in its deepest sense."[37] Under certain circumstances, Rudolf Steiner declared, he was prepared to work in and for the Theosophical Society; "his condition was only to be allowed such activity within the society that he considered his task: to let flow into European culture what illuminated the Christ mystery; what Western esotericism has become since the Christ event." (Marie Steiner).[38]

Within these theosophical connections, it is not known when and how Rudolf Steiner came across the book *The Transcendental Universe* by the English Christian and esotericist H. C. Harrison. Harrison's public lectures were published in 1894 in London, and three years later were translated into German; Rudolf Steiner had both editions. Harrison spoke and wrote as a "knower"; represented the esoteric teaching of the cosmic hierarchies[39] and the seven great secrets;[40] and dealt critically with Blavatsky's work, especially with her *Secret Doctrine*, which had appeared in 1888. He spoke about the secret knowledge of old occult schools, and maintained that long-concealed and protected knowledge had been justified in the past. He advocated opening now, to allow this knowledge to flow into civilization, at least partially—a process that had been begun in the second half of the nineteenth century by the Theosophical Movement.[41] Harrison's content, however (about the conditions of imparting spiritual knowledge and the spiritual path, including the "Guardian of the Threshold"), came from his own authentic inner experience.[42] He said about Blavatsky's publications, among other things, "Whether it was good or bad, she published an enormous number of reports regarding subjects that until recently had never been talked about, outside certain societies. These subjects are of such a nature that they recommend themselves to thinking people through their own merit, no matter from what source they come."[43]

"It is really not so important where she received her nearly encyclopedic knowledge. What we have to do is test it carefully, in the light of knowledge we already possess. For it cannot be denied that, although *Isis Unveiled* contains little that was not known before, *Secret Doctrine* brings very worthwhile news about prehistoric civilizations and religions; and it alludes to certain secrets whose existence would not be expected. A few of these have been tested by a process known to occultists, and found to be correct. Although perhaps not one person in a thousand outside the Theosophical Society reads the *Secret Doctrine* and perhaps one out of ten thousand is capable of separating the wheat from the chaff, people will, nevertheless, increasingly notice these as religious thoughts and gradually free themselves from atomistic illusions."[44]

Harrison regarded Blavatsky's presentation of the origin of the cosmos as especially significant: "As cosmogony they are, despite their mistakes, a worthwhile contribution to secret knowledge. Every European occultist must acknowledge that she has opened vast stretches of research areas, unknown until now."[45] By contrast, Harrison disapproved to a large extent of Sinnett's *Esoteric Buddhism*. He spoke about a book "which drew great attention when it appeared, but did not contain anything new."[46]

Blavatsky's *Secret Doctrine* appeared in German in 1899; Rudolf Steiner received it three years later, in summer 1902, as a present from Marie von Sivers. He wrote to her from London about his study of the book. Steiner read particularly the first part ("Cosmic Evolution") apparently with great interest, marking the book with numerous underlines, notes, and sketches. What Blavatsky wrote about cosmic evolution was for Rudolf Steiner exceptionally important—not in the sense of a primary source of knowledge, but as an object of comparison. Just two years after his lectures on the *Secret Doctrine*, he said in a lecture:

> We are not dependent on taking occult messages about the origin of the world from existing literature. People have forces that enable them to observe and research the truths themselves when they have developed these capabilities in the right way. What a person can experience in this way corresponds with what Mrs. Blavatsky brought over from the Far East. It turns out that also in Europe, occultists have preserved a knowledge that was handed down orally from generation to generation of teachers to students, and never entrusted to books. Occultists can therefore test what Blavatsky said in the *Secret Doctrine* against their own knowledge, especially against what they have

> acquired through their own capabilities. Thus, those who are trained in a European way, themselves examine the material in Blavatsky's *Secret Doctrine*. The content has been checked and confirmed, but it is nevertheless difficult for European occultists to make sense of it. One thing should be mentioned: European occult knowledge is determined in a quite definite way by Christian and Cabbalistic influences, and therefore has assumed a one-sided character. When a person accounts for this, and then goes back to the root of this knowledge, full agreement with what Mrs. Blavatsky has opened up for us is possible.[47]

Along with Rudolf Steiner, undoubtedly a man like Harrison was among the occultists investigating Blavatsky. Although Rudolf Steiner did not name Harrison[48] (for unknown reasons), Harrison evidently possessed old esoteric knowledge and independent spiritual experiences and insights.

*

Rudolf Steiner researched mostly in an original occult manner, and he did not lean on theosophical writings. This became apparent in autumn 1900 in Berlin, in the course of his first spiritual-scientific lecture cycle. From the beginning, his research concerned a broad field that stretched from Anthroposophy to cosmology and Christology. Rudolf Steiner always *compared* his own results with the statements of leading theosophists, as well as with "secret scientific" tradition; yet the absolute primacy of his own cognitive work stood the test. On November 9, 1905, Rudolf Steiner said in Berlin, indirectly answering Schuré's question to Marie von Sivers, "You find in my accounts of humanity's history, related in the essays "From the Akasha Chronicle," all that ever was taught and formulated *out of inner, mystical experience* in so-called secret schools about humanity's origin."[49] Rudolf Steiner described his reading in the Akashic

Record as reading a "living text," a spiritual history that comes about by expanding ordinary thinking to cosmic vision in the area of human perception, as "cosmic memory force."

Steiner's lecture cycle "Christianity as Mystical Fact" in winter 1901–1902 was based on research in "spiritual history," beyond material documents. Like all his "akashic research," this research was connected from the beginning with the knowledge of the Christ event and being.[50] In the process of compiling his "cosmic evolution," Rudolf Steiner found much that confirmed Blavatsky's statements; but he implicitly had to correct numerous accounts,[51] and expand and intensify others.

Originally, Rudolf Steiner hoped he could publish his cosmological book by 1904. However, the edition was much more extensive and time consuming than he originally had supposed. In contrast to Blavatsky, Sinnett, and other theosophical authors, Rudolf Steiner continued to follow and internalize natural-scientific research. Since his youth and the beginning of his studies at the Vienna Technical College, natural science had been one of the focal points of his interest, as well as of his life work. A year and a half after the 1910 publication of *Occult Science*, Steiner stated that in the book, "without its being noticed,"...the "results of all today's sciences, along with spiritual research" are woven in.[52] For Steiner, it was not just a matter of a acquiring individual scientific facts, and interpreting those facts in an authoritative context, revealed through occult research; it was also a matter of evaluating and transforming the foundation of these ideas. He had pursued this process methodically at the Vienna College, initially supported by an esoteric master. Steiner retained this way of proceeding, and continued it as he expanded his original field of spiritual research. He stated emphatically in 1924:

> In 1906 to 1909 when I described in my book *An Outline of Occult Science* the Earth in its earlier evolutionary stage as Moon, in its earlier incorporation as Sun, in its earlier

incorporation as Saturn; you will see that I did not stop with the Moon incorporation, but went further back to Saturn. All the initiates who had previously spoken about these things had stopped between Moon and Sun; actually they went back only to the Moon sphere. They were not interested, even sometimes uneasy, if a person had the impertinence to probe further back. They said a person cannot do that, because one comes to a boundary where there is a veil beyond which one cannot pass.

It was of course exceptionally important, and also interesting, to see the reason for this attitude. It was, you see, because such initiates (when one gets to know them well, one soon notices it) had a reluctance, had an antipathy against learning to know the imaginative forms related to the new natural science. If one confronted initiates with imaginations as they live in Darwinism, Haeckelism, and so forth, one could experience that they were quite unwilling, because modern people consider it childish, doltish and do not want to concern themselves with such things. If one presented them with Goethean imaginations, at first they were not so unwilling. However, if they found that a thinker expressed himself like a natural researcher of modern times, they dismissed this matter, too.

In short, a person could not approach these initiates with such ideas. It was only in 1906 to 1909, as I penetrated modern natural-scientific concepts in order to bring them into the soul region, where there are otherwise simply imaginations, that it was possible for me to penetrate to the time of Sun and Saturn. I did not employ natural-scientific ideas in order to gain understanding, in the way Haeckel or Huxley did. I used scientific thinking as an inner activity to go beyond the boundary where initiates of earlier times had stopped. Before the natural-scientific kind of thinking was in existence, a person entered higher consciousness inwardly only by penetrating the dream world with imaginations. For compiling my *Occult Science*, I attempted to accept the quite conscious internal idea world, which related otherwise only to external natural objects, and penetrate the imaginative world with it. This resulted in the possibility of penetrating into this whole chain of events: Saturn, Sun, and Moon. There a person could come to the point of researching, on earth, what old initiates had done.

The reason I talk about this path of knowledge is so that you can see how such things develop. You can say: that is something personal. But in this case, the personal is really quite objective. If there is criticism, it is because I wrote *Occult Science* like a mathematical textbook, instead of bringing in anything subjective; this whole process was written as I am describing it now, with mathematical coolness. But it is so. It has come about that one can carry the way of thinking existing since Copernicus, Galileo, and so forth—and which was so greatly intensified by Goethe—into the same soul condition that one otherwise has with imaginations. Therefore, a person can enlarge the area accessible to initiates; can push it back to the time of Saturn.[53]

*

"Anthroposophy is a path of knowledge that leads the spiritual in the human being to the spiritual in the universe."[54] Rudolf Steiner wrote *An Outline of Occult Science* out of his "I"; and he described the nature and reality of the human "I" in this book in a differentiated way. Later he repeatedly pointed out how much the central content of *Occult Science* is connected with a person's self-knowledge, and that study of the content leads to self-evaluation and self-assertion. The account of cosmic evolution in *Occult Science* was not an object and theme in itself, but occurred because of the human being; it started with

humanity, and led to humanity. Rudolf Steiner characterized his book *Theosophy* (the second part originally was intended to form the evolutionary content of *Occult Science*) as an "introduction to suprasensible world knowledge and *human determination*." In lectures Rudolf Steiner spoke about the methodical gesture of *Occult Science*:

> If such a book ... had been published in former times, it would have begun with an account proceeding from out of the starry expanses. My *Occult Science* proceeds strictly from the human being: In a certain sense, the human being is examined internally, and from there the world is sought. Humanity's inner being is expanded to old Saturn, old Sun, old Moon, and then to the future epochs of Earth development. ...When that is not accomplished in all its details, because the time for it has not yet come, it has nevertheless happened that the human being is primarily observed as a whole, from inside the heart, lungs, and so forth, so that by understanding the individual organs one gets to know the universe. Thus, today when a person studies the human heart, reads in the human heart, what is read there tells the person what the Sun is; it tells something about the nature of the Sun. A person learns, inside the heart, to know the being of the Sun outside. In ancient times, a person learned to know the being of the Sun, and by knowing the being of the Sun, knew what the human heart is. In modern times, one learns what the heart is, what the lung is, and understands the whole cosmos, the whole universe, from the human being.[55]

> *If we can understand ourselves by inner reflection, then we can also observe the cosmos; such perceptions deliver to us real cosmology.*[56]

Astronomer Elisabeth Vreede gave Rudolf Steiner the meditation:

> If a person understands the self
> The self becomes the world;
> If a person understands the world,
> The world becomes the self.[57]

In the times of the old mysteries, Rudolf Steiner said, the vision of revelation turned to the cosmos and from there back to the human being ("Earlier the heavens revealed to human beings what they needed to know for the earth.")[58] This consciousness and cognitive situation were transformed during the Mystery of Golgotha by the entry of Christ's "I" into relationship with the earth: "*Now humanity turns to the earth, because the earth is a creation of heaven.*"[59] Rudolf Steiner stressed once again, in 1923, that he drew much of his *Occult Science* from the "interior of humanity," out of the human constitution and the "Spirit of the Earth:"

> But the Spirit of the Earth speaks about the Saturn period, the Sun period, the Moon period of the earth, about the Jupiter period, and Venus period. The Spirit of the Earth speaks to a person about what it has preserved in its memory of the universe. Once a person's gaze turned outward to the heavenly expanses to explain the earth; now the person's gaze sinks into the human individuality, listens to what the Earth Spirit has to say in human nature out of the world memory; the modern person receives macrocosmic knowledge by understanding the Genius of the Earth.[60]

In this step Rudolf Steiner was much more advanced than Blavatsky and the theosophical forerunners, who worked and wrote primarily in the continuity of the old oriental mystery knowledge. By contrast, for Rudolf Steiner, everything was directed to the human "I", and thus to the Mystery of Golgotha as a conscious historical fact and turning point of first order.

*

Two years after writing the book, Rudolf Steiner recorded in a note to Edouard Schuré that, although Blavatsky's and Sinnett's cosmological writings exist in a distorted form, yet they possess a significant spiritual background; they came into being through the inspiration of high Eastern initiates. Rudolf Steiner applied this preparatory work to his own activity, to his task, "allowing what ... has become Western esotericism since the Christ event to flow into European culture" (Marie Steiner). In autumn 1907, in Barr, he wrote about the Theosophical Society and Movement:

> Their successful continued development in Western countries depends on the extent to which they prove themselves capable of taking up the principle of Western initiation into their influences. For Eastern initiates must necessarily leave untouched the *Christ principle* as central *cosmic* factor. Without this Christ principle, the Theosophical Movement would have no definite effect on Western cultures, which have Christ's life as their starting point. Therefore, revelations of Eastern initiation had to be placed in the West like a sect *alongside* the living culture. They could have a hope of success in evolution only if they destroyed the Christ principle in Western culture. This would be identical to eradicating the real *sense of the earth*, which lies in knowing and realizing the intentions of the *living Christ*.[61]

Rudolf Steiner wrote *An Outline of Occult Science* at the time (1909) when the Theosophical Society discovered Jiddu Krishnamurti, whom they would later proclaim to be the future "savior of the world." Rudolf Steiner's demonstration of the Christ activity in the history of the earth and humanity, which was also unfolded during 1909 in comprehensive lecture series, was in polar opposition to this. His book was compiled "in the knowledge and realization of the intentions of the *living Christ*" in preparation for Christ's reappearance, which would occur not physically, but in the spiritual-etheric world. Later Rudolf

Steiner said: "The occultist can point out how, since around 1909, in a clearly understandable manner there was prepared what will come; that inwardly we live since 1909 in a quite special time. Today it is possible, when a person is seeking for it, to be quite close to Christ; to find Christ in a different form than those in earlier times found Him."[62] On January 12, 1910, Rudolf Steiner spoke in Stockholm for the first time about the reappearance of the Christ being in the etheric. At the same time, the book *Occult Science* appeared, which dealt not only with the activity of the Christ being in the cosmos and on earth, but was itself really inspired by the Christ spirit. As Rudolf Steiner said in an esoteric class in Norrköping, Sweden, on July 14, 1914:

> ... From the beginning, all of *Occult Science* and our work has been founded on the knowledge of Christ; and it is inspired by the Christ being Himself. We always want to have that in mind, my dear sisters and brothers.[63]

Research into the history of the earth and of humanity's evolution required going backward in spiritual vision, "reading in the Akashic Record" as world memory. This path backward that Rudolf Steiner trod, however, was illuminated, acted upon, by the Christ impulse. In March 1914, he spoke in a basic lecture about the task of the "Christianizing" of human memory; and of the real "entry" of the Christ being into this specific soul sphere of humanity, as a cultural achievement of the future: "Christ will live in this memory (of humanity)."[64] Permeating thought and memory capacities with Christ's light leads to the strengthening and intensifying of memory. This is a process that belongs to humanity's future; to a large extent, it has already been achieved, in an exemplary way, by Rudolf Steiner. In his life work, he was preparing the path of salvation. In writing the Christ-inspired *Occult Science*, Steiner signified the manifested illumination of the Christ path, *with the help* of the Christ being, in his name, and with his support.

As Rudolf Steiner showed in numerous lectures in 1909 and at the end of the year with completion of the book, the history of humanity's and earth's development (from the past through the present into the future) was simultaneously the history of Christ's path—his gradual attraction to earth, his penetrating the consummation of the Mystery of Golgotha and its consequences—and the earth's further transformation to Sun existence. "Because Christ has entered into our memory, because Christ lives in the memory force, a person will know how Christ was active in the cosmos from outside the earth until the Mystery of Golgotha; how He prepared and passed through this Mystery of Golgotha; and how He worked further as an impulse in history."[65] Christ stands in the centerpoint of humanity's evolution, and He can be seen there:

> In the beginning was the memory;
> And the memory lived further;
> And the memory is divine.
> And the memory is life;
> And this life is the "I" of humanity,
> Which streams into humanity.
> Not one alone, but the Christ in the human being.
> When the human being remembers the divine life,
> Christ is in the memory;
> And the radiating memory life
> Will illuminate Christ
> In every impending darkness of the present.[66]

Rudolf Steiner spoke on July 31, 1915, in Dornach, about the living Christ being in connection with the saying, "I am with you every day until the end of the Earth period:"

> This means that what Christ meant to reveal to us was not exhausted with what is in the Gospels. He is among us, but not as one who has died; who once and for all time

> let everything that He wanted to bring to earth flow into the Gospels. He is a living entity bound up with earthly evolution. We can work through to him with our souls. He reveals himself to us, just as he revealed himself to the evangelists. The Gospel is not something that was once there, and then expired; the Gospel is a continual revelation. To a certain extent, a person who meets Christ, in looking up to him, awaits new revelations....
>
> Receiving Christ's revelation means obtaining from him information about the world. What is received, we must give back to the cosmos from the center of the soul. Therefore, what we have received as spiritual science, we may interpret as the Living Christ's revelation. It is he who tells us how the earth originated; how it relates to human nature; and what conditions the earth went through before it became earth. Everything we have as cosmology, what we give back to the world, he reveals all that to us. The continuing revelation of Christ is to feel oneself in this mood; to receive with inner spirituality from Christ the concentrated cosmos; to bring all this to the world with understanding. Then a person will no longer regard the moon as if it were a huge bowling ball or sphere shoved into the universe, dented and pocked by mechanical forces, and such things. A person who has received this understanding will know what the moon indicates; how it is connected with Christ, with the Yahve nature, and so forth: this is the continuing revelation of Christ. We must give back to the outer world what we have received from it.[67]

By conducting the research and writing *Occult Science*, Rudolf Steiner accomplished the task that had been the responsibility of the Eastern Theosophical Movement—that of transforming and advancing in the light of Christ the old mystery knowledge about the earth and humanity's development. By renouncing this process, old Eastern occultists, up to and including the Theosophists who succeeded Blavatsky, renounced the real "sense of the earth," which, according to Rudolf Steiner, lies "in the knowledge and realization of the living Christ's intentions."

*

"To receive from Christ the concentrated cosmos spiritually in one's soul, and as it is received, to give it back to the world"—this Rudolf Steiner sees as the initiate's present task at the advent of the new mystery period. Writing *Occult Science* was in this sense a social deed—passing on acquired initiation knowledge, real creative "world thoughts."[68] Passing on world thoughts to others, enables people to later give them back to the cosmos, a restitution that should be accomplished by individuals and the community in life and after death.

In feeling the need of YOUR grace,
Christ light of the world, I await
    forces
    opening gates of the soul.
To YOUR enlightenment
I will be peaceful within myself,
And thank YOU for YOUR gifts,
And give them
As YOUR offering to humanity.
I will be the
Instrument of YOUR words
With my soul's
    Best forces,
    Genuine depths,
    Inner respect.[69]

By writing *Occult Science*, Rudolf Steiner made it possible for many human souls to internalize and further transform the assimilation of the "world thoughts" contained in it. The goal was not merely "knowledge;" rather, the goal was the absorption of knowledge into the heart and will as the basis for a new morality and civilization, in gratitude to the creative hierarchies. In the last part of the book, looking both backward and forward at human cultural development, Rudolf Steiner wrote:

> The force of love must have its beginning in people of the earth. The "cosmos of wisdom" develops itself into a *"cosmos of love."* Love should come out of all that the "I" can unfold. As a comprehensive "paragon of love," the high Sun Being is represented in his revelation, which is characterized by the account of Christ's development. The seed of love descends into the human being's innermost core. From there it flows into the whole evolution. Just as the previously formed wisdom is revealed in the earth's external sensory world forces, in current "nature forces," so in the future, love will be revealed in all appearances as new nature forces. That is the secret of all development in the future: the knowledge a person accomplishes out of truly understanding evolution is a "seed" that will ripen as *love*. To the extent the power of love arises, an equal amount of creativity will be achieved for the future. There will be strong forces that lead to the above-mentioned end result of spiritualization, in what will come into being out of love. To the extent that spiritual knowledge flows into humanity and earthly evolution, an equal number of seeds capable of life will be present for the future. Spiritual knowledge changes into love through *what it is*. The complete process that has been described, from the Greco-Roman epoch to the present period, shows how this transformation will proceed and why the *beginning* of development for the future is made now. What has been prepared by Saturn, Sun, and Moon as enlightenment is active now in the physical,

etheric, and astral bodies of human beings; and it is represented there as the "wisdom of the world," internalized in the "I." Starting with the Earth condition, the "wisdom of the external world" becomes inner knowledge in a person. When it is internalized, it becomes the seed of love. Wisdom is the prerequisite of love; love is the result of knowledge, which is born again in the "I."[70]

*

"Whoever is acquainted with suprasensible research will observe in reading this book that an attempt has been made to maintain clearly defined boundaries between what both can and should be communicated currently from the area of spiritual knowledge and what shall be presented at a later time, or at least in another form."[71] Rudolf Steiner wrote *Outline of Occult Science* not just for the members of the Theosophical Society, or even just for their "esoteric school." On the contrary, it was an exoteric book for all interested people. He had to publish it, although he knew that the form he had found after much effort was a compromise. It was a compromise between what was necessary communication and concealment, which was just as imperative. Concealment was needed to protect some of the contents that either could not be mentioned publicly[72] or, at least, needed a different form of presentation. Steiner repeatedly pointed out in the years after the book's appearance that *Occult Science* showed only "sketchy indications";[73] was like a "charcoal drawing"[74] with sparse "indications in rough outline,"[75] especially in regard to the preliminary planetary stages of the earth. "The processes, beings, and their destinies are probably just as varied on Saturn, Sun, and Moon as on the Earth itself."[76] Steiner's choice of the word "probably" made clear he did not consider research on the planetary conditions "processes, beings, and destinies" to be complete. His presentation was not only an esoteric-exoteric compromise; it also signified a stage on his cosmological path of knowledge, a basic "sketch," of which further details should be added later.

Rudolf Steiner characterized the form of presentation that he chose in 1909 as "intellectually imaginative." He pointed out that in order to facilitate reception of the contents, he had to choose images according to the prerequisites of the time:

> I have already drawn attention to the fact that the description of the old Saturn period, and also the following planetary embodiments of our earth, as it is offered in *Occult Science*, is certainly not exhaustive. But for now, it must in a certain sense be sufficient to clothe what really matters in images taken from obvious and customary things, so that the public, to whom this book should also be presented, is not too strongly shocked.[77]

At the beginning of 1924, right after the Christmas Conference, Rudolf Steiner gave a lecture with quite a stylistically different description of earthly evolution. He said in that lecture:

> As I wrote *Occult Science*, I needed to bring the description of the development of the earth at least a little into harmony with the customary present concept. In the twelfth and thirteenth centuries, a person could have done this in another way.[78]

The compromise that Steiner finally found, which he had to make, *nolens volens,* was not easy for him; and he suffered from it. Only two years after *Occult Science* appeared, he unexpectedly gave five cosmological lectures in Berlin on "Evolution From the Viewpoint of Reality." To the members of the Theosophical Society (that is, to an inner circle), where he could speak differently, rather than out of "maya" and "illusion,"[79] he presented the essential events of the participating creative hierarchies.

In his preface to the fourth edition of the book, Rudolf Steiner wrote in 1913 about "how little the new revision corresponds to what it really should be as an outline of a suprasensible world outlook." He continued:

> It is noticeable to the author, in a number of places, how rough the accessible means of presentation proved to be, in contrast to what suprasensible research shows. Thus, more than one path could be shown in order to arrive at the concepts given in the book for Saturn, Sun, and Moon evolution. An important viewpoint regarding this aspect has recently been treated anew in this edition. However, the results regarding such things deviate so greatly from the outcome in the area of the sense perceptions, that attempting to shape the presentation exacts a continual struggle, for even an approximately sufficient expression. Whoever attempts a presentation such as is made here will perhaps notice that much of what is impossible to say in dry words is attempted through the *type* of description. The description is different for Saturn, for example, than for Sun development.[80]

Two years before, Rudolf Steiner had emphasized in his 1911 lecture in Basel:

> We learn what happened on old Saturn, old Sun, and old Moon, and what the task of the Earth is. When you read the descriptions presented in *Occult Science*, you will find the account for Saturn has an underlying emphasis that is quite different from that of the other planetary conditions. In describing the Saturn condition, you can feel how relationships are described with a certain austerity. You can feel that in the soul; and it is necessary to feel it. For the Sun existence, you can feel as if blooming, sprouting life was there. For the Moon description, you can feel as though

> a certain melancholic gloomy drought flows through the numerous concepts given. A sensitive person can perceive that, even in the sense of taste, even on the tongue.[81]

In this qualitative sense, there is more living in the book than appears on the surface, in the "seemingly incidental"[82] elements existing "between the lines"[83] that must be received *experientially*.[84] Rudolf Steiner counted on the active reception of the text and its contents, to which he continually urged, in a manner unusual for him. ("Read that in *Occult Science*, study it, look up in *Occult Science* what you want to know; remember we must reflect on these things.")[85] Rudolf Steiner knew how much depended on whether *Occult Science* really could find admission into human souls; into their self-knowledge and world understanding, as well as into the work of renewing various fields of endeavor. He published the book at the beginning of 1910 because it was directly required by the times, as well as by the Time Spirit. The book, including the limited form of presentation Steiner chose, belongs to the central Christ-Michael-language of the present. "In this *Occult Science* I went as far as it is necessary today for humanity's general consciousness."[86] Steiner hoped his readers and listeners would activate, ensoul, and meditate on the contents received. "It must advance ever further. What appears in *Occult Science* must be deepened and expanded."[87] The extensive descriptions of the anthroposophical training path included in this book were of methodological, groundbreaking significance—for oneself *and* for dealing with what was described in the other chapters of the book. In 1918 Rudolf Steiner said unexpectedly in a lecture:

> How many people come to me, describing something they have seen. Of course they have seen that. Imaginations are not so far removed from human development. "Was that the Guardian of the Threshold?" they ask. But it is not so easy to answer such things with a yes or no, because

> the answers include the entire development of humanity. However, answers will be given. I am now revising *Occult Science*, which will appear in a new edition. I will see that everything is included to answer such questions. All cautions, all limitations that a person should apply are precisely described in it. Feelings and emotions that a person should develop are described there. It is clearly stated, but one must read everything exactly. If I had presented everything that is contained in *Occult Science* in complete detail, I would have had to write thirty volumes. One must *think* when reading this book, and then must act accordingly; which one can do.[88]

It cannot be known, of course, whether the book has been received by many people in the qualitative sense desired by Rudolf Steiner. The sales numbers were exceptionally good, despite indignant public opinion.[89] Even in 1910, the year it appeared, three editions of the book were necessary. In a lecture in Dornach in 1922, Rudolf Steiner said, with a humorous expression:

> It is, after all, rare that such a book as *Occult Science* has done so well. It is difficult to read—*it must be difficult to read.* It is not formulated so that it steals into the soul in an obliging way—it is by no means travel literature! Since 1909 until now there have been 15 editions, which are all out of print. Anthroposophy really has come into the world....[90]

EPILOGUE: Christian Morgenstern

One of the most intensive readers of *An Outline of Occult Science* was the poet Christian Morgenstern (1871–1914), who became acquainted with Anthroposophy for the first time in January 1909. That month was the beginning of a cosmological-Christological lecture year, which Rudolf Steiner ended by writing *Occult Science.*

Although he was in the midst of a materialistic environment, Morgenstern's thoughts were in other directions. He had long been occupied with the question of the development of humanity and the earth. In his first book of poems (*In Phanta's Castle*, 1895), Morgenstern himself had written about the origin of Sun, Moon, and stars; about the cosmic-spiritual processes and their conditions—"Love is on all the stars." Ten years before meeting Rudolf Steiner, he entered in his diary, "The constant movement of all that is becoming; becoming itself is harmony, must be harmony. For whoever can hear it! To think it is divine!"[91] As early as 1891, the Morgenstern had written at age twenty:

> All of creation lies there like a book in whose leaves the eternal necessity is carved on the world plane with an iron stylus.
>
> Tremendous harmony resounds; we people are the notes.[92]

The concepts of world creation and its interrelationships were a consuming, life-long concern he pursued. Since his intensive study of the Gospel of John in 1905–1906, Morgenstern sought especially the secret of the Logos, of the creatively productive God; of his being and his work, which bear witness to his activity. Morgenstern longed for a new mystery wisdom and real insight into the conditions that lived in his sympathetic soul. "The creation always remained tragically incomprehensible, able to be grasped by feeling, but not accessible to thought; and it offered to a person little more than targets of despair," he wrote in his autobiographical retrospect on the period of his years-long search.[93] Christian Morgenstern was impressed that the "sense of life" exists in a "continually increased communion with being" or in a "conversation having the highest kind of mutual giving and taking."[94] Then he found both the historical structure and the future form of this "conversation" in Rudolf Steiner's 1909 cosmological lecture cycles, which he attended in Budapest, Dornach, Kassel, Kristiania (Oslo), and Munich with unconditional interest and great reverence.[95] Shortly after the beginning of the course *Spiritual Hierarchies and Their Reflection in the Physical World (Cosmos, Zodiac, Planets)*, which he attended in April 1909, in Düsseldorf, he wrote excitedly to his friend Friedrich Kayssler: "A cosmogony of the grandest kind is unfolded."[96] Later, Morgenstern wrote the poem:

> The mere desire of a great good
> Certainly is lofty human contemplation.
> However, it rises to full bloom only
> When grace brings a visionary awakening
> Of the cosmos' undiluted nature
> As spiritual art to consciousness.
>
> Then there grows from tremendous panoramas of creation
> Looking up to hidden creator spheres,
> Including self in their stages—there grows
>
> Sympathy with this world fate
> That nourishes more than deep heart desires
> And the highest gods called upon to share the work.[97]

In Rudolf Steiner's presentations, Morgenstern found the long-sought "starry script," as a Christianized cosmosophy that fulfilled his longing. For Morgenstern, Rudolf Steiner unfolded it as a message of a higher order, as one sent who spoke in the name of Christ:

He *spoke*. And as he spoke there appeared in Him
The zodiac, Cherubim, and Seraphim,
The sun-star, the planets moving
From place to place.

All that sprang forth out of his words,
Was lightning-quick, like a world dream, contemplated;
The whole heaven seemed to emerge
From his words ...[98]

Morgenstern studied the book *Occult Science* repeatedly; he read intensively, and just as meditatively; and he lived in the connections unfolded in the book—precisely as Rudolf Steiner had hoped. In carving out his inner path and his own poetic work, Morgenstern also drew "consequences" from what he received in this way. One year before his death, after a mutual study of *Occult Science* with Margareta Morgenstern and Mia Groddeck in Arosa (Chalet "Sonnenberg"), he composed the lines:

The earth is the centerpoint of the world.
Sun and planets were created for it.
They have positioned themselves around it.

After they emerged from the lap of the Thrones,
Old Saturn was the first existence to awaken
As warmth-sphere—so the prophets see it;

Then sank in world sleep and night
To re-emerge as old Sun,
As fire air (flickering 'twixt flames and embers)
Rejuvenated once more in enlivened spirit,
And fluid now, as old Moon,
The Sun thrusts both out in exaltation;

Brought back to the gods' dwelling
For the last time, to condense
Finally as Earth's initial structure,

Emanating, then fragmented and viewed
In Sun, Moon, and Earth, it becomes
The definitive world, home of the "I",

The Logos and the beloved fatherland.[99]

Christian Morgenstern internalized his own individualized Anthroposophy and its cosmology in the five years from 1909 to 1914 that his destiny granted him on earth. Rudolf Steiner said the writing of *Occult Science* was—like all of Anthroposophy—"inspired" by the Christ being, really "received" by Christ as a living Christ revelation. "It is He Who then tells us how the earth originated, how it relates to human nature, and what conditions the earth has gone through before it became earth. Everything we have as cosmology, which we now give back to the world, He reveals all that to us."[100] In a certain sense the Christ being lived in Rudolf Steiner's lectures and writings, and can be received and internalized through them. A few months after Christian Morgenstern's death, in Norköpping, Sweden, (the country where Christ's reappearance in the etheric was first announced), Steiner said:

> Christian Morgenstern, ... while he was connected with us in our anthroposophical stream, received what we have to say about Christ. In that, he received the anthroposophical training; in that, he connected this anthroposophical training with his soul. It really became the spiritual heart's blood of his soul. He received this training in his soul, so that this anthroposophical training contained the Christ as substance for him. He received it together with the Christ being. The Christ, as He lives in our movement, passed over into his soul.[101]

*

An Outline of Occult Science and the Mystery of Golgotha[102]

SERGEI O. PROKOFIEFF

The book contains the outline of Anthroposophy as a whole....

Everything that I have said since appears, when it is inserted into the right place in this book, as a further extension of the sketch made at that time.[103]

—RUDOLF STEINER

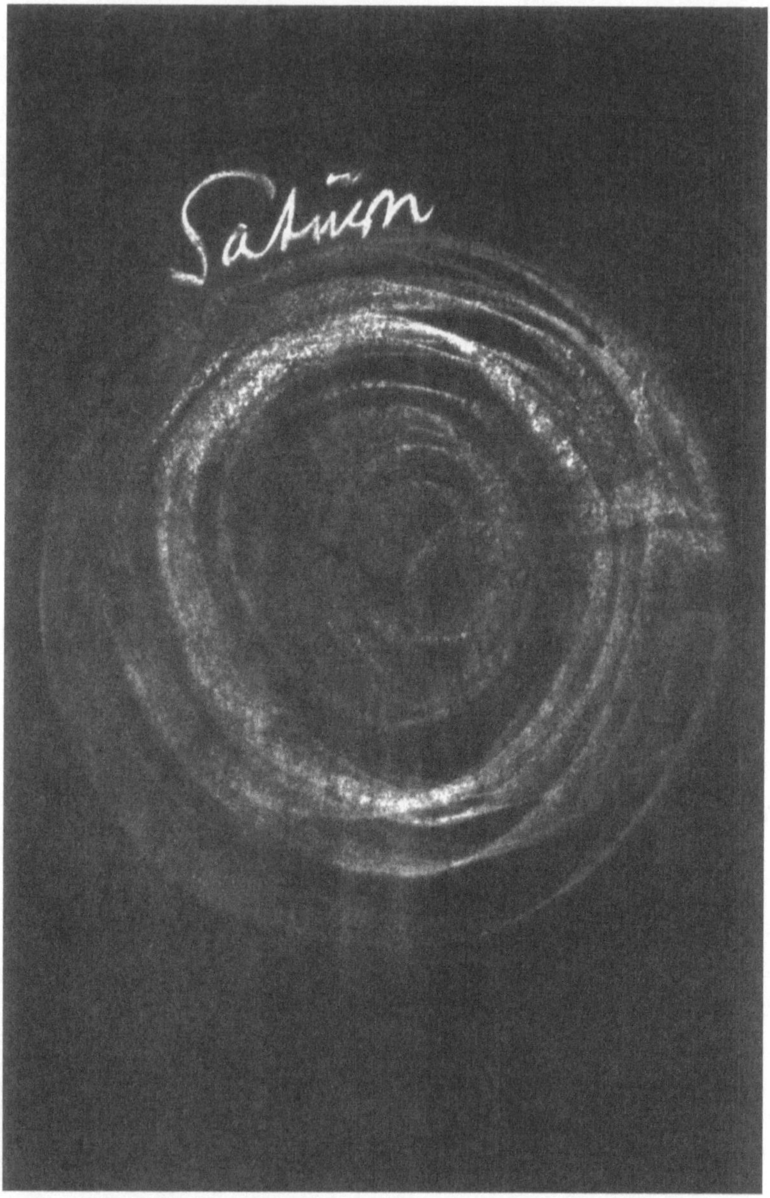

Blackboard drawing from GA 291

In Rudolf Steiner's book *An Outline of Occult Science* is a section that describes Christ Jesus' life on earth and calls attention to two noteworthy moments: the Baptism in the Jordan, and the death and resurrection on Golgotha—the "Mystery of Golgotha" as Rudolf Steiner calls it.

The book explains how the divine-cosmic-sun-being of Christ united with Jesus of Nazareth at the Baptism, and, in this moment, the Luciferic powers had to yield. Everything spiritual that Lucifer otherwise conceals from people, was manifested in Jesus of Nazareth. For the first time, it was apparent what the Luciferic powers had kept hidden from people since the Fall of humanity, so that they had no access to it.

During world evolution some beings remained behind on old Moon that became Luciferic spirits and unfolded their activity further on earth. If one wants to find a sphere of activity in the cosmos that remains untouched by the Luciferic powers, then one must go back to the evolutionary stage of old Sun. This means that a spiritual researcher who is not able to search back to the stage of old Sun has no possibility of understanding what once occurred at the Baptism in the Jordan. This is the reason why members of the Theosophical Society could not comprehend this event in the right way. In that group, the whole Christ event was considered only as the higher initiation stage of an earthly man.

How does one find the sphere that is not tainted by Ahrimanic powers? In order to do this, the spiritual researcher must search even further back, beyond the cosmic stage of old Sun. This is because the Ahrimanic beings, who are the ones who take away the possibility of understanding the Mystery of Golgotha in its deepest sense, remained behind on old Sun. If we want to comprehend spiritually the death and resurrection of Christ, we must go beyond the activity sphere of Ahriman; that means we must attain comprehension of the evolutionary stage of old Saturn. Ahriman's influence goes back only to the stage of old Sun. Therefore, we can really understand the Mystery of Golgotha only from the viewpoint of old Saturn, because that is where we find the origins of Christ's body, which at the Mystery of Golgotha went through death and resurrection.

Inasmuch as a person in the Theosophical Society—beginning with H. P. Blavatsky—was able to conduct research only as far back as the sphere of the old Moon, neither the Baptism in the Jordan nor the Mystery of Golgotha could be understood at all. That limitation later led to the absurdities that caused the separation of the anthroposophists from the theosophists, and the founding of the independent Anthroposophical Society.

These introductory remarks precede the real theme of this lecture, which from a spiritual-historical perspective maintains that the nature of the Mystery of Golgotha can be understood only from the standpoint of a new Christianized cosmology, as it is described in the book *An Outline of Occult Science*.

*

To draw close to old Saturn, one must approach in two ways what has just been said. Both approaches are taken, to begin with, from Rudolf Steiner's lectures and writings (reference will be made later to *Occult Science*). The presentation in these lectures forms a certain polarity. First, taking the description of world evolution as reported in the book *Cosmic Memory* and a few other lectures as a basis, one can understand the situation on old Saturn in the following way. The divine Trinity presides over all the hierarchies, and it includes the archetypal thoughts for creating a new cosmos. It is surrounded by the highest hierarchical spirits, the Seraphim. These have the ability to receive the thoughts of the divine Trinity, the plan of the future cosmos, from their hands, so to speak. The Seraphim conveyed this archetypal idea further to the Cherubim, who worked out all the details. The world plan originating in this way was passed on to the Spirits of Will, the Thrones, who began the real creative process through their cosmic sacrifice. They allowed a substance to flow out of their own being to the place where the old Saturn came into existence.[104]

As a result of this sacrificial creation, the beings of the second threefold hierarchy appeared. Of them, it was the Spirits of Wisdom, the Kyriotetes, who worked on the sacrificial substances of the Thrones and permeated this with their wisdom. From this wisdom there came into being a self-contained world organism, which the Dynamis then brought into movement. This creation was further differentiated into many individual, interrelated forms, which one can imagine visually as a fruit with sections, such as a well-formed blackberry. This task of differentiation was incumbent on the Exusiai, the Spirits of Form.

Right after that differentiation by the Spirits of Form, those beings who were to attain their "I" stage at this point (and therefore were in the center of evolution at that time)—the Archai or Spirits of Personality—appeared on Saturn. They began to reflect their consciousness in the warmth substance of the corporeality that had been developed. Thereby they rose to a state of "I" consciousness, and could then plant in these warmth bodies the archetypal seeds of what today we call our "senses." For the first time, there was a polarity of body and "I". The "I" needed an external sheath to achieve consciousness of self.

But the development went further. The Archangels are spirits who turned the predisposed sense organs outward and made them glow. When the sense organs began to glow, the exalted spirits, the Seraphim, could participate directly in the evolution of old Saturn. They implanted in the beings of old Saturn the first seeds of the Spirit Self. Then the Angels appeared on the scene by supplying these bodies with a sort of life; in this life it was also possible for the Cherubim to cooperate in further shaping old Saturn, and in providing the seeds of the Life Spirit there. Finally, a body originating in this way, which later formed the basis for the development of the human being on earth, was bestowed with a very primary, dark consciousness—such as minerals have today. At this stage, the spirits who began the creation process could also lay the first seeds of the Spirit Human into this body, which is what will come to completion at the end of evolution—including that of Earth and beyond, through its future stages of Jupiter and Venus—on Vulcan.

Thus, this process is based on a development that already bore at its beginning the seeds of its completion. This organic unfolding means that a person cannot gain a real picture, a true idea of the future (and consequently also not of evolution's final goal on Vulcan), if one does not know the nature of evolution's origin on old Saturn.

In what has been said so far, the stage of Saturn development has been characterized very briefly on a cognitive level. This approach is fully justified because in the process of studying we must, as spiritual students, necessarily pass through these cognitive stages. To make these complicated processes clear for readers, in his book *Cosmic Memory* Rudolf Steiner gives a short summary at the end of each chapter of what has been just described. This clarification is given because it is necessary at first to penetrate the description of world evolution strictly with our thinking, which signifies an important cognitive step on the path of modern initiation. Only then can a person move freely in the web of interconnected thoughts, as in a thought form, living into this world evolution.

One can also examine the whole process quite differently; that is, from the imaginative side, which is more internal. This second approach is, in a certain regard, in contrast to the foregoing. Here one proceeds from the assumption that a spiritual researcher who wants to investigate old Saturn clairvoyantly, stands at first before an absolute nothingness. There is neither space nor time—nothing that we can grasp with our thoughts or our imagination. What pervades the entire universe appears before us as a dark abyss. Standing at this world abyss, a person feels a great shock. This condition, according to Rudolf Steiner, is experienced by every spiritual researcher who arrives at the origin of old Saturn. In order to bear it, we need a great deal of help, which must have already come to us on the path of initiation.

In the lecture series "Evolution From the Viewpoint of the Essential,"[105] one can find, by careful reading, the crucial sentence in the first lecture, "What the person can initially only imagine becomes present to clairvoyance." (This refers to the primal origin of Saturn, which has been previously described.) The spiritual researcher experiences standing before this nearly incomprehensible reality "as a spiritual being, who feels united with the Christ being, carried by the Christ being."[106] This means that only those who "feel united with the Christ being" can actually venture to approach the origin of Saturn consciously. Confronting this original condition penetrated by Christ, one will experience how this world abyss is filled with something that at first cannot be defined, that is not yet substance. It can be described only by an analogy, as being similar to *will.* There is revealed in a powerful, moving picture a will that in its inner quality is *pure courage*—the courage to begin a new creation. Thus, the world abyss is transformed into an ocean of limitless cosmic courage. This is the true appearance of the Thrones, the Spirits of Will, coming into being in the universe.

One who now tries to produce this picture imaginatively within can experience how, in what at first seemed totally incomprehensible, there arises a mighty, increasing tension, a tension that develops from four sides but does not yet have space and direction. One feels as if a dark ocean flows on all sides, permeated as though with countless invisible flashes of courage. In the dark space on this stage of world becoming, for which practically no human words can be found to describe, still higher beings are revealed.

Rudolf Steiner helps us understand this new situation through the following image. Visualize a room in which a very wise man has been actively working for many years. Now one enters the room in the wise man's absence and can feel the atmosphere filled with great wisdom. This wisdom is not substance; physically it might be considered nothing, yet it can be experienced as intensively present. This is the picture of the appearance of exalted spirits, the Cherubim, in cosmic development. Their approach to evolving Saturn reveals itself from all four sides of the world periphery as mighty flashes in a limitless sea of courage.

Then a third element comes about through the increasing relationship between the Thrones (Spirits of Will) and the Cherubim (Spirits of Infinite Wisdom and Harmony): a great sacrifice is made. Now the Thrones sacrifice something of their own being, which then flows into the entire evolution. The Thrones are so filled with their inner creative activity, they want to make this infinite power available to other beings as well. From the depths of their own being, they bring a sacrifice to the higher spirits, the Cherubim. To clairvoyant vision, what they sacrifice looks like sacrificial smoke, which fills the inner sphere of old Saturn. This cosmic sacrificial smoke contains warmth, which is not yet physical at this stage, but is pure spiritual warmth. Out of this process, quite new beings develop: the Spirits of Time. This is the sublime moment in which time was born in our universe. Time exists as a sum of beings—the Archai, or Spirits of Personality—who incorporate in themselves the Being of Time.

These beings inhale, for the moment, only the soul-spiritual warmth substance of old Saturn. What they exhale is something totally different; it is something that has a vague resemblance to warmth as we know it here on earth. But it is not yet physical-sensory warmth in the customary sense; for initially it exists in the cosmos only as "free warmth," without any connection to objects that reflect or feel warmth or coldness. This reflection does not yet exist on old Saturn. Today a physicist can hardly form an idea of warmth that is not connected to an object, but exists only in itself. Yet the entire further development of Saturn (approximately from the middle to the end of its evolutionary stage) consists in the transformation of its existing spiritual warmth into physical-sensory warmth. It is the Spirits of Personality who inhale this Saturn substance as soul warmth and exhale it as physical-sensory warmth. By reflecting their being in physical warmth, the Spirits of Personality rise to their "I" consciousness. This breathing process becomes ever more intrinsic. By inhaling, these spirits experience their "I" consciousness; by exhaling, they shape their bodies (which consist of physical-sensory warmth) to ever greater perfection. Thereby their "I" consciousness becomes ever clearer and more comprehensive.

Thus, we see how a person can approach the original beginning of old Saturn quite differently—on the basis of the imaginative process. Rudolf Steiner gave the following imagination for this type of perception: one forms a picture of the mighty, flashing figures of the Cherubim nearing Saturn from all sides; kneeling before them, are the Spirits of Will, the Thrones, offering up to them the world sacrifice. (This was seen, movingly presented, in the Eurythmy performance.)[107]

Now we have before us two totally different approaches to the nature of old Saturn, and each is fully justified. In the first description, a person can approach the original condition of our cosmos in such a way that the intellect is used. Then too, a person can place the imaginative element more in the foreground, as is represented in the second description. At first, we can only place them beside each other, and cannot join them together internally without further processing.

If we consider on this basis the description of the same processes in *Occult Science*, we find there a third, totally different aspect that is represented in a singular way. Rudolf Steiner points out the special quality of this book in the last preface to the book, which he wrote shortly before his death. He wrote that the task he envisioned for himself in this case was to pour the concepts of world evolution attained by spiritual research in the suprasensory worlds into modern thought forms, so they would not lose their imaginative character. "In order to make such understanding (as is otherwise required for 'nature knowledge') really possible, the author of spiritual visions must pour forth correctly what was seen spiritually into thought forms, without losing their imaginative character."[108]

In what has been presented, two different approaches—one more cognitive and one more imaginative—were described in order to grasp old Saturn's coming into being. However, based on the one-sidedness of each approach, both are incomplete. With the book *Occult Science,* Rudolf Steiner created something that almost cannot be put into words. Yet Rudolf Steiner managed it. Because he was able to make a completely new connection between imagination and thinking, he could permeate his imagination with clear thoughts in such a way that the original imaginative character of his spiritual research was not lost. Thus, *Occult Science* became a singular work of art from which people could learn to fulfill the main tasks of our fifth post-Atlantean cultural epoch. With a thinking that (in the sense of the *Philosophy of Spiritual Activity*)[109] is brought to the greatest intensity and clarity, new, free imaginations must be achieved that will neither get lost in thinking nor extinguish it, which would lead only to intellectual abstractions or nebulous imaginations. Out of this work of art comes a fully new quality in which both poles (thinking and imagination) merge harmoniously with one another and continually blend.

What does this accomplishment actually signify? It is the first step in the modern suprasensory experience of connecting thinking and imagining into a unity in a unique way. Thus, one can experience *Occult Science* as a great training book for what must be achieved especially in our time; what Rudolf Steiner called the new intellectual clairvoyance, which people must develop during the fifth post-Atlantean cultural epoch: to experience Christ consciously in the etheric realm. Rudolf Steiner added: "Progress occurs only when people develop a higher intellect, not only for themselves, but also for carrying into the astral world. Through such *intellectual clairvoyance*, sophisticated people can and will approach the visible etheric Christ ever more and more clearly in the course of the next 3,000 years."[110]

What we need in preparation for meeting the etheric Christ are not thoughtless imaginations or shadowy webs of abstract thoughts; but just these two polar attributes—the sharpest thinking and the power of free imagining. These must connect in a new, indivisible unity, fructifying and intensifying each other. Only where these forces merge to form a fresh capability in people, and thereby become a new, suprasensory organ of perception, is it possible for the modern, free person to meet the etheric Christ in a legitimate way and to truly recognize him. The special contribution of *Occult Science* for our time lies in helping people unfold this new capability in themselves, to perceive Christ in his etheric form ever more consciously.

However, world evolution went even further. After old Saturn, was old Sun. On it, the human being, formerly consisting only of a physical body, obtained the ether body. Now matter separated for the first time, creating "above" and "below." Below, a thick, gaseous substance was formed; above, light arose from a process of refinement.

On the next cosmic evolutionary stage, old Moon, the human being received the astral body, whereby a still stronger polarization occurred. Above, the sound or chemical ether emerged; below, a watery element was formed.

With the Earth stage, this process reached its greatest differentiation: the human being received the "I". From this point forward, the human being experienced conflict between the life ether and physical body, which increasingly took on death-mineral components. In paradise, in the primal condition of Earth and Moon, these two poles were connected. The original paradisiacal body had been still fully penetrated by life ether, which was why the human being had been at that time immortal. Then the decisive moment of world history took place: the higher hierarchies allowed the opposing forces into humanity's development.

To attain freedom, it was necessary for the human being to dip into the material element more deeply than originally had been planned. The so-called Fall of humanity occurred. The freedom available to human beings today was obtained along with great loss. First, death entered into humanity's development as a result of the weakening of the life ether forces coming from nature. These weakened forces could not prevent the physical body from the Fall. Second, human beings lost direct connection with the divine-spiritual world, which they had still possessed in the paradisiacal condition. Since then, humanity has been increasingly dependent on only sensory-material nature.

For this reason, we human beings now exist in a painful polarity. On the one hand, we have our liberated "I", which increasingly has been deserted by all good forces. On the other hand, the connection to our spiritual home, to the world of the hierarchies, has been lost. Out of this loneliness we look back on the body, which produced our "I" consciousness on earth through a reflection process, and observe this mortal body continually and inexorably decaying during earthly life. Already with the first breath of the newborn child this death process starts, and it continues throughout life. The forces of death finally win the upper hand over the slowly dwindling forces of the life ether, which can no longer keep the physical body alive.

One must look clearly at the drama of the situation that has come about in this way. One must observe oneself as an "I" abandoned by all good divine-spiritual powers, and must gaze continually into the abyss of death. If one tries meditatively to envision this repeatedly, one will experience in the soul something like an echo of what occurred in the Mystery of Golgotha on Good Friday. Then one can microcosmically understand what Christ Jesus, out of his divine freedom, shouldered for all humanity. Good Friday is the time when the crucified Son of Man, deserted by all divine-spiritual forces, looked into the abyss of death, and out of this experience spoke the poignant words: "My God, my God, why have You forsaken me?"[111]

A total eclipse prevailed in this moment on the hill of Golgotha. Out of the darkness resounded these words, which were simultaneously the words of all humanity, words of the despair of each human "I." The "I" was, to be sure, on the path to freedom, but it felt itself increasingly deserted by the spiritual world.

The people—Roman soldiers, educated persons, and high priests—who gathered around the cross, ridiculed Him: "If You are God's Son, come down from the cross."[112] They shouted, "Let's see if Elias will come and help Him."[113] But help did not come. Nothing came. Only the despairing words resounded in the total stillness of earth and heaven: "My God, my God, why have You forsaken me?"—the words of the human "I" left alone in the face of death, looking at the dying body.

With the resurrection, the opposite occurred. Then the "I" of the Son of Man through the Christ in him, connected with his origin in the spiritual world out of his own power. That power became accessible henceforth as a human force to all people.[114] Through the resurrection, this "I" connected with the highest spiritual world, which is also the world of absolute morality. Out of the force of such morality (which then was taken hold of by the "I" with its human forces provided by freedom), death of the physical body was finally overcome. Thereby, in this body a new life force lit up; a new life force, which was no longer the original power of natural life ether belonging to humanity from the beginning of earth development.

After the Fall, that etheric body had not been able to avert human death; but the new life force was totally capable of conquering death. One can also say that in the resurrection for the first time a phenomenal inversion of world-historic dimensions occurred. Christ Jesus' "I" achieved a connection with the highest spiritual world; his "I" internalized this connection to such an extent that it was placed as a seed, as a possibility for all people to achieve such a connection in future Earth evolution.

From Christ Jesus' resurrection on, this seed lives in each human "I," carrying the potential to achieve a new, free union with the highest spirituality of the world. Out of this connection, the seed can create the moral forces that act in a transforming way, even down to the physical body, so that it overcomes death. In each human "I", this seed waits to be grasped consciously and be brought to completion.

How can this knowledge actually be obtained? Rudolf Steiner describes that quite specifically. To understand the process better, we must turn once more to the development of old Saturn. A person will never understand the nature of the human "I" without being familiar with this oldest evolutionary stage of our cosmos. While we can readily understand today that the physical body originates out of nature that surrounds us, we may ask whether we are able to imagine an environment from which the human "I" can also be understood. Rudolf Steiner responded to this question in this way: If one could take the "I" in its true being and place it before oneself like the external physical body and if one could find the environment on which the "I" depends just as the physical body relies on what can be seen from outside through the eyes (in other words perceived through the senses), then one would come to a world characteristic, to a world tableau, that simultaneously penetrates our outer environment and is invisible in it, still today; this is the world tableau of old Saturn. This means whoever wants to know the "I" in its world must be able to see such a world, to see the old Saturn period."[115] Therefore, the human "I" can be understood only out of the being of old Saturn. As the youngest member in the human being, the "I" is today in the *first* stage of its development; that is, it is in the stage comparable with old Saturn in world evolution.

How can this comparison be useful? By asking what was the most important purpose of the development at that time, we determined that the very first substance that emerged from the cosmic sacrifice of the Thrones was warmth; in the primal beginning, this warmth, was not physical-sensory but a pure spiritual warmth. The entire Saturn development was necessary to transform this warmth gradually into physical-sensory warmth. The way that happened is connected with one of the most burning questions of every thoughtful person; the question that approaches one from science, art, and religion. How can morality and natural science be reconciled? Or to express it differently: how can knowledge and belief, nature and spirit, external and internal be re-connected with one another? Where is this connection between the world of morality and the world of natural laws to be observed in human life?

To answer these questions, there is no other way than to take old Saturn into consideration and to look quite precisely at how the transition, described earlier, from spiritual warmth to physical-sensory warmth, once took place there. If we can grasp that, we obtain an idea of what actually happened during the resurrection on the hill of Golgotha. Of course, it is possible to go on simply believing in the resurrection; but to understand it, a person must know how the moral-spiritual passes over to the physical-sensory, grasps hold of the physical, and fully transforms it. This transformation can occur only through the highest spirituality. Only the "I" that is connected with the whole spirituality of the cosmos receives thereby the inner force necessary to transform matter. Only on this basis can death really be overcome, ensuring the human "I" immortality in the spiritual world.

One can now actually be in a position to understand what happened at the time of Christ and recognize that the seed for this inner development lies, since then, in every person; it waits only until more and more people gradually choose to go the same path microcosmically that Christ once accomplished macrocosmically. The key to understanding these connections correctly lies in observing the transformation of spiritual warmth into physical-sensory warmth as it was archetypically completed on old Saturn.

How was it possible for Christ, from the Baptism in the Jordan, on through the following three years, to unite himself so intensively and existentially with the body of Jesus of Nazareth (down to its mineral component, where the death forces are situated in the human being), that it became possible to overcome death through resurrection? For this, after Christ's "I" had dipped into Jesus' etheric body, Christ passed through all the elements of the etheric body—and then also the physical body—in order to arrive at the solid mineral substances; that is, to the origin of the death forces in the human being (the skeleton). For only out of the realm of death could the resurrection occur.

Now let us look more closely at the steps on this path. First, Christ had to pass through the three kinds of ether of which Jesus of Nazareth's etheric body consisted: the life ether, the sound or chemical ether, and the light ether. As Christ advanced to the last one, the transformation occurred. With that, the next stage, the fourth, was prepared to connect Christ with the warmth ether in Jesus' body, then to accomplish the further decisive step; that is, the transition from spiritual warmth to the physical warmth of the human body.

Then the path went further, through all the basic elements of the physical body. After Christ's divine "I" had taken hold of the physical warmth in Jesus' body, and brought it under control, this process also occurred with the "air body," and later with the "water body" in the bodily sheaths of Jesus of Nazareth. Not until Golgotha was this process completed with the mineral component of the physical body; that is, with the bones of the human skeleton. Therefore, Rudolf Steiner says that Christ was, and remains, the only being on earth who brought the mineral substance of the bones under the power of his "I", and thereby became the Master of Death. "It is indicated to us that through this mastery of the bones, there came into the world a force that really is able to overcome death in physical matter. The bones are the cause of human death because the human body was so created that it incorporated the hard bony mass so that humanity is involved with the mineral element of the earth. Because of that, death became inherent in humanity. It is not without reason that death is represented by the skeleton."[116]

The path to taking hold of the bone structure of Jesus of Nazareth, which was for Christ the greatest conceivable sacrifice, was consummated for the salvation of humankind. This whole process of the ever closer connection of Christ with Jesus' body (as Rudolf Steiner describes it in lectures about the Fifth Gospel) was connected with pain and suffering that would be almost unimaginable for an ordinary person. Christ voluntarily accepted this suffering, as he relinquished, little by little, his divinity, and become completely a human on earth.[117]

When we now try to understand this path of Christ's moving through the etheric and physical sheaths of Jesus of Nazareth—understand it not only from the spatial-spiritual viewpoint, but also from the temporal-spiritual viewpoint—we find the following. From the temporal-spiritual perspective, during the three years of life in the body of Jesus of Nazareth, Christ had made his way from the Earth (life ether), through the old Moon (sound ether), and the old Sun (light ether), to old Saturn (warmth ether). Christ did this to obtain from this primal past of our cosmos, the forces with which he, in the body of Jesus of Nazareth, could achieve the transition from spirit to matter, or from the moral world to the natural world. Thus, for Christ the further path was open from then on to take hold of the physical body. Seen chronologically, this means advancing from the immeasurable distance of old Saturn through the stages of old Sun (air body) and old Moon (water body) to the mortal Earth body of the human; and in this process, mastering the pure mineral substance of the bones and permeating them with the whole power of his "I." Only on the basis of the path described here, penetrating the human skeleton with Christ's "I" force, could the resurrection from the realm of death take place on Easter morning.

From what has been said, it follows that when we want to understand in this way the path of Christ to his Ascension; that is, to the completion of the Mystery of Golgotha; we need the whole content of world evolution back to old Saturn, as Rudolf Steiner describes it in *Occult Science*. Without thoroughly comprehending this world evolution, the secret of the Mystery of Golgotha in its entire significance will remain inaccessible to us forever.

If we succeed in grasping the above-mentioned path of Christ through the entire world evolution, as is possible today by studying spiritual-scientific accounts; then we will also understand and be able to duplicate consciously, what Rudolf Steiner communicated as the present result of Christ's sacrificial path at the Turning Point of Time. In the lecture of December 18, 1920,[118] Steiner described how we can today duplicate the second part of this Christ path—from old Saturn to the present—in a microcosmic way; we can work together with Christ on building the future of our cosmos (including the cosmic conditions of Jupiter, Venus, and Vulcan).

Let us imagine that an individual would consciously give the "I" an inner "jolt," a strong awakening movement, and thereby, would turn toward a high moral ideal. All the while, this individual would neither remain at the level of mere cognition, where an ideal is abstractly grasped in thinking, nor revel in lovely images of desire, but would be really filled in one's whole being with this ideal. If such a person went farther—imbued with the strict training of *Occult Science*, so that thinking would be endowed with the capability for free imagining, and this individual gained a new organ (or center of power)—then this person would be in a position, based on this capability, to kindle the greatest enthusiasm for the chosen ideal. Today, however, people have tragically nearly lost this wonderful capacity for enthusiasm.

Regarding old Saturn, a person especially needs the capacity for enthusiasm to visualize properly the mighty imagination of the Thrones kneeling before the Cherubim, and time emerging from their sacrifice as a community of new beings—the Spirits of Personality. Rudolf Steiner mentions in this connection how all that happened on old Saturn was contained and surrounded externally by the Seraphim: "The Seraphim wrapped it all up in a cloak of enthusiasm that rayed further into the universe."[119] Here we catch sight of the highest spirits, the Seraphim, who cover this occurrence in a mantle of their enthusiasm for a new creation. The Seraphim clothe the entire being of old Saturn in this cosmic enthusiasm. Rudolf Steiner emphasizes especially that enthusiasm is the only capacity in humanity through which we can carry in ourselves an echo of what the highest spirits at the beginning of world creation experienced: limitless enthusiasm for the beginning of a new world.

At the time Rudolf Steiner was alive, people's capability for enthusiasm was quite weak. He gave an example of how much more lively people were at the time of Goethe. To be sure, he doesn't give specific names, but one could very well imagine Novalis, Schelling, the Schlegels, and Tieck, who all, even in their youth, gathered together to listen to a new poem or a philosophic treatise from one another. Then it might have happened that they derived such great enthusiasm for what they heard that if someone today could have eavesdropped on the scene, he might very well have thought all those young people had suddenly become crazy. Enthusiasm lived very strongly in them—even for the most minor of human creations. Every individual creation, no matter how great or small, is worthy of true enthusiasm—a poem, as well as the cosmic creation of old Saturn.

What happens with such enthusiasm? In a certain sense, we all know. It makes a person warm. At first only emotionally, but then when the enthusiasm increases further, the emotional warmth gradually changes at a particular moment to physical warmth. There occurs a real wonder, which bears the rudimentary force of true white magic. Perhaps it is actually the greatest wonder that a person can experience in the physical body, becoming warm not only emotionally but also physically through enthusiasm.

To clarify what is meant here, let us turn to Rudolf Steiner's lecture "The Nature of Art."[120] It is concerned with two women in an icy landscape at sunset. One feels only how cold it is. The other, by contrast, feels the cold, but also experiences the beauty of the surroundings. Through the enthusiasm that fills her soul in this moment, there unfolds a creative, artistic force that becomes in her a new source of warmth, which enables her to resist the external coldness. This is the great wonder, often unnoticed, that we encounter almost daily, especially when we grasp internally with our "I," the corresponding ideal itself.

However, this transformation of emotional to physical warmth goes further. What happens here is described by Rudolf Steiner out of his spiritual research in the lecture of December 18, 1910, which was mentioned earlier. As this process begins in us and gradually becomes stronger, this enthusiasm-warmth stream gradually imbues not only our warmth body, but also continues its activity in our air body. As the process works further, enthusiasm becomes a source of light. Thus, we achieve the step from old Saturn to the inner experience of old Sun.

This process unfolds even further. Through the same force of enthusiasm, now the water body becomes a new source of sonorous musical impulse. New harmonies arise in us that can be active in the chemical composition of the metabolism. Thereby, we experience the condition of old Moon.

Finally, this process also takes hold of the suprasensory part of the solid physical body. Enthusiasm lays the finest seeds of a new life there. Now the present condition of Earth is reached; we can connect here directly with forces emanating from the Mystery of Golgotha, which since then have been working further in the whole Earth evolution. United with the Christ force, which is able to work in a transforming way down to the mineral bone structure, this new life in the human being can also overcome in the future, when it has fully developed, the forces of death down to the physical body. Thus, we can experience and celebrate the inner resurrection. "That is the living force which is able to transform the bones back again; that means to gradually guide what will occur in the future mission of Earth evolution into spirituality."[121] In another lecture, Rudolf Steiner also calls this path, which begins with enthusiasm for everything true, beautiful, and good, the path of will to Christ.[122] Here, the inner aspect of this path has been described.

Today we are not yet able to fully consciously assimilate the threefold activity of the enthusiasm stream described. According to Rudolf Steiner, this process has a decisive significance for the whole cosmos after a person's death. What happens esoterically here on earth in the air body, water body, and even suprasensory parts of the physical body is preserved carefully in the human components: in the astral body, the seed of light; in the etheric body, the seed of tone; and in the suprasensory parts of the physical body (supported by the etheric body), the seed of a new life. When we have become free of physical matter after death, then our astral body begins to shine in the spiritual world; our etheric body begins to sound; and we carry the seed of a new life out into the cosmos, as a witness that the resurrection forces have started to become active in the human. Rudolf Steiner expresses this in the following words: "You sense in this place what life, which is poured out into the world, really is. Where the sources of life reside"—which can also overcome death. "They exist in what stimulates the moral ideals active in the human being. When we allow ourselves today to be illuminated by moral ideals we should tell ourselves that they pour out life, tone, and light, and become capable of *creating worlds*."[123]

What does it mean to be "capable of creating worlds"? When we carry the new light into the spiritual cosmos in this way, we lay in it the seed for future Jupiter. Insofar as our being begins to sound after death, new harmonies of the spheres arise out of this resounding. That music builds the basis for future Venus. When we carry the seeds of new life into the spiritual world, they gradually become the force with which we will create on Vulcan in the far distant future. Out of the resurrection forces that originated in the Mystery of Golgotha, this new cosmic creation will come about. Since Golgotha, these forces are available to every person and can be used for effective inner development.

As in the era of old Saturn, the Spirit Human was prepared by the Thrones, so also in human beings today, this far-distant future of the Vulcan stage exists in embryonic form. If one asks why we are able today, after death, to create out of our own being a basis for the whole world future (for Jupiter, Venus, and Vulcan), one must turn back to the beginning of our cosmic development, to old Saturn, to answer this question. Old Saturn is the cosmic origin of this wonder, wherein spiritual warmth became physical warmth. Here lies the determining key to understanding the Mystery of Golgotha. As on old Saturn, the spirit of matter (as physical warmth) came about for the first time, so it took hold in the Mystery of Golgotha on the path described earlier. Christ passed through the sheaths of Jesus of Nazareth into his physical body, and transformed it into pure spirit, "Spirit Body,"[124] which bore the power to defeat matter, and the death connected with it. Thus, the basis for the whole future evolution of our cosmos, including Vulcan, was created.[125]

We have the possibility to participate, if at first only simply and minimally, in the new creation through the force of enthusiasm in the human soul, which is like a last echo of the mighty jubilation of the Seraphim. (Fyodor Dostoyevsky wrote of this in an artistic premonition.) We can thank Christ's deed on Golgotha that we are able to participate in this creation, and this knowledge must become ever more conscious. The "I" of the Son of Man, the god who became man, internalized the entire morality or spirituality of the world, and thereby prepared humanity for the possibility of reaching the goals of Jupiter, Venus, and Vulcan in the future. All of that lives in us today. But we can grasp this only from our individual "I"s, through freedom; we must give ourselves this "jolt" toward the spiritual world, and toward the new ideals that flow to us through spiritual science. In this regard, Rudolf Steiner says: "When we consider spiritual science as a source of the moral, then we can be most enthusiastic for what is moral, which works out of spiritual-scientific knowledge, but is at the same time the source of the ethical in the higher sense."[126] Then we achieve through spiritual science the "resurrection forces"[127] because we live in their stream and will be creative microcosmically in the same way Christ Jesus was macrocosmically creative, by creating the resurrected body at the Turning Point of Time.

The possibility for this creative transformation has been given objectively to human beings since time of Christ. So this path can be followed consciously; the decisive transition from moral to natural, and back from natural to moral, must be really understood. For this, we need the complete contents of *An Outline of Occult Science*, in which the wonder of transforming the spiritual into the physical on old Saturn, and the physical back to the spiritual in the Mystery of Golgotha, is described. The cosmic dimension of this event was then turned by Christ into a new, purely human capability. It will unfold in us when we are able to take up the stream of the resurrection forces in ourselves. For only the resurrection and its consequences lead us to the future Jupiter, Venus, and Vulcan, and, thereby, to the last goal of the entire world evolution. This world perspective can be achieved only when humanity takes up the Christ impulse in freedom; only when humanity creates the will to allow the spiritual seeds that were planted through the Mystery of Golgotha to arise in the individual "I" of all human souls.

This is the broad view of *An Outline of Occult Science*. Without this book, the Mystery of Golgotha in its cosmic dimension would remain unintelligible for people. All seven chapters of the book are necessary for complete understanding of the reality of the resurrection so that a person can learn out of the free "I" to act, ever more, in the sense of the resurrection impulse.

*

Returning now to the third aspect of Steiner's presentation of old Saturn, we can make a further discovery on the basis of what has been said. One relives the experience in question here, more strongly when one, as a non-German, strives to learn the German language. This need not be in a school or university, but simply for oneself, just to learn out of the necessity of reading Rudolf Steiner's words in the original. If a person has read *Occult Science* several times in translation, and later reads it in German, then through this venture (by no means an easy one), one discovers the following.

By studying *An Outline of Occult Science*, one acquires not only the German language in general, and Rudolf Steiner's specific expressions, but also something quite different. During the process of reflecting on that experience and then reading the book again, it is revealed that the language in the book is, in reality, a totally new and quite individual language. I am firmly convinced that out of all of Rudolf Steiner's works, a person can learn this special language best by studying *Occult Science.* I venture to say that this language conforms, above all, with the account of world evolution from old Saturn to Vulcan, as it is described in this book. A person learns thereby not only to speak another language, but at the same time, with its help, to understand increasingly the whole world and humanity in their earthly and cosmic development. Now one no longer goes blindly through the world, but can be certain through this understanding. A person comes into real spiritual communication with the whole cosmos and all of its beings. If one accomplishes this through personal experience, then one knows what this new language actually means. Every person who learns the quite special language in *Occult Science* can come to this decisive experience. (This is also possible when one reads it in another language.)

Rudolf Steiner explains it this way. "With the language—even if it seems to be very abstract—through which we hear about Saturn, Sun, Moon, and Earth ... and about various other secrets of evolution, through this so-called doctrine, we acquire a language in ourselves into which we can pour the questions we want to pose to the spiritual world. When we learn in our souls to speak properly in the language of this spiritual life, then ... it will come about that Christ stands by us and gives answers."[128] Continuing, he says, "Therefore, we should not seek mere training, but we should look for a language to acquire spiritual science and wait until we find the questions in this language that we may pose to Christ. He will answer; yes, He *will* answer! "—that is the singular Christ language of the present. [ibid., italics by Rudolf Steiner.] We find the language of Christ where human thinking rises to imagination and unites with it so intensively and consciously that, with time, it begins to speak in one's own soul.

At first, perhaps a person will find this language is difficult to learn. But it must be so; it is not a simple, customary language, but that of Christ. Also, imaginations of world evolution carried in thought are not easy to understand, but they show us how Christ himself sees and guides the entire evolutionary process. It is the language of the spiritual world, which comes about in the light of the Mystery of Golgotha, and which encompasses equally both the world on this side and the world on the other side of the threshold. What *archetypically* occurred in the Mystery of Golgotha will become a new capability with which, and from which, we can learn this Christ language today.

*

Let us now try to summarize the whole process. On the basis of what has been said, a person begins to see the way in which *An Outline of Occult Science* is a Christian book. A person experiences how this book develops cognition further, and then enlivens it; how in this thinking, imaginations start to stream like the blood streams in the body. Through study, we approach increasingly nearer to Christ, until we actually meet him. But the new capabilities achieved in this way can unfold further. If, despite all difficulties, a person recognizes and learns in this book the new language of Christ, then a higher, inspirational element is introduced. Now we are also able to hear Christ's answer to the questions we pose to him. When we follow the path of enthusiasm that has been described for all that is beautiful, true, and good in the world, and thereby we gradually deepen the force of enthusiasm through spiritual science, then we will one day realize how this path has its origin in the Mystery of Golgotha; or more precisely stated, has its origin on Easter morning, in a world jubilant about the beginning of a new creation.

Thus, we grasp through our engagement with *Occult Science* a new *thinking* that leads to true imaginations; we learn a new *language* with which we can hear Christ's words; and we tread a *path* that connects us with the spiritual world in a new and conscious way.

Therein lie the three archetypal qualities of a Christianized "I," which can be comprehended through this book: how an "I" that is conscious of its connection to Christ thinks, how it speaks, and how it finds the path to the source of a new creation.

As the Christ figure is found in the center of the whole universe, so the Christianization of the human "I" stands in the center of human evolution. Therein exists today the message of the modern science of the Grail, which is hidden in the secret of the Mystery of Golgotha, and is thus the nucleus of the entire world evolution from old Saturn to future Vulcan. Through intensive work with *An Outline of Occult Science*, one can make this secret manifest. This is the present path to Christ.

2.
The First Goetheanum and Its Christological Foundations

Preface by Sergei O. Prokofieff

PETER SELG

Rudolf Steiner and the Building of the First Goetheanum

SERGEI O. PROKOFIEFF

The Nature of the First Goetheanum and the Mystery of Golgotha

Johannes Building, March 1914

Preface

RUDOLF STEINER WROTE in the book *An Outline of Occult Science* that with the Johannes Building—later renamed the Goetheanum—Anthroposophy appeared visible in its entirety.

The building was conceptualized by Steiner as an unparalleled synthesis of the arts. It was realized, with many helping hands of both artists and lay people, not in symbolic forms but as a purely artistic composition.

In ancient times the master-builder Hiram called many different peoples together to construct the great Hebrew mystery temple in Jerusalem. In a similar way, Steiner gathered together people in Dornach, Switzerland, during the portentous time of the First World War. People came from seventeen countries (including countries that were fighting as enemies in the war), to work in freedom and love out of the source of esoteric Christianity, to build collectively an edifice for the spiritual life of the future.

As "House of the Word," the first Goetheanum was a revelation in the present of the creative Logos forces working through the building's forms and colors. It would become a place where, in the sense of the "new Christian mysteries," human beings could learn to know and experience themselves in connection with the spiritual cosmos. The building was an effective answer to the question of what is the true being of humanity.

Reproduced here (in slightly edited form) are the two lectures that Peter Selg and I gave on the occasion of the conference "The Christological Foundations of the First Goetheanum" at Ascension 2009 in Dornach.

This was the third of four conferences pertaining to the Christological foundations of Rudolf Steiner's life and work. The first (in 2007) was dedicated to the book *The Philosophy of Spiritual Activity [The Philosophy of Freedom]*. The following year, a conference was held focusing on the book *An Outline of Occult Science*. In 2010, this series will be completed with the conference entitled "The Christological Foundations of the Christmas Conference of 1923–1924."

SERGEI O. PROKOFIEFF

Goetheanum, Dornach
September 2009

Rudolf Steiner and the Building of the First Goetheanum

PETER SELG

Few of life's fairy tales have greater significance than the story of this building—and the building itself.

—CHRISTIAN MORGENSTERN[1]

Dear Friends,

In his biography about Ehrenfried Pfeiffer, Alla Selawry wrote concerning Pfeiffer's connection to the first Goetheanum:

> Pfeiffer loved this building, which conveyed to him an unearthly beauty and harmony. Its architecture and the sculptural form of the interior space, the cupola paintings, and the special glass windows that cast their transparent lights and shadows on the carved wooden pillars speak directly to people and awaken new kinds of forces. They open an effectual suprasensory spiritual world. Meditatively observed, they serve to train the imagination. The color-flushed walls do not screen the surroundings, they offer a harmonious soul world. The building reveals the periphery and unites the human psyche with the world spirit. At the same time, the building incorporates an essential aspect of Rudolf Steiner's being. In this monument, his entire life work, art, philosophy, and spiritual science become alive.[2]

The first Goetheanum, according to Alla Selawry, *incorporated* an essential aspect of Rudolf Steiner's being; that is, his work as well as his life. Dr. Ita Wegman remarked about the connection between Rudolf Steiner and the vital secret of the Dornach building in an article that appeared a few months after his death:

> A mystery exists in his being both the constructor of the artwork and Rudolf Steiner! How does one produce a work of art? The god in him built geometrically, out of etheric substances, a building around him; and he stood in the middle of this edifice. Then he needed only to erect

> this artwork externally, out of material substance, and it was completed on the physical plane. The "Word" shapes the architectural contours etherically, so that physical forms result from these geometric-etheric shapes and are produced artistically in physical matter. This is how the Goetheanum arose out of Rudolf Steiner. His Word, which heralded Anthroposophy, built the Goetheanum etherically: Rudolf Steiner's concentrated Word and his own etheric body were conjoined with the artwork, were inseparably connected with it.[3]

Rudolf Steiner was without doubt the first and best worker for Anthroposophy. By creating the Goetheanum, he wanted to erect a real *home* for it—and at the same time to build a home for people who seek Anthroposophy on earth. Rudolf Steiner spoke about "constructing for the anthroposophical cause,"[4] a "veritable building;"[5] and he applied himself completely to its achievement. The Goetheanum, according to Ita Wegman, originated *out of* Rudolf Steiner; out of his being, his "Word," through the commitment of his life forces; from the sphere of his imaginative forces, his "devotion body."

Rudolf Steiner's "Word," which "heralded Anthroposophy," did not belong to him personally in the sense of ownership or possession; nor was it the bearer of his personal opinion. Rather, Rudolf Steiner served the "Word" denoted by Wegman. He once said that the Goetheanum building in all its forms is *"an incorporation of the spiritual being to whom we are attached."*[6] When Louis Werbeck thanked Steiner as the initiator of the Christmas Conference, Steiner resisted to a certain extent and directed his glance to the "spiritual being" in whose service he worked with and for the Goetheanum. In answering Werbeck, he said:

> But, my dear friend, what occurred here [during the Christmas Conference], I know it, I may say it, because it is said in full responsibility considering the spirit who is,

> should be, and will be there, the Spirit of the Goetheanum. I have allowed myself to speak in his name during these days about many things that might not have been presented so strongly if it were not to honor the Spirit of the Goetheanum, invoking the good Spirit of the Goetheanum. So allow me to accept these thanks in the name of the Spirit of the Goetheanum, for whom we wish to act, strive, and work in the world.[7]

Rudolf Steiner did not refuse, but accepted Louis Werbeck's thanks. However, rather than attributing the gratitude to himself, he received it vicariously "in the Spirit of the Goetheanum's name, for whom we wish to act, strive, and work in the world." Rudolf Steiner represented the intentions of this Spirit and was its "mediator." This included representing and mediating in the difficult times and situations that arose in the course of the building process. About his successful work with Edith Maryon on the Group sculpture (the Representative of Humanity) in the Goetheanum, Rudolf Steiner said in retrospect: "What really happened there? It was not a matter of doing something together so that just any cooperative result was achieved. We could accomplish the work only in the way I had to do it; *as it had to be accomplished according to the intentions I had to represent.*"[8]

This spiritual law of "coming into existence" was engraved in the Dornach Goetheanum building; the spiritual law provided the special signature and consecration of the building; its focus and its brisance—until the hour of its destruction, its death, and beyond. The following discussion covers some motives and internal incidents of this development, which belong to the fateful history of Anthroposophy in the twentieth century.

*

The initiative for constructing a central building for Anthroposophy and for creating its corresponding form did not emanate from Rudolf Steiner, although he had previously stressed the importance of artistic creation for the future of civilization. Rudolf Steiner started working with Marie von Sivers in 1902 on the arts of speech formation (*Sprachgestaltung*) and recitation, and wrote on November 25, 1905, in a letter to her:

> This should be our ideal: to create *forms* as the expression of inner life. For in a time when we cannot observe the creation of forms, spirit must necessarily vaporize itself into insubstantial abstraction, and truth must be confronted with the purely tenuous sense of vacuous material aggregation. When people really are able to understand forms—for example, the birth of the soul out of the Sistine Madonna's ether clouds—for them, there will soon no longer be anything material that is devoid of spirit.[9]

At the Theosophical Society's Whitsun Congress in Munich during 1907, Rudolf Steiner was responsible for the artistic arrangement, the interior decoration of the hall, and numerous other elements whose significance he stressed emphatically.[10] In a report about this event, he said in Berlin: "One can effectively *build* theosophy; one can construct it architectonically, with regard to education and the social question.[11] The "building" of spiritual science was understood not as the construction of a house (or "building"), but as a cultural effect. Again at the Christmas Conference of 1923–24, following the mantra spoken while "laying the foundation stone" of the General Anthroposophical Society, Rudolf Steiner said: "The building shall be erected on this foundation stone, whose single blocks will be the work accomplished in all our groups by individuals outside in the wide world."[12]

An offer was made immediately at the 1907 Munich Congress to endow the spiritual-scientific teacher with his own building; or rather, to build a "temple" for his "Word." Rudolf Steiner reacted cautiously; "temple building" was only tentatively included in Anthroposophy's functional intentions for the twentieth century. Marie Steiner-von Sivers wrote: "Rudolf Steiner ... resisted this [request for "temple building"]. He imagined a building for humanity; a House of the Word, which should serve the science of the spirit."[13] A year and a half later, after inaugurating plans for the first Goetheanum, Rudolf Steiner stated explicitly:

> The entire building idea, the whole Dornach edifice will not be a temple, but a place in which people come together to receive suprasensible knowledge.[14]

After the destruction of the building on New Year's Eve 1922, Rudolf Steiner wrote in retrospect:

> To one who entered through the main portal, the entirety should have said in an artistic way: "Know the true being of human nature." Thus, we wanted to create the building to be a home of knowledge, not a temple.[15]

And so, from the beginning, Rudolf Steiner strove for a "home of knowledge," a place that would serve the "science of the spirit"—a real *academy*. Based on suprasensible knowledge gained through research and teaching, it would have an effect on civilization. The Munich friends' theater building projects, conceived to satisfy the requirements of the mystery dramas, by no means went far enough for him. The future academy—as a unifying place of science, art, and religion—should enable new dramatic art, but this would not be its only, or most urgent, goal. In one of the early discussions concerning the Munich building plans, Rudolf Steiner said he would rather establish a bank than construct a theater[16]—"one can build it [spiritual science] architectonically, with regard to education and the social question..."

The Munich initiative group that formed a core for a "Johannes building" clung unswervingly to their agenda, but extended it in the directions of Rudolf Steiner's aim. (The building received its exotic name from the artist "Johannes Thomasius," a central figure in the mystery dramas.) The "Johannes Building Association" was formed in April 1911. The following October they expressed in a letter to Theosophical Society members:

> The idea of an academy for spiritual science is the obvious outcome of receiving the treasure of spiritual knowledge appropriate for out time. It is an unavoidable conclusion.[17]

At the initiation of the Stuttgart branch house in November 1911, Marie von Sivers also emphasized that despite local member buildings, one should not lose sight of the real goal: constructing an *academy for spiritual science.*[18]

*

In the context of historically representing the development and objective of the first Goetheanum, Rudolf Steiner wrote at the beginning of 1923, shortly after the building's destruction:

> I considered myself only as a person commissioned by those responsible for the building's purpose. I believed I should concentrate my forces on developing the internal spiritual anthroposophical work, and gratefully accepted the initiative of creating its own place of activity. However, in the moment in which the initiative approached its realization, for me the artistic arrangement was a matter of inner spiritual work. I had to devote myself to this creation.[19]

Indeed, Rudolf Steiner devoted himself to the "artistic arrangement" of the building with love, as "the initiative approached its realization." It was an exceptional work process, an occurrence of external as well as "internal spiritual work," from which the manner of the necessary "arrangement," or rather, the artistic design to be created, could emerge. Repeatedly, Rudolf Steiner showed that the building concept could occur only in executing the work; in the artistic process; in "fulfilling creation." This he provided completely, despite his limited time, considering the given conditions, possibilities, and limitations.

> When something must be tackled, then it must be undertaken as well as a person is able at that point of time. When one performs such an objective, one learns to know the real laws of one's existence.[20]

Rudolf Steiner actually took charge of the Dornach construction project in 1913. He conceptualized the entire building; personally selected the spot on the property for the foundation stone; held the ground-breaking ceremony; and three days later completed laying the foundation stone "when Mercury appeared in Libra as evening star."[21] Rudolf Steiner had deliberated deeply on the decision to build, as well on as his connection with the Munich initiative; but he agreed in the end. Later, he said the building must be "tackled"; it was the right time, and it was desired by the spiritual powers. In 1917 in Berlin, Rudolf Steiner described how in the future it will be increasingly necessary to consult the spiritual world, particularly the Christ being himself, when we are faced with important decisions, especially about establishing something new. Steiner said:

> ... The time will come with Christ's appearance, with Christ's existence, when people will learn to consult Christ not only for their souls, but for what they want to establish here on earth through their immortality. Christ is not only a ruler of humanity, he is a human brother who wants to be asked, especially in future times, about all the details of life. By contrast, today people simply put into motion what they want to establish. Today actions are carried out for which people seem to be a long way

> from putting the question to Christ. When something occurs today, we must ask ourselves who poses the question, what does Christ Jesus say about that? Who asks? Many people say they do; but it would be blasphemous to believe they ask; to believe that in the form it is presented today, the question really is addressed to Christ. Yet the time must come, it is not far off, when for what they want to establish, immortal human souls will place before Christ the question: shall it happen or not? When human souls see Christ near them as a loving companion in the details of life, they receive not only comfort and power from the Christ being, but also information about what should happen. Christ-Jesus' realm is not of this world but it must be active in this world, and people must be the tools of this realm that is not of the earth. From this point of view, we must observe today how rarely the question is posed that must be asked of Christ for individual deeds and events. However, humanity must learn to consult Christ.[22]

There are many indications that, regarding construction, Rudolf Steiner asked the Christ-Being the momentous question: "Shall it happen or not?" And received an affirmative answer. Therefore, specific efforts could be begun in Dornach. The day for laying the foundation stone arrived.

Steiner gave a mighty speech, consciously and emphatically invoking the hierarchies and describing the spiritual misery of the time in which the building would be erected.[23] Rudolf Steiner recited the "cosmic Lord's Prayer" from the Fifth Gospel for the first time in the course of his address. Then he departed for Norway to present lectures about this new testimony of the time of Christ. According to Andrei Bely, his presentations about the Fifth Gospel[24] formed the spiritual sheaths of the newly inaugurated building. Even after his return from Norway, Rudolf Steiner continued these lectures in various German cities. Later

Christoph Lindenberg wrote, fittingly, about the Christological connection of the lectures and the building.

> The developing building was veiled in the spiritual atmosphere of a new Christian revelation. Whenever Rudolf Steiner returned to Dornach, he had once again "in the outside world" borne witness to the Christ deed and led people out of their depths to a new experience. ... Through Rudolf Steiner's interaction with the building, there emerged in the structure's periphery a supernal landscape destined to determine its atmosphere and nourish it in the spiritual.[25]

The activity of laying the foundation stone encompassed a serious pledge: "that we on this day, in which we feel our souls united with what we have placed symbolically into the earth, engage ourselves in what we correctly perceive as humanity's spiritual stream of evolution."[26] The "spiritual stream of evolution" about which Rudolf Steiner spoke in this way was inherently connected with the Fifth Gospel and the future activity of the Christ impulse. The connection included also the preparation for Christ's reappearance in the etheric[27] and the urgently needed spiritualization of every area of human civilization in the age of technical materialism. The building begun in Dornach on September 20, 1913, the intended "Free Academy for Spiritual Science," was to provide this development, and to function in a correct way (meaning a contemporary way) to imbue culture with Christian principles in the sense of Michael. When Rudolf Steiner said in London on May 2, 1914, "Michael can give us a new spiritual light,"[28] the cupolas of the academy had already been built in Dornach.

The building, and the decision ventured for it, were a milestone. One day before laying the foundation stone, Rudolf Steiner wrote to Alexander von Bernus: "... For me this means, in an occult sense, a responsibility that weighs heavily on my soul."[29] In laying the foundation stone, Rudolf Steiner referred to the necessity of continuing to battle in a great spiritual fight, "which is a fight imbued with the fire of love."[30] Two days later, he indicated in Basel for the first time that the Dornach building would be a central "irritant and annoyance" for the enemies of Anthroposophy.[31] Rudolf Steiner had united his existence and task with the destiny of the building; in taking over responsibility for it, he inseparably involved the sphere of his life forces.

*

On September 20, 1913, all members of the Anthroposophical Society looked to Dornach. All branches were punctually informed in their respective towns and urged to accompany the process of laying the foundation stone with concentrated attention on that moment "when after a two-thousand-year deprivation, once again, an earthly mystery center was dedicated," as Michael Bauer wrote to his friend Christian Morgenstern.[32] At the beginning of 1914, half a year later, many young members and friends traveled to Dornach in order—for a shorter or longer period—to help. Among them were the Russian artists Andrei Bely, Assja Turgenieff, and Margarita Woloschin.

Rudolf Steiner had repeatedly emphasized that constructing the "Johannes Building" was exceedingly urgent, and spoke on various occasions about the necessity of completion by August 1914. Early in 1914, from Dornach and other towns in the surrounding region, 250 people were already working on the building, its intended form becoming more visible from week to week. The Russian painter Margarita Woloschin wrote about her arrival and joyous local reception (by Max Wolfhügel and Hans Strauss).

> They greeted me in the same way blessed spirits might welcome a newly arrived soul in paradise.[33]

Then the collaboration of the newcomers, received in this way, began. Shortly afterwards Woloschin noted in her diary:

> Should one jot down an entry now, or should what one experiences here remain in the soul, as a seed for the future? What is now worked into wood will disappear after some decades like these diary pages; and yet the secret of future centuries is concealed in what happens here.[34]

Margarita Woloschin reflected about the difference in the written notations and artistic *processes*, the "what happens here." Although living in anticipation of an ephemeral monument, she experienced in the process of work an element of the future, a "secret of future centuries." Essentially, stability was not the completed work; rather, it would be the activity of having brought the work into being; the devotion and cooperation of the individuals; the "building of an anthroposophical cause"; not the structure, but the constructing itself, as work in a community.

*

During this construction work Rudolf Steiner appeared absolutely present at the scene of action. His appearance on the construction site came as a surprise to many old and young anthroposophists. One knew him from lecture halls, from his books, from the inner scope of the esoteric school, from esoteric-cultural initiatives, as well as from personal conversations. Now, however, one saw him active in building, in practical work, and in all kinds of weather. "...in the rain in high boots, on hot days in sandals, a white work coat covering his street clothes, greeting people graciously as he hurried by, holding a sketchbook, a plasticine model in his hand." (Assja Turgenieff)[35]

Rudolf Steiner was seen not only "hurrying by;" one met him also at work, as early as 1914, carving—competently, devotedly, and without pause.

> Every half hour we had to take a break, had raw fingers; and it looked as though a mouse had gnawed on the wood. However, he stood for hours on his box, calmly and rhythmically hitting the chisel, looking briefly from time to time at the little cast plasticine model. As though in conversation with the wood or eavesdropping on what was taking place he stood there entirely engrossed in work with the form progressively being pared out of the massive wood. (Assja Turgenieff)[36]

Absolute interest in the work and acting in its service could be experienced in Rudolf Steiner's exemplary, orientation to the future. "He stood there entirely engrossed in work..." Without doubt, Rudolf Steiner personally lived, in a traditional Christian sense, what he had developed many years before in his lectures about the "fundamental social law" and the significance of human work.[37]

He later said, in his memorial speech for Edith Maryon, "See, my dear friends, it is a question of an entirely new interest arising: enthusiasm for the task itself. Such people are preoccupied only in the work, and nothing more than achieving it. Whether people are in agreement or not, the job must be done; the work must be possible."[38]

The activity in Dornach was important; it served a great goal. It went far beyond the Anthroposophical Society and existed in the "signs of the times," in what the Time Spirit supported and expected. People had to contribute their individual capabilities; however, personal characteristics receded in view of what was to be objectively performed through the individual and the community. "That the work was there: that was your goal," Rudolf Steiner wrote about Edith Maryon and her exemplary attitude.[39]

Much could be learned, even in an artistic sense, from Rudolf Steiner's way of working. Margarita Woloschin (born Sabaschnikov) recorded in her diary:

> Doctor Steiner works on the capitals very attentively, very carefully. He holds the chisel in his hand and hits it lightly with the hammer. In concentration and gratification he appears to listen inwardly to something beautiful. After awhile he says, "Think about the surfaces; the edges will occur by themselves, one must not begin with them; one should not know in advance how the edges will appear. You must be curious about the edges; not about *what* kind of edge will occur, but *how* it emerges. Being curious can be very helpful. A person must think that one doesn't make a boot, but a foot. The form should emanate from the inside out through its own power. ... Think about the flowers, study the plants! The etheric forms of people and animals are corrupt; in plants they are pure. When you study flowers, the movement of their surfaces in space, then you will be able to understand the etheric body."
>
> As we departed he asked: "Frau Sabaschnikow, can you live into these forms?" "Gradually," I answered, not wanting to express that I had long perceived these shapes as something related to the depths of the soul. "Oh, they will certainly please you when you sense them within you." And he repeated: "One must think about the surfaces, sense the flowers in space."[40]

In his book of collected poetry *Contemplation*, Christian Morgenstern published this verse in 1910:

> Don't say: this cannot be imagined,
> Cannot be conceived! One day
> A person receives definite impulses
> And descends to the sources.[41]

Even years before, Rainer Maria Rilke wrote in his *Book of Hours*:

We are workers, apprentices, journeymen, masters,
We build you, you towering nave,
Sometimes there comes to us a serious wayfarer,
Mingles genially with our hundred artisans,
And shows us, trembling, a new skill.[42]

*

Rudolf Steiner not only worked in an exemplary way on the Dornach building, as a "serious wayfarer," from the "sources" of artistic activity, and demonstrated new "skills,"[43] he also gave lectures about the architectural ideas of the building. These briefings in the carpentry shop, which dealt with the building's special structural design questions, began in June 1914. They were, according to Marie Steiner, an "introduction into the workshop of his artistic spirit."[44] The lectures took place under makeshift conditions, in the building's work atmosphere. Chairs were carried into the workshop for the older members; all the other listeners took their places on woodworkers' benches and boxes, on piles of boards, and on the ground. The sister of Assja Turgenieff, Natalie Turgenieff-Pozzo, who also came to Dornach as a volunteer in her youth, wrote:

> We liked the unusual lecture atmosphere: white boards and colorful clothes. Dr. Steiner enters, he looks around, because he is never indifferent to the surroundings. He sees the color combinations, observes the groups of people, and sends greetings in all directions. He notices everything, the auditorium amuses him. These lectures were like a joyful science, light and active. From afar one often took him to be a young person.[45]

Rudolf Steiner spoke about spatial forms, pillars, and ornaments; about aesthetic laws of form and colors. On June 17, during the dedication of the glass studio, he also elaborated on the inner attitude for work on the building; on the necessary "feeling for work." He said:

> ... I believe that a good, healthy feeling is when we continually sustain the perception of not being equal to the task through all of our activity. For only in this way will we attain the highest achievements possible. We will start to reveal our spiritual-scientific knowledge in the artistic way possible in our time, and with our means, by realizing that we are hardly equal to the actual task. It is my opinion that every time we enter our construction site we should feel as though surrounded by an aura that inspires us to do our best with our ample powers and abilities. For in view of what should be accomplished you cannot do enough; even if you do your best it is by far not enough.
>
> Essentially, an indefinite feeling, a vague premonition that a great task looms about us, should motivate us upon entering this construction site.[46]

The building project was immense, and the task of "envisioning" new forms and "creating" them physically was more than complicated. The co-workers' attitude, their internal conviction, was important. Failure occurred when a person indulged either in artistic pride or in resignation: over-estimation of self or despair. Ideally, the soul needed to be centered between the poles of temptation and failure. The "healthy perception of not being equal to the task" connected with the individual's maximum initiative. Application of this initiative could advance to become the Christian ethic of the building—in its erection and later activity as "Free Academy for Spiritual Science." Rudolf Steiner spoke about the "necessary development beyond everything personal," and called the edifice an "educational means beyond everything personal."[47] Achieving the high ideal of the "Johannes Building" required an appropriate inner mental attitude. At the same time, the architecture itself was instructive to the individuals; it was a "means of educating" the spiritual community and its members.

*

Rudolf Steiner continually visited the artists who were cooperating on the building in their studios, displayed interest for the individually accomplished work, and encouraged people to continue their efforts. His interest and advice were important and strengthening. "After such discussions, every one of them was deeply convinced he or she was the only one who understood the Doctor and worked as he wished" (Assja Turgenieff).[48] All the while, Steiner left the artists free. He was not the "owner," and his co-workers were not "laborers." They did not merely carried out his ideas, his specifications, for creation; rather, they were themselves free, creative individuals, "friends" in the Christian sense (John 15:15). Margarita Woloschin wrote about an unexpected visit by Rudolf Steiner to her studio in November 1914.

> He appeared suddenly as if from behind my back. "Can you paint this?" He held a drawing of the Egyptian initiate with an angel and an archangel above him. I asked: "Doctor, how shall I paint it?" He simply replied: "I want you to remain quite free."[49]

Replying to Margarita Woloschin's requests, Steiner ardently discussed with her how to implement the theme artistically; if she hadn't had the "I" presence to ask, this explanation would not have been forthcoming. In this way, Steiner "gave the artists their heads," and granted them full freedom, knowing well this freedom for creating could be misused, which often happened. He interfered in undesirable developments only sporadically. In a report by Assja Turgenieff, the following situation can be taken as an example.

> Among us it was customary to refer to the Glass House ... as the "House of Justice" until Dr. Steiner strictly resisted it. In the future, people would think the Glass House was not his work—the most dangerous symptoms were contained in such things: in the future the name Rudolf Steiner would (like Shakespeare) be made into a general term for many individualities in order to extinguish his personality—we have often heard this statement from him.[50]

The situation in the Glass House was complicated, and Assja Turgenieff withdrew from it, even though Rudolf Steiner had chosen her for the glass work. The people working there had only a very limited understanding of the "intentions" Steiner "had to represent." They considered his sketches simply as "stimulations" for their artistic freedom, their own style of interpretation, and design abilities. Steiner didn't intervene, and so Assja Turgenieff sought different work on the building and finally became involved assisting with the Group sculpture.

*

Rudolf Steiner worked further with great intensity. The necessity "of finding ideas for the building that brought him in the right way into the spiritual world," determined his activity and its content and goal. "Here everything is a unity, everything lives, and everything is concretely received from the spiritual world," he said to Margarita Woloschin, about the construction site.[51] The actual "receiving," however, was achieved in the process of the physical work: the moving, the seeking and finding, with many unexpected departures ("By performing such an action one really learns to know the actual laws of one's own being ...").

In a later lecture, Steiner spoke about his sculpture at the foot of the stairs in the Goetheanum:

> You can believe it or not, but it is true. I believe when a one ascends and enters the auditorium, one must have a specific experience. I tell myself that the person who goes up there must have the sensation that "There inside, I will be secure in my soul; there is tranquility of soul, to receive the highest truths to which a person initially can strive." Out of this conviction, I obtained the arrangement of three semi-circular channels in three consecutive perpendicular spaces. If one goes up these stairs, one can obtain this feeling of tranquility. It is not simulated—certainly not—but only afterwards, I remembered that the three semi-circular canals in the ear also correspond to these three consecutive chambers.

In this way, the building arose in its form, hand in hand with the emergence of eurythmy. Rudolf Steiner said in retrospect, "In all probability eurythmy could not have been found without the work on the building."[53] In another place he wrote from the opposite perspective: "I know I have created the form of the building out of the sentient soul condition from which eurythmy images also come to me."[54]

Steiner said of the building that the "actual laws of its being" were initially found in the process, in the actual implementation of plans, with its many inflections and developments. These developments were not predictable, even for Steiner; they stemmed from the work itself, the exterior and interior work. Many different people participated in this work—not only in manifesting the forms that had already been found, but also in the process of discovery. Once, Steiner sought out in the playground and thanked a Stuttgart Waldorf School student whose handwork forms had stimulated him to solve a building task.[55]

Steiner spoke repeatedly about the help he received from another child, Theo Faiss, who died at an early age in Dornach because of a tragic accident on October 7, 1914.[56] At the beginning of 1915, three months after the child's death, Steiner reported about the building's changed "aura," in which the imaginative forces of the deceased child lived. Steiner spoke about helping forces, inspirational forces, resulting from turning his attention to the etheric body of the deceased child. These forces, connected with the structure's aura, helped him to discover "ideas" that positioned the building "in the spiritual world in the right way."

As well as Theo Faiss, other anthroposophical friends of the building also went unexpectedly into the spiritual world. Among those who belonged to the nucleus of those who took initiative for the building was Sophie Stinde, who died unexpectedly in November 1915. Rudolf Steiner worked with the support of these deceased people, with their assistance and help, in overcoming the gulf that divides the living from the dead. He described this support in various lectures as a social cooperation beyond the threshold of death, and as being essential in this epoch, which dawns with Christ's reappearance in the etheric. Steiner achieved this coming of Christ in his work; he realized it in anticipation and preparation. Future Christianity was part of the mystery temple in regard to the site being created; in regard to the content and goal of its artistic representation and spiritual teaching. But more than that, future Christianity actually lived in the construction process, in its evolution. The structure was made possible with the aid of sacrificial contributions, with the help of a new social milieu. This sacrifice comprised the donation of material goods and monies, and even more meaningful, the contribution of the spiritual world, including the contributions of the deceased individualities whose destinies were connected with the Anthroposophical Movement. "We thank our dead friends, that they are among us; and that we are united with their forces, which can perform work for the spiritual cosmic culture incumbent upon us" (Rudolf Steiner).[57]

*

Many of the volunteers and artists who came to Dornach in early 1914 were young, and they knew little at first about all of these processes. They experienced pleasure from the new art forms and the beginning of mutual creative work, and joy from sharing a common spirit and from Steiner's working presence at the building, whose form developed from week to week. Individual experiences were different; nevertheless, a stratum of destiny was touched with their involvement in collaborating on anthroposophical work, in particular, their depth of will. Steiner said at the dedication of the Glass House that the construction site should be entered with a certain inner attitude. "Something like an indefinite feeling, like a general premonition, that a great task hovers over us, should enliven us when entering this construction site." Assja Turgenieff wrote in her recollections:

> A strange atmosphere often overcame one on this hill. It was all so new, so young, pointing so far into the future; and yet one encountered places that appeared as familiar as old friends and relatives: a few scaffolding bars, a ladder alongside, heaps of sand sacks, wheelbarrows, a chalk pit with its scoop ... Where have I already seen that? It was as though images from past times, separated by a thin layer of air, reflected in the present ... or was there a curtain, which one only needed to draw aside a little, and quite different impressions would appear? Great sublime structures from old and ancient times! We stood around him many times, working together on the great project. In nightly dreams one or another of these images became more tangible.[58]

Rudolf Steiner hoped for a corresponding experience in the social-forming force. The co-workers in Dornach could become a community in peace and freedom, provided they knew the deeper reason for being there; in the sense of the mystery dramas, the reason in respect to destiny. The "building of the anthroposophical cause" was the work of a community; of "our work,"

Steiner said repeatedly. It must be possible to create unified work through harmonious efforts together, he said, as he handed the first sketches for the small cupola to Margarita Woloschin and her colleagues in late autumn 1914.

At this time, the World War I had already begun. The building was by no means finished when the war began on August 1, 1914. For years, Steiner had spoken about this threatening war and the coming catastrophe, not as a prophet, but to foster other developments in the consciousness of the operative forces. Both the building and its community existed in connection with gearing up for peace. On June 17, six weeks before the war started, Steiner said at the dedication of the Glass Studio:

> When the ideas of such art works find successors in culture, then the people who go through the doors of such artistic works and become impressed by what is expressed in the design forms; when they have learned to understand the language of these art works with the heart as well as with the intellect, then these people will no longer do wrong to their fellow human beings, for they will learn love from the sculpted forms. They will learn to live together in harmony and peace with their fellow human beings. Peace and harmony will flow into hearts through these contours. Such structures will be law-givers. What otherwise cannot be achieved by external presentations, will be attained by the forms of our building!
>
> My dear friends, no matter how many people today speculate about getting rid of criminality and delinquency through external establishments, in the future, true healing from evil to good for human souls will come from the bona fide art of this spiritual aura being sent into human souls and hearts, so that—if they allow the aura to work on them out of what emerges from architectonic sculpture and other forms—when these human souls and hearts are prone to lying, they stop deceiving; when they are prone

to disturbing the peace, stop shattering the equanimity of their fellow human beings. Buildings will start to speak. They will speak a language that people cannot even suspect today.

Today people meet in congresses in order to negotiate world peace. They believe what goes from mouth to ear can really bring about peace and harmony. But congresses do not create agreement and serenity. Peace, harmony, humane conditions will be able to circulate only when the gods speak to us. [...] My dear friends, art brings about the organs through which gods can speak to humanity.[59]

In this connection, Rudolf Steiner described the building intended in Dornach as "law giver"; whoever fully understands and lives with this building, learns to not lie or do wrong. In Dornach a *social architecture* developed, in the form-language of the building and the relationship and harmony of its elements, as well as its effect on the people. Steiner envisioned that successors would emanate from the building in the future:

... When everything is completed that is being done on this hill, with this spirit of love, which is always the essence of real artistry; then from this hill, from what supports it, the Spirit of Peace, Spirit of Harmony, Spirit of Love will radiate into the world. Then it will lead to the possibility that what is created on this hill will inspire successors, so that a great many centers of such earthly-spiritual peace, such earthly-spiritual harmony, such earthly-spiritual love will prosper in the world.[60]

Two weeks after the beginning of the war, Steiner spoke again in this sense, in the carpentry shop:

Our building abounds in composed thoughts and in peaceful work. In these times when everything seems to

> be shattering, we want to strive to be a group that fosters and cultivates peace and harmony in every heart, so that every person has the best thoughts about another person, without envy, without discord. That will be the only thing that makes it possible during the impending painful events to continue what must be set forth. For our work must and will be continued despite all mounting obstacles. What must happen will occur in the sense of our movement.[61]

Eight years later, Steiner formulated a cultural text for the Act of Consecration used in the Christian Community..."O Christ, you said to those walking with You, 'I stand at peace with the world; this peace with the world can be with you also, because I give it to you."[62] Steiner impressively taught and lived such a peaceful "relationship to the world" on the construction site, at a time when the search lights from Istein Klotz reached the Dornach hill every night and the thunder from the cannons in the Vosges Mountains could be heard.

Rudolf Steiner stressed on September 19, 1914, that it was the task of the Johannes Building, "to guide human souls to be on the earth together harmoniously."[63] He had said three months earlier at the dedication of the Glass House that people "will learn love from artistic shapes." Now he indicated that the individual building forms should be regarded as written symbols of a "divine language"; as creations that are grasped and penetrated by the life of the Christ impulse. "... that one sees in these forms how the Spirit who communicated with the earth through the Mystery of Golgotha, streams through it." Christ wants to speak in the "House of the Word"; he seeks, beyond all division of folk and nations, an expression, a revelation through the speech of the higher hierarchies. "And this building shall be the mouthpiece!"[64]

Steiner depicted the Pauline experience of "Not I, but the Christ in me," as the central and deepest experience that people would have in the Johannes Building, or Goetheanum. The architecture was a companion, a training path to the higher "I"—and its crowning was to be the sculpture of the Representative of Humanity, in the small cupola in the east, in which Christ stands between the adversary powers that he overcomes through the substance of his love.[65] The experience of this temple as a mystery center of the future should help a person to advance to a deeper layer of being; and with this, at the same time to advance to an understanding of the other person, who lives from the same forces. "Humanity emerged from a unity, but past earthly development has lead to segmentation. In the Christ-Imagination, above all, an ideal is contained that counteracts all separation, for in the person who bears the Christ name, also live the forces of the High Sun Being, in which every human "I" finds its primeval basis."[66] Thus, the building was predisposed to support social development and the creation of peace in a Christ-centered way, as the "Representative of Humanity."

In the following four years of the war, Steiner continued to work on the building, with ever fewer assistants. He noticed every detail of the creation, as well as each person who participated in the work in the various circumstances of life, from the cleaning lady to the artist.

> Once, in winter, in the cold and dust, Dr. Steiner came to our work, climbed as usual onto the ladder and the stacked boxes that formed a rickety scaffold, answered our questions, deciphered the movement of forms for us. But this time, he worried that we probably had cold feet, and he sent us electric heaters. He cared for both the healthy and the sick. He sent a doctor, made inquiries, and often visited the sick himself. The years passed in quiet work. In the distance we heard the cannons. (Natalie Turgenieff-Pozzo).[67]

Together with one of the doctors who came from the Ukraine, Henrietta Ginda Fridkin, Steiner attended to the illness of the workers who had mental crises and other life situations characteristic of the hardships imposed by the times. Steiner's devotion to life extended to all the beings in the environment of the building as well, from the old grey spaniel that waited for him daily, to the new-born kittens in the carpentry shop, and many more. "One thought about the old theocratic belief that a part of the Shekinah, the Glory of the Lord, imbues everything, and therefore a person should honor all creatures!" (Adelheid Petersen)[68]

*

From the beginning, even before the outbreak of the war, Rudolf Steiner paid special attention to every one of the day laborers, who performed the major physical work on the building. They came from around the Dornach area, and were not anthroposophists. Workers had long been dear to Steiner's heart; his past teaching activity in the worker training school in Berlin in the years around 1900 had been important to him.[69] But class distinctions, discrepancies, and difficulties were still generally active; and even in Dornach, tensions occurred between anthroposophists and those who bore the real burden of the physical work. The workers represented a different social position, and they repeatedly encountered resentment. In a later, retrospective report, one wrote:

> We workers lived in a quite different social strata than the "artists" did, who busily carved or chiseled; and the "members," who walked around in flowing purple garments to "meditate" and to light the 12,000 candles illuminating the cupola, and so forth."[70]

Numerous workers had doubts about the anthroposophists' social attitudes and intentions. Although, after the end of the war, the Anthroposophical Society publicly advocated for new social impulses and for the "threefold social organism," particularly in Germany and Switzerland, these things had been little apparent on the construction site. ("A slight tension existed: shouldn't the social impulses, of which much was spoken in the 'threefold time,' be valid especially at the Goetheanum?")[71] Their doubt and the tension extended to the monumental building that they were erecting with their hands, which was neither an apartment building nor a school; neither a kindergarten nor a hospital—its social commitment and appropriateness were, therefore, questionable.

> What purpose should the temple serve? The unusual shapes, the pictures of humanity's history in the cupola paintings, the extraordinary drawings (stars, angels, demons) in the glass windows: we should help erect something like this. But wouldn't it be appropriate that we possibly also understand what is represented there?[72]

Finally, the workers begged Steiner for a meeting in the carpentry shop. After he listened to their criticisms, worries, and questions with great composure, he decided to hold lectures about anthroposophical spiritual science for the workers—they would take place after the breakfast break, as part of the paid work time. He admitted no other listeners to these lectures, which he developed from the audience's questions; and he spared no pains to represent the contents of Anthroposophy in a direct way.

> Dr. Steiner spoke to us ... quite frankly, freely, and plausibly about things like the two Jesus boys, which then, at least in my vicinity in Dornach, was discussed extremely secretively, and to a certain extent, only whispered even in the members' circles.
>
> But *how* he spoke to us had a very special style: clearly, distinctly, simply, with almost extreme or drastic examples, but always fully stating the deepest substance, not

> instructing by "popularizing." One cannot really describe it. One could perhaps say, he spoke as modestly as a comrade. And yet we often had such enormous respect, most of us had palpitations of the heart; often it was discussed for days who should ask a question and what it should be.[73]

"...modestly as a comrade."— Steiner's appearance, his disposition, and the manner in which he represented the new spiritual science were immediately believable to them. There developed, gradually and soundly in the workers, a consciousness for the task to which they applied themselves; increasingly they took part in building with all their hearts. Assja Turgenieff wrote: "It was staggering to observe the resonance of these lectures, the quietly collected earnestness with which these people went back to their tasks."[74] Steiner was pleased that many of the workers found a connection to Anthroposophy, to "building the anthroposophical cause." In this way, the Goetheanum came into being in the difficult years of the war and the time afterward as the site of a new society and community; not without repeated crises, but, still, in the sign of peace.

Starting in autumn 1920, Steiner held lectures in the building. Among these was the fundamental course "Cosmology, Philosophy, and Religion from the Anthroposophical Point of View." He later wrote about these lectures:

> I went into all of my lectures, and came away from them, with an inner thankfulness in respect to what the building of the Goetheanum had brought about.[75]

At that time, Sophie Stinde had already been in the spiritual world for seven years. While on earth, and later from the spiritual world, she had "initiated" the building with her friends, and cooperated in its development. Just one day after her departure from earth, Steiner said, on November 18, 1915:

> To us, who profess to be faithful and loyal to the spiritual worlds, belong those who have only changed the form of their being; despite their having gone through the gates of death, as true souls they are united with us as our most important and significant co-workers. The veils that (in many cases) surround those who are embodied in the physical life, gradually drop away; and the souls of these, our dear deceased, are—we know this to be a fact—in our midst. Just now we need such help. We need such help, which is no longer cherished from the physical plane, such help which is no longer taken into consideration because of the constraints of the physical plane. When we have a deep, intense belief in the advancement of our cause in world culture, then it goes without saying that we are fully conscious that those who have once belonged to us and are now working among us with suprasensory means from the spiritual world; they are our best forces."[76]

*

The destruction of the building on New Year's Eve 1922–23 did not come as a complete surprise; nevertheless, it was a blow that Rudolf Steiner and the Dornach community barely survived. The wooden building was not destined for eternity; and on various occasions Steiner acknowledged that he expected the building would have a limited life span. However, the adversarial forces had their effect early in the scheme of things, and brutally. The Anthroposophical Society was far from being conscious of how dangerous the situation actually was; and the destructive potential increased from year to year. Steiner continually pointed out the danger, and what it was necessary to do. He urged every member to strive for maximum awareness and complete engagement, as well as the Anthroposophical Society itself. Yet, little effort was made; and even in November 1922, one month before the fire, Steiner stated in Holland that the "right heart" for the Goetheanum was scarcely present any longer. The worries about its completion and its maintenance were essentially left to him alone. Economically, politically, and socially, the years after the war were difficult; and the Anthroposophical Society was weak. In the Hague, Steiner said:

> It would, of course, be highly desirable that care for the center in Dornach not lapse, but that friends are found who dedicate their assistance.... The moment the Dornach center collapses, then everything will break down. I wish this situation to come to consciousness because in many cases it has not been pursued. Actually—I must say—it has become an extremely difficult problem for me: a crushing concern.[77]

The substance of love and sacrifice was built into the Goetheanum, "a site of love in the midst of furious hate."[78] The Goetheanum was surrounded by aversion and rejection, and its protection through the community of anthroposophists was ineffectual. It was set on fire, and became the tragic victim of total destruction in one single night.

Ita Wegman wrote that Steiner was connected with the Goetheanum through his etheric body, or life body. "His Word, which proclaimed Anthroposophy, built the Goetheanum; Steiner's concentrated Word and his own etheric body were bound up with the art work, were inseparably united with it." Ita Wegman made this diagnosis as Steiner's physician. She was exceptionally close to him in the two and a half years following the fire's devastation.[79] He confided much to Ita Wegman during this time, including the secret of the building and its connection with him. After the destruction, this connection emerged even more clearly. "One who was connected with the building in love, felt the merciless flames painfully penetrating the feelings that had flowed into the destroyed forms, and into the work attempted therein."[80] The attack on the Goetheanum was directed, not only against the site of Anthroposophy, but also against Steiner himself, as its spiritual center. Steiner survived the night of the fire, but emerged a changed person. "Compared with other people, I am already as if dead on earth," he often stated. "My "I" and astral body direct the physical body and supplement the etheric" (Ita Wegman).[81] Connected with the physical, Steiner's life body was affected by the attack. He had created the Goetheanum with the help of this body; and with it everything was connected until his physical extinction, his dissolution from the earth. To a certain extent, Steiner's formative forces accompanied this path, which was the aspect of destiny into which he consciously entered.

The Goetheanum was "dead" or rather had "died away," as a real "life being," as Steiner often stressed. He spoke of a permanent funeral in the heart, an "Anthroposophy become homeless"[82] and an irreplaceable, dramatic loss.

> The cupolas were covered with northern slate from the Voss slate quarry. The blue-grey gleam in the sunlight combined with the wood color presented a unity that many people welcomed sympathetically as they made their way up the Dornach hill to the Goetheanum on a clear summer day.
>
> Now they encounter a heap of rubble over which a low cement ruin towers.[83]

Continually, Steiner pointed to the tremendous pain from the loss, "for which there are no words"; the Goetheanum was destroyed in the physical world, in the sensory sphere of human existence, in and for which it had been constructed.

> The entire being of this monument was oriented to its *panorama*. The memory hurts immeasurably. One *remembers* it in soul experience, which clamors for the *vision*. But the possibility of beholding it has been removed since New Year's Eve.[84]

Steiner spoke about the obliteration of the Goetheanum as an "irreplaceable loss." The central "means of representation" for the Anthroposophical Movement,[85] a "House of the Word," was irrevocably gone. In all of its forms and shapes it was aligned with the Christ impulse in the twentieth century, and thereby also with Michael and his manifestation. It was possible, to be sure, to hold further lectures after the fire and to work through the Word. However, according to Steiner, something was destroyed and taken away that would never return; and the loss extended beyond the words of (internal as well as public) speech. Once, he said about the lost operative organ of the first Goetheanum:

> I would like to say that it had become possible to speak to the whole world through the purely artistic forms of the Goetheanum architecture. Certainly, people in our present time who lack a sense for what Anthroposophy can offer through words, also have little feeling for the artistic forms they perceive in Dornach. Yet one must say that the sympathies in our present time correspond to a time once when the eye was more easily directed to what could be seen than the soul through its inner activity to what was heard. Thus, the Dornach building greatly enhanced the possibility of speaking to human beings about the spirituality that humanity needs today. Through the Goetheanum's visible shapes and clearly recognizable handwork, an infinitely greater number of people actually received communication about the secrets of the spiritual world, than previously could have been reached through spoken words. Once and for all, through the Dornach Goetheanum, people—particularly those with sufficient good will, who looked at this Goetheanum and the Anthroposophy behind it without prejudice—could experience that Anthroposophy is not sectarian in its nature, but rather addresses the great task of our age that consists of receiving the resplendence of a new spiritual light, henceforth accessible to humanity, and

> imprinting it on human culture and civilization. Attending a single, randomly selected meeting, under certain circumstances even unbiased people could speak of a sectarian movement. Yet considering the diligence with which it was attempted in the Dornach building and its art forms to avoid every traditional symbol, every allegory, and to allow the anthroposophical impulse to stream forth in pure, actual art, it was not possible for people of good will to speak of an anthroposophical sect. People had to realize that Anthroposophy fosters something of broad human appeal, not something strange and different; rather, seeking for the present what is universally human in the area of mental reflection and creation. The Goetheanum, which is so tragic to behold as a ruin, was a powerful means of expressing the Anthroposophical Movement's true nature. We attempted to introduce this general impulse into every single form, into every single image of the structure. We tried to provide pure art, because pure, true art is profoundly part of the anthroposophical impulse. Precisely through the Goetheanum, even for people who had no interest in the Anthroposophical Society, the concern of the Anthroposophical Society for the divine could be communicated.
>
> This is how things were for nearly ten years. That became impossible, henceforth, in one single night.[86]

The "genuine cooperation of science, art, and religion appropriate for the world,"[87] that occurred in the first Goetheanum had been intended to mitigate the "obliteration" of the human soul in the age of materialism. This intention came to a tentative end with the "death" of the building. Steiner had pointed out in Basel on May 5, 1914, during the initial building period, that a "divine impulse of spiritual culture," most preciously connected with the building, might flow into humanity as a being who "can maintain the balance" in the "service" Ahriman will perform."[88] For Ahriman and Lucifer had no access to a place that aimed to support the new, future human capabilities. Among these new capabilities, not the least was that of developing "karmic perception,"[89] at the dawn of the Michael epoch. "Anthroposophy as a striving to Christianize the world..." All that, prepared in the contours of the building, lived, thanks to long work, for the individuals and the community—"that became impossible in one single night."[90]

*

In Kristiania during May 1923, a few months after the building's destruction, Steiner spoke for the first time about how after Christ's Ascension the apostles mourned the physical withdrawal of the being who had walked with them for three years and forty days. About the inner situation of the apostles (when, after the Ascension, all visible observation of the one who was the "I" of humanity was removed), he said:

> There was a point of time in the life of Christ Jesus' students when they said to themselves: "We have seen Him, we can't see Him any longer. He descended from heaven to us on the earth. Where has He gone?" This point of time in which the apostles believed they had lost Christ's presence is recorded in the Christian Ascension festival. It is said that the High Sun Spirit who had become the human Jesus of Nazareth on earth had disappeared from the apostles' consciousness. After Christ's apostles had this experience, they were overcome by tremendous grief. This grief could not be compared with any other sorrow experienced on earth. In the old mysteries, when people celebrated the sun cult and had laid the god's image in the earth so that it might rise again after several days, something like this great grief came over their souls concerning the god's death. But even

> this sorrow could not be compared in magnitude with the mourning that engulfed the hearts of Christ's apostles.[91]

However, the suffering in remembering, the incomparable grief of the apostles, was the prerequisite for a new birth; it made possible the Whitsun event, following a difficult time of ten days, in which the apostles, according to Steiner, went about "quite deeply heartfelt" [feeling things deeply in the heart] and thought with "inner force" about everything "that Christ had ever said to them."[92]

The archetype of the apostles' grief lived in the anthroposophical community surrounding Steiner after the burning of the Goetheanum removed all sight of the building. "The *memory* hurt unspeakably." After its inauguration, the Goetheanum had "lived" only two and a quarter years on earth. It had lived as the site of eurythmy and speech formation; as the site of Steiner's spiritual-scientific lectures, spiritual research, and training; as the site for developing capabilities for self knowledge (essentially "I" preparation) in a mystery center. Steiner's lectures and discussion in the year 1923, which dealt with the Anthroposophical Society, its situation, and crisis, were a call to go about "quite deeply heartfelt"; to comprehend the loss of the Goetheanum; and to concentrate on those tasks placed before the spiritual community in arousing the "Christ impulse" in the destiny of the twentieth century. Without his addressing the Christological prerequisites of this self reflection in a direct way or making the relationship of the situation to the "Ascension" publicly known, it lived as a concealed secret in the background of events.

The first Goetheanum was a "House of the Word." In 1923, Steiner said that "word" in the anthroposophical context has a different definition than in the usual present-day sense.

> Words can be interpreted as really being requests. In Anthroposophy, strictly taken, every word when it is

spoken in the right sense is a request, a devotional prayer that the spirit may descend to people.

From such a prayer the building in Dornach was carried out.[93]

One year after the destruction, with "the frightful image of the burning Goetheanum in the background,"[94] and after the grief and "unspeakably painful memory," finally, a new birth became possible; and the possibility came through Rudolf Steiner. The devotional prayer "that the spirit may descend to people" enabled the inauguration of the spiritual foundation stone at the Christmas Conference 1923/24. This event had its prototype in the world-historical Whitsun in the sense of the active—and continually active—Christ being. "And, lo, I am with you always, even unto the end of the world." (Matthew 28:16-20, KJV).

Softly on delicate feet it approaches,
Before sleep like a fluttering:
Listen, oh soul, to my counsel,
Let luck and comfort smile on you—:

Those bound to you in love,
Will always remain near you,
Truly entwined with you they will
Encircle you with small and large orbits.

They will rely on you
Unrelated, like you to them,—
And awakened to beholding
You will in emulation serve them![95]

—Christian Morgenstern

The Nature of the First Goetheanum and the Mystery of Golgotha

SERGEI O. PROKOFIEFF

Above all, this was necessary: to one day execute a building, which in all of its forms is an embodiment of the spiritual being to whom we are devoted.

— RUDOLF STEINER[96]

DEAR FRIENDS,

On December 31, 1923, at the end of the Christmas Conference, Rudolf Steiner commemorated the burning of the first Goetheanum. On this occasion he said: "Directly connected with the fire that evening, was everything to which our Goetheanum building should be devoted."[97] Reflecting on the event of the previous year, Rudolf Steiner spoke these words, and they make us aware of two things: that the words really signify that Steiner spoke for the last time in the first building and that something singular was expressed in the content of the last words resounding in that edifice, which only a few hours later would be taken away from the earth.

Steiner was an outstanding and prolific speaker. That fact is demonstrated in his collected works by the stenographs of over 6,000 lectures he held in his lifetime. His last lecture in the first Goetheanum is of singular significance.

We have already heard in the lecture by Peter Selg that this Goetheanum, or Johannes Building as it was originally called, emerged quite out of Steiner's spirit. In all its shapes and colors it represented Anthroposophy in a visible form. When Steiner spoke in this temple directly from the source of Anthroposophy, his speech, his word, was quite special, for it accorded in full harmony with these contours and colors, with all the thoughts embodied in the building. Like the building's forms, Steiner's speech had a living, organic character. Today, when we read the written shorthand notes, we might have problems with the length of the sentences and their many subordinate clauses, with the sentences' quite singular *organic* formulation, because in the computer age we have increasingly lost the ability to think and speak in such a way. But in this speech, containing Steiner's particular sentence structure, one can experience the same quality manifested in the formation of the first building—what is expressed in the movement of the architrave; in the rhythmic sequence of the capitals; in the colors and forms of the glass windows; and in the paintings in the two cupolas.

All of that wove and wafted naturally through Steiner's speech. Especially in the capitals and motifs of the architrave, one could discover the prototype for the main idea interwoven with various subordinate clauses, which at the end of their ultimate development returned on a new level to the original thought that had been introduced at the beginning. When readers conscientiously try to connect their own soul with such a precept and experience it inwardly, they finds themselves not in the past, but in the future—emerging out of the spiritual present.

One can hardly find appropriate words to describe what it signified when Steiner, surrounded by these special forms, spoke in such an individual way. His words corresponded to the living metamorphosis of the capitals, the architrave, the etched glass windows, and the manifold paintings with their flood of colors in both cupolas.

Having all that as a background, we can turn our attention to the last words Steiner spoke in the first Goetheanum. For these words, the very last lecture, are a real legacy; they are what the master builder wanted to give the architecture to take with it on its cosmic path. This is the same path that every person treads after death: the path into the vastness of the universe where the spirit of the cosmos penetrates, moves, and enlivens everything we see in the star studded heavens—all orbits of the planets, all spiritual regions of the fixed stars, the entire zodiac.

In his last lecture there on December 31, 1922, this unparalleled dramatic and tragic evening in the history of the Anthroposophical Society, indeed in the spiritual history of humanity, Steiner invoked the Spirit of the Cosmos, the great cosmic spirit, from the lectern that was placed on the line of demarcation between the large and small halls.

What did Steiner speak about in this lecture? He spoke about the future of humanity when the human being will be an eyewitness in the great temple of the cosmos; about the future in which the entire cosmos with all its planets and fixed stars will become the great temple of the universe. As free beings, humankind will abide sovereign and independent in this cosmic temple, and will celebrate an activity in which they summon the Spirit of the Cosmos so that it can be present and active here on earth. The human being, performing a cosmic transubstantiation, a spiritualization that extends into the earthly substance—that is the image of the future that Steiner placed before the audience at the end of this lecture.[98] It was a tremendous future perspective, which he then concentrated into a two-stanza mantric verse and wrote on the blackboard with his "starry script," as Marie Steiner called it. The blackboard with the verse written on it also fell victim to the fire, and dispersed into the spiritual cosmos with the entire building.

I would like to begin my actual presentation now with these words that Steiner spoke at the end of this last lecture in the first building, and wrote on the blackboard.

> There approaches me in earthly activity
> The physical image presented
> Of the stars' heavenly beings:
> I see them transforming themselves lovingly into will.
>
> There penetrates into me in fluid life
> The physical force developed
> Of the stars' heavenly deeds:
> I see them transforming themselves wisely into feeling.[99]

What do these words mean? Primarily, they point to something we all know very well in daily life: our nourishment. Three times a day we ingest the solid and liquid elements of food. From the path of modern spiritual knowledge, we can detect even more in this: in the solid food, we see the image of the twelvefold starry cosmos; and in the liquid food, the image of the moving stars, the seven planets. As Steiner describes, when we rise through the stages of imagination, inspiration, and intuition into the spiritual world, we thereby strengthen our "I," so that it unites with the Spirit of the Cosmos. We receive this Spirit of the Cosmos into ourselves; then, we can transubstantiate the material substances received into our bodies, and join them consciously with the spirituality of the zodiac and with the spirit of the planets, that is, with the Spirit of the Cosmos. And thus, we take the first step to spiritualizing the whole earth.

The integral reality of *cosmic communion* reveals itself to us in these simple mantric words, which harmonize with all the forms of the first building and bear a tremendous perspective of metamorphosis, that is, the spiritualization of the earth.

Proceeding from this last thought, one is amazed to discover the following: when one entered the original building from the west, the entrance to the hall was across from a large human face etched in the red window. Although a person could rightly interpret this representation in various ways, one way is certainly in harmony with the words that were last spoken in the building: This window was the face of the future human being; the person who stands consciously in the Temple of the Cosmos, observing the cosmic communion in which the human being unites the spiritual cosmos with human physicality. This spiritualization is performed out of the human being's free "I"; the transubstantiation is performed in the human body, which leads to the beginning of the transformation of the entire earth. This depiction of the human being as participant in the Temple of the Cosmos, represented in the red window in the west of the Goetheanum, indicates Anthroposophy's greatest mission in the world, which as we will see, found its artistic revelation in the ideas carried out in the first Goetheanum. In this regard, for the last time surrounded by all the colors and contours of the first building, Rudolf Steiner said: "All that is our relationship to the world, primarily recognized in human beings as cosmic ritual, is the beginning of what must happen if Anthroposophy is to achieve its mission in the world."[100]

Then, one entered the hall with the two times seven pillars, which expressed world development through the seven planetary spheres. The path led foremost through what forms the second part of the cosmic communion: the inner transformation of fluids, the juices of the human body, by spiritual planetary forces. Precisely that was also brought to expression in the configuration of the first Goetheanum's hall. The twelvefold nature of the fixed stars, the zodiac, was found beneath the small cupola. The zodiac is another part of the speaking, weaving, acting Cosmic Spirit, a force active in the expanses of the fixed stars with which we can and must spiritualize, transubstantiate, the solid elements of our nourishment.

If we look, in this sense, at the first Goetheanum in its entirety, we can say that this building was truly erected according to the nature of cosmic communion. Its purpose was to show people the way to this exalted goal. The building concentrated the secrets of the cosmos and brought to life what every person can find in this temple of new spiritual activity. (Although it wasn't a temple in the usual sense, it was based on a temple archetype.) The building was intended to enable the lofty ideal of humanity's development: the individual's participation in the Temple of the Cosmos, connecting with the earth in a new way out of the free "I," conscious of the seven planetary forces, which could be experienced in the hall and its forms, as well as the forces of the zodiac, which shone toward the viewer from the hall under the little cupola.

Thus, by entering the first Goetheanum, every person could experience, consciously or unconsciously, the essence of this cosmic communion as the great goal of earth evolution. One can also say that Rudolf Steiner revealed to us precisely this original thought, this deepest secret, in the last moment of this building's existence on the earth, in his closing words, the mantric verse with which he ended the last lecture.

Continuing an imaginary visit to the original building, gazing from west to east, one can envision the Group sculpture, the Representative of Humanity, (although it hadn't been installed yet), which was also depicted with the same motif in the painting on the eastern part of the little cupola. Steiner repeatedly said that a person must never enter the first Goetheanum without imagining the Group in its place in the east of the small cupola. What came toward us there?

Let us again turn our imaginative gaze to the starting point in the west: one stands here before the entrance to the Temple of the Cosmos. In front of one in the hall is the entire perspective of the seven planets, and in the small cupola's hall, united in the circle of the zodiac, the infinite starry worlds. Then from the east of the building, appearing to come toward one from the area beyond the zodiac, beyond the infinite worlds of the fixed stars, the Representative of Humanity, Christ. He comes from our humanity, the original habitat of our "I." In this moment we do not gaze at the zodiac (where the astral, animal forces of the zodiac rule), but beyond the zodiac.[101] We look directly into the area of the spiritual world from which, in Christ, the World "I", the highest archetype and model of every human "I," came to the earth and became human.

Thus, in the first Goetheanum, we look up to our original habitat beyond the visible cosmos. From this original place, a figure of what we experience as the most important for forming the kernel of every person's being, our individuality, our "I," approaches us. The entire future perspective of this "I" appears to us from the east; comes nearer to us through the world of the fixed stars and on through the world of the planets. It speaks to us the words that Steiner spoke just one year later, in the introductory lecture of the Christmas Conference: "That is what I am as human; as god-willed human on earth, as god-willed human in the cosmos."[102]

In connection with this building, another point should be mentioned. The central figure appears from the east—in this regard the east signifies the spiritual world—forming the balance between the polarities. We have the feeling that the entire structure is erected within this balance: the load-bearing and supporting forces, the plant-like metamorphosis in the hall and the crystalline shapes in the theater, the curved arch elements that rhythmically transform into solidly formed lines only to curve again—everywhere this architecture has emerged from balance. Whenever something threatens to become Ahrimanic, it is balanced Luciferically, and vice-versa. This symbiotic compensation creates a free space in the middle, causes a streaming toward the center, which is the true revelation of the figure approaching us from the east. In this building, the initial step pointing to the future is achieved by a purely Manichaean element: overcoming and thereby transforming the Lucerferic and Ahrimanic forces of evil.

It is not surprising that the adversaries retaliated with the horrible, destructive reaction that completely demolished this wonderful architecture on New Year's Eve 1922. We must generate the courage to observe the specific forces that caused this destruction. Steiner has explained it to us. After the fire, in esoteric classes during 1923, he described it in Kristiania in the north, then in Dornach in the so-called "Wachsmuth-Lerchenfeld Group."[103] He spoke because we must realize that the forces that wiped out the first Goetheanum then, are also active in the world now, corrupting humanity's spiritual life, destroying human freedom, and infiltrating politics, where powerful inhuman interests play a decisive role.

Steiner spoke in those esoteric classes about the two polar streams opposing the correct, free development of humanity, at that time (which still holds true, as well, today). On the one hand, he pointed to certain secret societies in the west that have corrupted some Free Mason movements, and have enabled them to achieve their claim to power in world politics. Of course, one can disregard the antagonists, and concentrate on the structure of harmony and beauty. However, Steiner specifies, in tracing the evolution of the world, that development, which was burst asunder by this faction, is proceeding with gigantic steps toward the abyss. The Masonic order is one of the dark occult streams active in the world today.

On the other hand, working from the other side is a polar stream, placed in world-historical opposition to the first stream. That is the Jesuit order, which since its establishment, aims to suppress human freedom with a system of spiritual exercises that subjugates people to the god of the Old Testament. Instead of striving for the freedom of the Christian world, for the Christianity of the new world, the order seeks to return people artificially to the condition existing before the Mystery of Golgotha. This is exaggerated by misusing the founder of Christianity's name through Western atheistic permissiveness, which excludes human freedom and value.[104]

On the public stage of world events, these two occult streams maintain the strictest opposition. However, Steiner reported in the above-mentioned esoteric classes that these opposing streams were united in harmony at least once. The result of that unity was the burning of the first Goetheanum.[105]

We ought to look at these two streams not only in this narrow sense, but also must consider all of humanity. For example, the first stream is active wherever interests of certain groups monopolize general human concerns, in politics and human relationships. And furthermore, we are faced with the second stream where human freedom is not recognized and valued. These are the forces that brought death to this wonder of the world, the first Goetheanum. Rudolf Steiner was conscious of this.

In the Goetheanum auditorium nearly two years before the fire, Steiner read from a secondary Free Mason journal a statement filled with irreconcilable hate, that this "wooden mousetrap" in Dornach needed only a spark of fire so that the pompous model would perish.[106] We see the intention of the adversaries was there, was already present in the world. Steiner had made people aware of it quite a long time before the fire. Steiner told us all that. Although he continually stressed the agitation that emanated from the Catholic priest Max Kully, who lived near the Goetheanum,[107] and how the Jesuits' aspirations stood behind this agitation,[108] his way was to leave people free. We anthroposophists—the first Goetheanum belongs to all of us, including those who sit here in this auditorium—we were sleeping, just as the apostles in the garden of Gethsemane slept. While we were sleeping, this building had to leave the earth. Despite this great tragedy, its leaving was really something quite unusual, even something wonderful.

Steiner always spoke about the colors and forms of the architecture; of their being larynxes which had been built for the gods, so the gods could speak to humanity. Through the building, which stood on earth for ten years, the gods turned ever more distinctly, ever more perceptibly to humanity.[109] These forms that dissolved in the fire were received, transformed, into the spiritual world. At the same time, the relationship between humanity and the gods was reversed: in this tragedy gods no longer spoke to humanity, but humanity conversed with the gods.

The object that had emerged from people's handwork through human love was now sacrificed to the gods as an offering, as the most wonderful fruit of the earth. In the sea of fire, the organ suddenly began to sound out, accompanied by an indescribable play of colors from the melting of the metal. The hierarchies, among whom even the highest were present at the time, revealed themselves in this sea of fire in the tones and colorful melting of the metallic components of the organ. Steiner later indicated in Holland that people with spiritual eyes could experience how the beings of the first, the highest, hierarchy—thrones, cherubim, and seraphim—were present in this melting metal[110] and received the sacrifice from human hands, the sacrifice of love, offered from earth to heaven.

Connected with this New Year's Eve tragedy, there is even more to ponder. For instance, the question has often been posed: what was the situation with the consecration of the first Goetheanum? Steiner expressly alluded to this at the first academic course in September 1920. He said that neither this academic course, nor any other major events would comprise a dedication, the real consecration, of this building in the esoteric sense. In order to perform such a consecration, one must wait until each word resounding in the building would be expressed in harmony with the forms and colors of the architecture.[111]

How long would Rudolf Steiner wait for that? A sacrilegious hand had already laid the fire between the double walls, and in this last world-historical moment, Steiner could wait no longer. It was of the utmost importance that the building not cross over into the spiritual world without being dedicated. If that had happened, the Goetheanum would never have been able to fulfill its task, neither on earth nor in the cosmic expanses. The tragedy demanded that the building have its dedication.

What happened in this decisive moment at the last lecture in the first Goetheanum? Let us try to imagine the situation quite precisely and concretely. Steiner stood in the center of the building. He spoke so that his words were united in absolute harmony with all the forms, colors, and floods of light filling these rooms. He spoke as never before. There are recollections about this evening; that after the lecture, when people left the building, they suddenly realized under the night's star-studded heaven that Steiner's words about this mighty cosmic ritual, which had just resounded in the hall, had united with the whole cosmic surroundings, whose archetype this building was.

In his biography, Heinz Müller remembered this singular lecture by Steiner, and shared the following. "The festivity, the forcefulness of his speech escalated during the course of the lecture. One had the feeling that here a great initiate was celebrating the cultus of the future, the cosmic ritual of humankind. After he had spoken the verse [the cosmic communion] one more time,

Steiner stepped in great modesty to the side of the podium, so that it was taken for granted that nobody would applaud, which was always customary at other lectures. Both verses remained, written in his lovely longhand, on the two blackboards as we, deeply moved, old and young, exited into the clear, starry night of New Year's Eve."[112]

Having spoken in this way, Steiner was simultaneously in this building and in the Temple of the Cosmos. He was the celebrating priest who summoned to earth the Spirit of the Cosmos, this all-encompassing Spirit who ensouled the planetary spheres and served, one could also say inspired, all the regions of the fixed stars. In the truest sense of the word, to be filled with spirit means that one is penetrated by seraphic enthusiasm,[113] which is active wherever sacrificial substance (here the cosmic communion) builds the foundation for a new creation. This Spirit of the Cosmos was present in the structure. All around (if the walls of the building had been transparent, those present would have been able to perceive it), the fire already blazed, for it had been laid several hours before, long before Steiner had begun this last lecture.

In the afternoon, even before the eurythmy performance, eurythmists heard in the cloakroom strange noises they couldn't identify.[114] These noises came from the fire, which was spreading between the double walls, and in the huge rooms between the inner and outer cupolas. In fact, it was consuming the entire periphery of the building as Steiner spoke the mantric words, and then wrote them on the blackboard at the end of his lecture.

What does this image tell us? A sea of fire invisible to people, but visible to all the gods, and standing in the middle, a free individual celebrating in the Temple of the Cosmos, invoking the Spirit out of the expanses of the universe. Spirit and fire! What is indicated by this image, which was a reality at that time? It reminds us of the words by John the Baptist, who announced, "I indeed baptize you with water; but one mightier than I cometh ... He shall baptize you with the Holy Ghost and with fire" (Luke 3:16, KJV). A baptism with fire was received by the first Goetheanum, in the last moment of its earthly history. The Goetheanum entered the spiritual world, not undedicated, but as a consecrated sacrifice. Out of a free deed, out of an elevated human being's deep devotion, a sacrifice of love was offered to the gods. The sacrifice was baptized with the Spirit of the Cosmos—and with fire. Fire, which has cleansed everything since the beginning of time on old Saturn; fire, which builds the bridge between the physical world and the world of spirit.[115]

Here, in the deepest sense, and one might say in complete seclusion, Rudolf Steiner, face to face with the spiritual world, performed a Manichaean deed. By his deed, the terrible attack of the adversaries was transformed through the free will of a human being into a new blessing. As a result of dedicating, or baptizing, the Goetheanum, the subsequent "esoteric impetus" of the Christmas Conference was able to penetrate the whole Anthroposophical Movement.[116] This Manichaen consecration was achieved by Rudolf Steiner, not only in the merciless course of personal destiny, but for the karma of all humanity.[117]

The connection with a spiritual Christ baptism was confirmed by Steiner during the Christmas Conference, one year later, in the memorial lecture referred to earlier. There he disclosed a mighty perspective about the teachings of the Rosicrucians, who in the past were recognized by their students from the mild look and light in their eyes.

Rosicrucians described to their students how the human being is connected with the first hierarchy through the physical substances of the body, which, despite the astonishing relationship to the hierarchies, on this level, is nothing more than simply mineral matter. Through the fluids of the body, the human being is connected with the second hierarchy, where one experiences the self as having a sleeping plant nature. Through the air essence in the body, the human being is connected with the third hierarchy, where, like the animals, humanity does not progress beyond a dreamlike sleep. Only when one, out of the "I," grasps the element of warmth, of fire in the self, does a human being comprehend something the self can experience as an "I" being, as a free being on earth.

In this way, the Rosicrucian master revealed to the student the decisive secret of how to build out of the "I" the inner bridge from the physical to the spiritual fire, and thereby from the physical to the spiritual world.[118] As Steiner expressed it, Rosicrucian students went away from their master with deep satisfaction, for they knew the deepest secret of human nature in its relationship to the spiritual world. Then out of this inner satisfaction, out of this peace with the world, their eyes began to shine. In this way, Rosicrucian students themselves gradually became masters.

Steiner continued in his lecture that at the time the Goetheanum had been burning, one year earlier, these Rosicrucian masters, who knew the secret of fire in its connection with the nature of the human "I," were in attendance. They were present at the fire, not physically, but in spirit. In relation to this burning Goetheanum, they served as—here is Steiner's decisive word—advocate for the Spirit.[119] A true baptism with fire and spirit!

When we reflect on the words with which Steiner closed the last lecture in the first Goetheanum, the words of cosmic communion, we can ask how it was possible that these words were spoken within the stream of the new mysteries? On an earlier occasion this year, I have already spoken extensively about this.[120] It was possible only on the basis of events at the time of Christ; the occurrences on Good Friday. What do we find on Good Friday, when we look at the events of that day with the help of Steiner's statements from the Fifth Gospel? Here we find, among many other things, something that is also a type of cosmic communion, the mighty communion of the entire earth planet. First the earth received the blood flowing from Christ on the cross; and thereby also the earth received the forces of his etheric body (which are always connected with flowing blood; with all fluids moving rhythmically in the body). Then this bloodless body was removed from the cross and laid in the grave. As we know from

Steiner's accounts, an earthquake opened a fissure in the earth, which received this special body.[121] Thereby, the cosmic communion of the earth was accomplished through the blood and body of Christ.

We can ask, why did the earth need this cosmic communion? This question has also already been discussed here in a different connection.[122] The earth needed these fluid and solid substances because at the time of Christ it had reached a point where a new connection with the Spirit of the Cosmos, with the spirituality of the planets, with the spirit of the fixed stars had become necessary. In a spiritual sense, our earth originated from the world of the planets and fixed stars. The earth was born at the beginning of its planetary evolution under the direction of zodiacal forces; it was connected with the Cosmic Spirit during its innumerable periods of evolution. In ancient Atlantean times, earth inhabitants still could witness this Spirit everywhere in nature processes. The inhabitants spoke about the "TAO," which resounded to them from all processes, objects, and beings of the world. The earth at that time was quite permeated with this Spirit. If everything had remained that way, the earth never could have been the place where the human being would become free. Therefore, one could say the earth had to make a sacrifice. It had to separate itself from the Spirit of the Planets and the Spirit of the Fixed Stars—at least at a certain level of its existence. For this reason, present day science must weigh, measure, and count everything in the cosmos, because it has become as though dead for human experience. Because the earth sacrificed its relationship to the cosmos in this way, humanity could become free beings on it.

Then a time came when the earth's independence had advanced so far in relationship to the cosmos, that it needed a new connection with the universe for its further development. Without this new connection, the earth's spiritual transition to the cosmic condition of Jupiter would not be possible in the future. Through Christ's blood and body, the earth can receive the Cosmic Spirit anew. As Steiner describes it, during the three years of his life on earth, Christ Jesus was continually connected with the Spirit of all seven planets. Also, in Christ's body, all the spiritual forces of the zodiac's twelvefold nature were continually active during the three years.. Steiner says that throughout his earthly life, Christ was under the influence of the Spirit of the Cosmos; that is, the Spirit who weaves and is active in the world of the planets and in the world of the fixed stars. "Christ was always under the influence of the entire cosmos; he made no step without the cosmic forces working within him"... "The Spirit of the Cosmos" worked through and in him (GA 15, Chapter III). In the course of the three years, this Spirit imprinted, on the one hand, Christ Jesus' singular body from the world of the fixed stars; and on the other hand, imprinted his special blood from the world of the planets. Then on Good Friday, through Christ's blood and body, this Spirit of the Cosmos was connected with the earth anew, so that earth could one day reach the Jupiter condition, and thereby be a place of further activity for humanity. In order to attain this goal of becoming Jupiter, the cosmos of love, our earth needed the loving sacrifice of Christ's blood and body—along with the etheric forces of the planets and the spiritual force of the zodiac.

Only because the earth had received the cosmic communion at the time of Christ, could Steiner pass on to us the mantra, as the last words in the first building. The two verses of the mantra described how the cosmic communion could cooperate, through the reception of earthly nourishment, in transforming the earth to the extent of really transubstantiating its substance. As a visible symbol of this process, which is simultaneously a true expression of the reality standing behind it, the first Goetheanum had been built, so that every person who entered it might experience something of this cosmic communion.

Then this building was taken away from us. (We will come back to this event again later.) What happened after this tragedy in the history of our movement? Our movement in no way came to its conclusion, to its end. There followed an answer from the highest powers, as in every true sacrifice, when it is accepted by the spiritual world. As a result, an enhancement came, in infinite perspective, for which we have a macrocosmic prototype at the time of Christ.

After the anxious, desperate atmosphere of Good Friday, the mood of Easter morning dawned as a new heavenly light. This is the mood of starting into a new future, which one can describe with the sentence from the Apocalypse: "Behold, I make all things new" (Revelation 21:5, KJV). In our human language, there are almost no words to describe the Good Friday mood of Christ's apostles; the most important, the holiest, the most exalted they had, was taken from them in death—the sun of the world disappeared for them like a sun eclipse. Three days later, on Easter morning, with the dawn of the physical sun, there occurred for them the lighting up of the spiritual sun, and a quite different mood, the feeling of starting again in a new world.

In the same way, in this microcosmic, and nevertheless human history, the macrocosm of our movement is reflected. There was a desperate, depressed mood on January 1, with the most important, most visible center of the Anthroposophical Movement, having been taken in a single night. Margarita Woloschin, who arrived in Dornach on the morning after the fire, immediately walked up the hill. She described that she could see only the foundation, which still remained. Everything above was covered in fog, and so it seemed to her as if the building was perhaps still there. But it was no longer there...[123]

Think of Steiner's indomitable will! He carried out everything that had been planned for January 1, despite the fire and the sleepless night. Just imagine how the whole hill was still covered in smoke and fog, yet Steiner's next lecture took place in the totally devastated carpentry shop, where everything was still wet because people had feared it could also catch fire. Like a symbol of the whole tragedy, the sculpture of the Representative of Humanity lay outside on the earth in the snow; an unimaginable, additional pain for Steiner.[124] He spoke in this first lecture after the fire, entirely out of the eternal presence of the Spirit, and as though sealing the tragic event. He read the words from the Free Mason periodical about the "wooden mouse trap" in which it was said that at some point, a fire would be laid. Now the deed was done—the fire had been laid—the building was no longer there. Steiner read these words without comment.[125]

Where were the students who could have prevented this catastrophe from happening? They were widely dispersed. Their consciousness and spiritual presence were not sufficient to prevent it. Thus, Steiner stood quite alone during the night of the fire; occasionally one or another of his students came to him. Yet everything continued the next morning without interruption. Let us transport ourselves there, and witness as in a true picture what occurred then. In the ravaged carpenter's shop, the Three Kings play was being performed. The chairs that had been arranged in a hurry, were out of alignment. Steiner sat in the front, in the middle of the first row. The angel opened the play with its proclamation. Suddenly the actress couldn't speak any more; she began to cry. Then she composed herself, spoke a few more words; and then cried a long time, perhaps several minutes. Steiner sat calmly in the first row, not interrupting the tears, and waited until, after a lengthy time, the actress collected herself again and the play could continue.[126] What does this earthly image reveal to us? I believe it gives us a true picture of what was happening in heaven. It was the picture of the crying angel—if angels really can cry—whose larynx was removed from the earth. One can imagine the angel had spoken to humanity for years through the architecture. Suddenly that was no longer possible; the spiritual world could not speak to human beings any more in this special way.

Let us compare, dear friends, this difficult, depressed mood with the atmosphere of the Christmas Conference one year later, the atmosphere of the inauguration lecture, which has already been mentioned. Then the great difference becomes clear at once. Steiner said at the end of the lecture that what he expected above all from the people who had come to this conference was not wisdom, was not clever thoughts and future plans but atmosphere, atmosphere, and again atmosphere,[127] as well as enthusiasm for a new beginning. One should not forget that all the participants had to pass by the ruins on the hill each morning as they went into the carpenters' shop, where the lecture was held. Yet, at the Christmas Conference nothing of this shadow was experienced; it was only the pure joy of a new creation. "Behold, I make all things new!"

These two moods, taken together, create an image, a reflection of the atmosphere that macrocosmically constituted the transition from Good Friday to Easter morning at the time of Christ. This image also belongs to our movement, to the development of the new mysteries in the twentieth century.

How did this phenomenal metamorphosis come about, from the first Goetheanum to the Christmas Conference? Within our movement, this metamorphosis is comparable with the transition of the Good Friday mood into the atmosphere of Easter Sunday at the time of Christ.—How did it come about? To this question, Steiner gives us an answer that is so modest one almost overlooks it. The answer occurs at the end of the short cycle, held at Easter, 1924, in Dornach. It was the last Easter which this great Easter initiate (one might say) would spend here on earth. At the end of the fourth lecture, which was the last, Rudolf Steiner said briefly (without naming the actual event], that what was taken from all humanity one year before through the fire had become a deed of the cosmic expanses. The cosmic expanses are where the wisdom of the Spirit, indeed the Spirit itself rules; this deed had returned and could be accepted again by one (here he did not name himself, but spoke in the general "we" form; yet, everyone knew who was meant) who had the possibility to accept the deed; and that was naturally only himself alone.[128]

Rudolf Steiner could then enable this Spirit to be active on the earth. He represented and manifested it further, so that out of this "good Spirit of the Goetheanum"[129] (meaning the "esoteric impulse," "esoteric impetus," about which Steiner often spoke), everything was able to develop at the Christmas Conference and afterwards. The second Goetheanum, the Michael School on the earth, karma lectures, biodynamic agriculture, and much more, developed from this "good Spirit." In the last part of this presentation we must ask a further question. We must ask what could have happened if Steiner had lived even longer?

We have already seen how this building forms a connection with Good Friday, with this great communion of the earth; and how this great communion found its expression in the mantric words that were first engraved, if even in another way, in the forms and ideas embedded in the first Goetheanum building. Still a further connection can be found with this building, not only with Good Friday, but also with Easter morning; and it is directly associated to our present time, as we will see at the conclusion of this lecture.

Let us look once again at the events of Good Friday, at which the cosmic communion of the planet earth was enacted: Christ's blood and body were received by the earth. We have its microcosmic consequence in the meditation of the cosmic communion given by Steiner on December 31, 1922. On Easter Sunday, the two substances appear in the resurrection in a fully metamorphosed form, as though having gone through a process of macrocosmic transubstantiation.

Steiner reports that Christ's etheric body, which was connected with the blood, became the compressed etheric body of the Risen One; it could be visible physically,[130] and the apostles visually perceived him. The resurrection body emerged on Easter Sunday out of the reconstituted phantom of the physical body. As on Good Friday, the body and blood of Christ had dissolved into the earth, so on Easter Sunday, they appeared again in a metamorphosed form, bearing the purely spiritual components of the blood and body.[131]

It is not surprising that in this mood of the Christmas Conference, which was a real Easter atmosphere (beyond the event of Good Friday, of which the last lecture in the Goetheanum reminds us), we also can find a way to the reality of the resurrection. Details mentioned on another occasion[132] explain how the Foundation Stone Meditation, when we understand and apply it correctly on the way to modern knowledge, can lead to a meditative experience of the resurrection body; and how the seven rhythms of this verse lead to experiencing, grasping, and uniting internally with what Steiner described as the Risen One's etheric body compressed to physical visibility. Thus, the Foundation Stone Meditation and its rhythms are central to the Christmas Conference, and throw light on the new mysteries for us.

This future perspective, which at the same time is a real Easter perspective, can also be discovered in the first Goetheanum in a quite singular, special way. This is because (as already mentioned) it is closely connected, not only with Good Friday, but also with the events on Easter Sunday.

To identify this even deeper significance of the first Goetheanum more precisely, one must first answer the following question. What happened further with Christ's body, with his blood, after they were received by our earth on Good Friday? This secret can be disclosed with the help of spiritual science. With the blood, the earth received the forces of Christ's etheric body. These forces lived on in a metamorphosed form after the resurrection, as the compressed etheric body of the Risen One. Out of these forces a new etheric sphere is formed around the earth. One time, Steiner also called this sphere the "ether ring." The further history of this etheric body is connected with the earth becoming a new sun; it builds the sphere of our earth's becoming sun.[133]

What happened with the totally spiritualized substance of the physical body? This substance lives on in the earth as a phenomenon, which causes a process of gradually transforming physical matter. In its mineral substances, physical matter will become "light-colored," and later, will become totally transparent, on the path to the future unification of our earth with the sun. As the result of the resurrection since the Mystery of Golgotha, there are two spheres: the etheric sphere around the earth in which the earth begins to be a new sun and a second sphere (growing as though out of a seed from the divine body received by the earth) in which the mineral sheath of the earth will be increasingly spiritualized and transparent—two Christ spheres! Christ is active in both spheres since the Easter event, and is still active on into the future. Christ's activity comes out of the past and into the present, for the future, to prepare the earth from both directions for its last transubstantiation. This has been accomplished so that we human beings, thereby, can collaborate; can cooperate as free beings.[134]

From these two spheres (which we can identify as a result of the dual occurrence on Easter morning with reference to Christ's blood and body); one can say that out of these two spheres involving the compressed etheric body and the phantom body of the Risen One, two decisive events occur in the present. Out of the first sphere, proceeding from the etheric body of the Risen One, there is the appearance of Christ in the etheric. Out of the second sphere (although one should naturally not think of these as separate entities)—where the divine body was received by the earth through a kind of cosmic communion, and the material is since involved in the process of spiritualization—out of this sphere Christ is active today as the Lord of Karma. In karma there is also a kind of transubstantiation; that is, the spirit takes possession of matter and totally transforms it. Transubstantiation and karmic activity, Rudolf Steiner says, have the same nature and origin.[135] Where karma is active, transubstantiation always occurs. Where transubstantiation occurs, karma is transformed. Expressed in another way: out of transformed matter, which will eventually become pure light, new karma emerges in the world.[136] This does not come any more from the past, but increasingly develops the future.

Thus, we are involved with two great Christ events in the present: The activity of the etheric Christ and Christ as the Lord of Karma. Their starting point was at the time of Christ (with the divine blood and the divine body, which then became the compressed etheric body and the phantom of the Risen One). These events now extend into our immediate present, and lead us from there to the future of Earth evolution.

When we envision this fact, we can recognize it in the Goetheanum's glass window motifs. First of all, in the central motif of the red glass window in the west, there is the face of a human being who represents the new, free human being celebrating in the Temple of the Cosmos, in the sense of Rudolf Steiner's last lecture in the first Goetheanum. Then we observe in the large hall, in the southern green window, how the path of modern initiation is begun with overcoming the Luciferic powers; and correspondingly in the northern green window, the Ahrimanic powers are overcome. In the north, the blue window shows in a lemniscate movement[137] the spiritual forces of the planets, which participate in the pre-birth development of the human etheric body. Correspondingly, in the southern window are seen the spiritual forces of the zodiac, which underlie the physical body of the human being. Thus, to the spiritual student are revealed the secrets of the human being in space, otherwise concealed by Lucifer and Ahriman. In the two violet windows the secrets of time are disclosed, which otherwise are kept hidden by Lucifer (in the mystery of birth in the southern window); and Ahriman (in the mystery of death in the northern window). The entire path culminates in the two rose windows (more accurately, the color is actually "peach-blossom"), in which the Christ's twofold appearance in the present is represented.

Let us consider the two Christ representations in more detail. On the northern side, he appears out of this Ascension-etheric sphere of the earth, which can be represented properly only through the germinating and sprouting nature around humanity. Here Christ appears in the etheric, and his revelation is a blessing for human beings. In this representation the human is led by a guardian angel out of that sphere to this encounter, which was created at the time of Christ by the compressed etheric body of the Risen One, so that Christ can be revealed to humanity in our time.

Now let us look at the southern window. There we see matter first in its present condition, in which it is penetrated by the forces of death (the skull on the left in the central motif, and the motif on the left side). Then we see the motif on the right, in which earth material, everything firm, the mineral, is lit up, illuminated, permeated by the spirit; so, where death appeared earlier, now only good spiritual beings preside. It can gradually become clear that this second Christ-sphere was formed by the resurrected body at the time of Christ, after the earth had previously received the substances of the divine body; we human beings can participate freely in the process of its spiritualization. If we do this, we no longer experience the first building standing before us—it becomes transparent. It will become a wonderful cosmic face, the face of a human being who is willing to work on this creation of Christ in the earth freely and consciously with other people.

We see represented in the central motif of the rose window in the South the appearance of Christ as Lord of Karma, which is the culmination of the modern initiation path. The human being sits (sitting is the best position for meditation) and meditates, so that a conscious relationship can be established to Christ's resurrected body. Thereby the death forces in the meditant will be gradually overcome. If these death forces are transubstantiated, then the being appears who has brought about this transubstantiation— the Lord of Karma, Christ. In this way, Christ is experienced in the heights of modern initiation through intuition, as is described in the book *Outline of Occult Science*. In the timeless Christ being, the past (the time of Christ Jesus); the present (his appearance in the etheric); and the future (the spiritualization of humanity and the earth by the Christ force) are inseparably joined together. Above all, the two main forms of Christ's appearance in the present, pointing to the future, now stand in front of us in the glass windows of the auditorium of the second Goetheanum, as they were originally present in the first building in a much more powerful and impressive manner.[138]

On the basis of what has been said, to conclude, let us turn once again to the configuration of the first building. Let us comply with Rudolf Steiner's wish that we never enter the first building without imagining the Representative of Humanity (the Group sculpture) in the east, in the small cupola. If we do this, then we can experience how the unfolding of all forms and colors of both rooms moves toward the Group sculpture. Also the two forms of the present Christ-appearance on the rose windows with their inner connection to the events at the time of Christ Jesus point to the *central figure* that comes toward us from the east. It would not be right to say that this figure is the Christ during his life in Palestine, or the Christ as he meets us in the present as the etheric Christ, or the Christ of the future who descends to us from the heights of modern initiation. He is all of these at the same time, in the single form of his timeless presence, as Rudolf Steiner represented it personally from his inner viewpoint in this sculpture.

Christ is forever connected with us only in his eternal presence, which encompasses at once the entire past and future.[139] Because the human "I" attains its full reality in the present, it therefore finds the possibility of finding Christ in itself. As world "I," Christ meets the human "I" in the moment when (in the human "I") time comes to a standstill, becomes eternity, and unites "one's own "I" with the world "I."[140]

That is the spiritual condition indicated in Richard Wagner's *Parsifal* with the words, "Here, time becomes space" (Act I). Thus, the first Goetheanum was a new space, born out of the stream of spiritual time, in which a conscious meeting with Christ can take place in the present.

One could say: as the Mystery of Golgotha gives to the entire human and earth development its highest meaning, so the figure of the Representative of Humanity (the Group sculpture) gives to the first building, and hence to all of Anthroposophy, its meaning. For the Christ being stands imperturbably in its center. That is, among other things, the first Goetheanum's declaration to us. It is a shining message from the Christ being and Christ activity, not only out of the past; not only into the future; but above all, here and now, in the full conscious present of the "I".

This presentation concludes as once again the words of the cosmic communion resound—the words with which Rudolf Steiner ended his last lecture in the first Goetheanum.

There approaches me in earthly activity
The physical image presented
Of the stars' heavenly beings:
I see them transforming themselves lovingly into will.

There penetrates into me in fluid life
The physical force developed
Of the stars' heavenly deeds:
I see them transforming themselves wisely into feeling.

3.
Christ's Reappearance in the Etheric in Relation to the Fifth Gospel

Preface by Peter Selg

Peter Selg

Rudolf Steiner, the Fifth Gospel
and Christ's Reappearance in the Etheric

Sergei O. Prokofieff

The Mystery of the Resurrection in the Light
of the Fifth Gospel

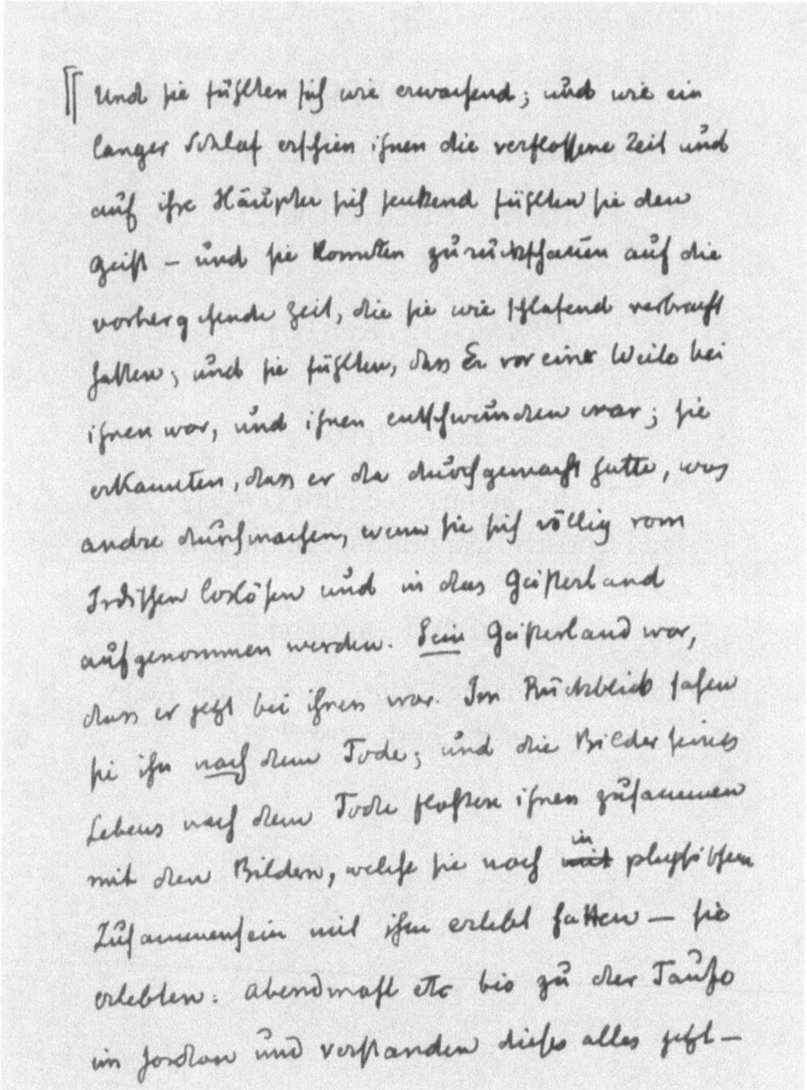

Und sie fühlten sich wie erwachend; und wie ein
langer Schlaf erschien ihnen die verflossene Zeit und
auf ihre Häupter sich senkend fühlten sie den
Geist – und sie konnten zurückschauen auf die
vorhergehende Zeit, die sie wie schlafend verbracht
hatten; und sie fühlten, dass Er vor einer Weile bei
ihnen war, und ihnen entschwunden war; sie
erkannten, dass er da durchgemacht hatte, was
andre durchmachen, wenn sie sich völlig vom
Irdischen loslösen und in das Geisterland
aufgenommen werden. Sein Geisterland war,
dass er jetzt bei ihnen war. Im Rückblick sahen
sie ihn nach dem Tode; und die Bilder seines
Lebens nach dem Tode flossen ihnen zusammen
mit den Bildern, welche sie noch ~~mit~~ in physischem
Zusammensein mit ihm erlebt hatten – sie
erlebten: Abendmahl etc bis zu der Taufe
im Jordan und verstanden dieses alles jetzt –

The awakening of the apostles (Whitsun).
Entry in Rudolf Steiner's notebook regarding the Fifth Gospel.
Rudolf Steiner Archives, Dornach

Preface

Europe has struck dead
The eternal Christ
With written symbols.
Reawaken Christ anew.

— Rudolf Steiner, notebook entry1

In response to a request by many people, the two lectures Sergei O. Prokofieff and I gave during the Easter Conference 2009 at the Goetheanum on the subject of "The Fifth Gospel and Its Significance for the Present and the Future" are published here.

The text is consciously printed with minimal modifications, to retain the verbal character of direct speech, with consideration of the specific community of people who were gathered in the auditorium. In the bibliography, further studies are suggested in which many of the motifs in both lectures are treated in a more extensive and detailed way.

Heartfelt thanks are extended to Ruth Andrea and Ute Fischer for helping with the typing and correction work!

Peter Selg

Ita Wegman Institute,
Arlesheim, Switzerland
May 2009

Rudolf Steiner's Lectures about the Fifth Gospel and Christ's Reappearance in the Etheric

Peter Selg

Dear Friends,

I thank Sergei Prokofieff for making this conference about the Fifth Gospel possible at this time and place. It is quite special that we are united at Easter in the Goetheanum, to speak about, and reflect together, on the deep secrets of the Fifth Gospel and esoteric Christianity. Especially in the days of Holy Week and Easter, human memory is called upon in a special way to internalize the processes that happened at the time of Christ Jesus, and to connect them with the present and future.

I am speaking this evening about Rudolf Steiner's lectures from the Fifth Gospel, in relation to what he described as the most essential event of the future, the "great secret of our age";[2] the occurrence of Christ's reappearance on earth in the etheric realm.

As we are here together at Easter 2009, we are heading collectively toward the year 2010 in a threefold iteration of the 33-year cycles that have elapsed since 1910. That was the year in which Rudolf Steiner began to speak intensively about Christ's imminent reappearance, starting with a lecture in Scandinavia, in Stockholm. Steiner called that coming event a development of human soul capabilities—*natural* human soul forces. According to Steiner, humanity is about to make a great "leap," which already began in 1899, and now is increasing dynamically. People's natural soul capabilities—not only those called forth and intensified by esoteric development, but also the natural soul capabilities of all people—will unfold to the extent that they will penetrate more and more into the sphere of the life forces; into the area of the etheric. Steiner said it will be increasingly possible for people to perceive in the etheric, and with it also the concretely *formed* etheric; that is, the etheric body of nature beings, people, and even greater beings, while maintaining human "I" consciousness.

In ancient times, people saw the etheric in an imaginative way, but they had to lose the perceptive capacity to gain, to develop, their "I" consciousness consolidated in themselves in detachment from the world. However, Rudolf Steiner said that we live at the dawn of an epoch where people with attained and sustained "I" consciousness will discern once again the etheric life sphere. This dawning epoch, as Steiner described, is lengthy. It began in the first part of the twentieth century, and will last more than 2,500 years, so that humanity actually will have a great deal of time to unfold, develop, and strengthen the new soul capabilities. Two thousand five hundred years sounds reassuring. Steiner's statements show us that apparently he much relied on the fact that what was to begin in a rudimentary way in the twentieth century, would actually occur, be perceived, and be protected. Steiner often spoke about the years 1930 (or 1933) to 1940 (once he extended that period to 1945)[3] as being decisive years for this beginning. He also referred to this time, oddly enough, as the darkest epoch of the twentieth century. We can see the truth of that statement in retrospect. Ever again, Steiner pointed out how much would depend on people's not "crushing" the inner experiences that would develop and the phenomena that would appear during these years; these experiences would need, rather, to be protected and promoted.

In his lectures, Rudolf Steiner asked how we will notice that people are awakening to the etheric; he answered by sketching the spiritual future. He said there will be more and more people having "anticipatory" experiences, so that they etherically envision the events of coming days. People will unconsciously begin to look a little into the immediate future, which has something to do with the etheric; they will essentially draw the near future into the present, catch up with it, live in it imaginatively. At the same time, they will find out that by performing an act, even by just setting in motion an intention to act, making a resolution for the future, a picture-experience arises in them. This could be an image that, on the surface, has nothing to do with their intended or performed act, but depicts what they eventually will have to do as karmic compensation for this act. According to Rudolf Steiner, people will experience a karmic, destiny-compensating future aspect in acting, or even just in intending to do something. People will be quite otherwise absorbed in the future force of their own being, in their conscious and social forces. They will not only act but also behold in anticipation, the compensating, correcting result of their action.

This development, Rudolf Steiner said, will point ahead in time and will draw the future into the present, yet it will also include the past—the past will also exist in the present in a heightened way. With an elemental power, something like a karmic recollection, a remembrance of destiny, will arise in a person; the person will sense a "terrible thirst" for karmic reminiscences. In this regard, Steiner described, remarkably, that these soul capacities will be present, but the experiential content will not necessarily be present. People will get into great difficulties. Because of their soul forces, they can and *must* increasingly remember the last earth life, but because of the circumstances of their past life, they find no point of departure for memory—because that earth life extended without depth. For, not by any means will everything be remembered, but only deep, existential experiences connected with the real human "I." For this reason, Steiner said, Anthroposophy is there—among other things—to help us live through our experiences more intensively; and to help us recapitulate our experiences at night, before sleep begins. Then we can remember the experiences later, and our future memory capacity will not fall into a void.

People will also develop a new relationship to time. They will naturally develop new soul capacities, but must learn to deal with them. In connection with this etheric awakening, this growing into the etheric, approaching humanity in a way quite new, will be the figure who has accompanied history for at least 2,000 years—who has been present for 2,000 years in the earth's atmosphere, in the earth atmosphere's etheric realm. Now that humanity is developing toward the etheric, it will therefore also move toward him, toward Christ. Steiner said in his lectures during 1910, that Christ's reappearance from the circumference of the earth is only conditionally a "coming"; it is much more a state of humanity's growing toward him. "Christ will appear again, because people will raise themselves up to him in the etheric heights," Rudolf Steiner said.[4] The "exalted etheric figure" of Christ, according to Rudolf Steiner, will be perceptible to people.[5] This perception is the prerequisite for much more, especially for a strong, very intensive connection with the Christ being himself. In his lectures in 1910, in some intimations in the preceding years, and in much that followed, Steiner made clear that all of Anthroposophy was and is a work of preparation for this human occurrence. It is an event that will and must be consummated, independently of whether people long for it or not; of whether they have a relationship to confessional Christianity or not. It is not a question of confession or religion in the narrow sense. Rather, it concerns human perceptive ability overall in the area of life forces, in the area of the etheric, and for that reason also in the area of the temporal, time rhythms, the "time body." A person will experience past and future differently in the present. People will also experience the "temporality" of humanity, and the representatives of humanity whose work is "soul inspired in world rhythms," as it is expressed in the Foundation Stone Meditation.[6]

Rudolf Steiner hoped that in the Anthroposophical Society those who were his students would pass through an awakening process, so they would be prepared for this coming time. This, however, means that at the same time, they would be in a position to understand the soul phenomena occurring—and this understanding, to be sure, would be not only for themselves. Steiner said that in the twentieth century, there would come people who have these spiritual observations, pictorial experiences, etheric previews and karmic reviews, as well as Christ experiences. These people would need understanding and help, so they would not be committed to psychiatric hospitals as "insane." According to

Steiner, here lies an essential task of the Anthroposophical Society: "so that these first subtly appearing abilities do not pass people by unnoticed and disappear without a trace; so that gifted people are not considered dreamers and fools, but are understood and supported by a small group of people who in this context prevent human misunderstanding from brutally killing these tender beginnings."[7] There exists a danger of "suffocating," an actual physical danger, to which Rudolf Steiner repeatedly pointed; he connected it with his indications about the essential years 1930 or 1933 to 1945. As already has been emphasized: although the soul experiences will develop over a period of 2,500 years, Steiner attributed an essential, if not crucial significance to the destiny of the "pioneer group" in the 1930s and 1940s of the twentieth century.

A review of the century reveals in a shocking way that these rudimentary experiences really happened, often in the most dreadful places—in the Nazi prisons and concentration camps—precisely in this time, in the years Steiner had named. People were tortured and murdered; others, a few others, escaped only at the last moment. Later, they reported about their experiences, including some very spiritual experiences. Rudolf Steiner spoke about "suffocating"; and death by gas, by excruciating suffocation, was the destiny for millions of people, primarily those of Jewish background. Nobody knows about them, knows what martyrdoms they went through, in the most horrible way, at the hands of Ahriman and his hosts. Those were the years in which, according to Steiner, the essential future steps actually should have been taken.

In the same lectures, Steiner also spoke about the effects of the other adversarial force, who is also antagonistically working against humanity's advance and future. In the 1910 lectures, he continually warned about false "Christians," about false "Messiahs," about the misuse of spirituality that will also occur, and continually increase. Christ proclaimed this on Tuesday of Holy Week on the Mount of Olives, speaking about his future return to four of his apostles. "And then if any man shall say to you, lo, here is Christ; or, lo, he is there; believe him not: For false christs and false prophets shall rise, and shall shew signs and wonders, to seduce, if it were possible, even the elect. But take ye heed: behold, I have foretold you all things." (Mark 13, 21-23, King James Version)[8] Along with the danger of "killing," "suffocating," and "stamping out," therefore, is the danger of false, blinding, and concealing spirituality that is deceptively clothed in Christianity, in the framework of pure delusion. Anthroposophists, students of spiritual science, Steiner said, have a task to protect and support people who have etheric experiences. At the same time, anthroposophists need discerning judgment for what the true coming of Christ is; and for what is alien to him. The appearance of the Christ being in the etheric is a subtle, continually endangered process. In other words, the appearance of the human being in the etheric, in Christ's sphere, is threatened today, and will still be threatened long into the future. The years 1930 to 1940 (or 1945) were determining stages on the path, and witnessed the powerful burgeoning of evil. But the process continues, along with the threats to it from right and left.

*

The "coming" of the etheric Christ is actually an ascent of human beings toward Christ. At the same time, however, it is certain that, as of the twentieth century, the Christ being also turns toward people in an intensified way. This meeting has lived for a long time in Christianity, not only as a hope, but as a concrete promise. Precisely on Maundy Thursday evening, on which we find ourselves today, this stream of the former covenant still lives. Christ spoke on Maundy Thursday evening to the apostles about the future. Rudolf Steiner stressed that the proclaimed, predicted love of Christ will come; but it will not come without people's cooperation. In this connection, Steiner spoke very clearly about his own task; about the task of anthroposophical spiritual science. He connected it with the task of

John the Baptist: to prepare people to perceive that realm of heaven—the Christ realm—and to make possible his coming through this perception.[9] For this coming is not by any natural law; it takes place only to the extent its path has been prepared. One can recognize Steiner as a figure, as a spiritual being, who had to open up the way to Christ in a very special way.

The devotion of people to the coming Christ realm must be specific; there must be a purely expectant atmosphere; mere hoping and begging is insufficient. In 1912, two years after the first great announcement of the coming Christ, in Cologne and then one week later in Berlin, Steiner named specific soul capacities people must develop to allow, to make possible, further devotion to Christ. Christ will not reappear in a physical body; instead he will appear in "sheaths" corresponding to the elements of a corporeality; these sheaths must be co-created by people. Many of us know both of these lectures,[10] having considered them in study groups and in inner, meditative life. However, we must continually reawaken to the content of these remarks by Steiner, to understand Christ's future "body" formed out of people's soul forces. The future "astral body" of the Christ being will be formed from the feelings of astonishment and wonder that people develop for the spirituality of the world and creation. When these forces successfully light up in people's souls all over the world (having been supported rather than suppressed through education), they will create a force of attraction for the Christ being. Or seeing the reverse perspective: then it will be possible for Christ to merge with these forces, to use them in a certain sense as his "astral body."

We live in a time when the most massive attacks are made on children's souls, on the forces of reverence and wonder they have brought with them; these forces of reverence are intended to be further unfolded on earth, in the family and elsewhere. Yet, in spite of these attacks, many children still have these hallowed forces of wonder. The future of the children and the future of all humanity and the earth, depend on encouraging these attitudes and capacities. Steiner did not speak in these Cologne and Berlin lectures about the child's forces of wonder; he spoke rather about mature, ripe reverence and wonder for world secrets, for the spirituality of the creation. But there must be preparation in early childhood for adults to develop these capacities of wonder and reverence; preparation for these Christ-guided, Christ-permeated forces.

The other pole Steiner mentioned, which corresponds to Christ's physical "body" and develops in an emotional-spiritual regard, involves individual impulses of conscience that can live in a person. When these impulses grow strong, an energy sphere develops that can be directed toward Christ, and into which he is able enter. Experiencing Christ's coming in the etheric, therefore, is by no means dependent only on a capacity of simple perception. This experience is inherently connected with, and dependent, on people's morality; every advance in spiritual development is, and must be, moral. The centerpoint between feeling wonder, astonishment, or amazement and the individual impulses of conscience corresponds to the sphere of the life body, the etheric body. In this regard, Rudolf Steiner spoke about forces of sympathy and compassion:

> ... Every time a feeling of compassion or shared joy is developed in the soul, an attraction force is formed for the Christ impulse; Christ unites himself through compassion and love with people's souls. Compassion and love are the forces out of which Christ forms his etheric body until the end of earth development.[11]

Thus, as Steiner emphasized, a statement of the Bible becomes very real: "Inasmuch as ye have done it unto one of the least of these my brethren, ye have done it unto me." (Matthew 25: 40, KJV). Until the end of earth development, Christ will form his real life body out of people's concrete compassion and love; out of compassion and love forces. This in no way exclusively applies to the Christ being, or even only principally; it applies to the compassion we show to others, to fellow human beings, to the co-created, to the "You." Only then, in showing compassion, can one truly recognize and worship Christ as the representative of humanity; only if one is actually in a position to see in each concrete "You" a high, even a supreme, Christ-endowed, Christ-connected Being. "Inasmuch as ye have done it unto one of the least of these my brethren, ye have done it unto me."

Altogether, Steiner's 1912 Cologne and Berlin accounts are important for our theme: the coming of the Christ being in the etheric and, accordingly, the realization that Christ in his etheric body is inherently connected with the task of first forming this etheric body in a certain way as humanity's deed and achievement! People must grow toward Christ, not only as observers, but as knowing, feeling, and acting beings. Steiner once said that Christ pervades humanity with moral force.[12] At the same time, the possibility for this depends on whether a spiritual morality permeates and determines our thinking, feeling, and willing. We need spiritual morality to determine and support the forces of reverence, loving participation, and conscientious action in the world. This development can and must happen, said Steiner; the decisive question of the future is a moral one. According to him, we live at the dawn of a new epoch, the time when this moral development must succeed. The coming of, and the connection with, the etheric Christ will have consequences in many areas of peoples' lives. Our connection with the dead, our relationship with those who have preceded us into the spirit and accompany us with their forces, will become much more real and effective. Also, our self knowledge will grow. Poised between past, present, and future, we will become able to form our lives and our life relationships responsibly, with the help of Christ, the future Master of Destiny. Christ supports and organizes life in a progressive way—*if* people want this, if they prepare themselves for it, if they live in pursuit of this coming realm. It is now the dawn of an important time, an important developmental stage in humanity; at the same time, we are close to—or in the midst of—the abyss. Steiner also stressed this aspect repeatedly. It is not simply a matter of lovely soul capabilities and impressions; it is a matter of abilities that are urgently needed because the other forces—the forces of the abyss—will attack with great strength. In the midst of the 1910 lectures mentioned earlier, in these various statements about Christ's coming in the etheric, Rudolf Steiner made the first allusion to a pending Fifth Gospel.

*

It was during the time after Easter on April 18, 1910, in Palermo, Sicily. The stenographic notes of the lecture are sparse. The theme was Christ's coming in the etheric, and Rudolf Steiner spoke about a Fifth Gospel. A postscript appended to the lecture states that Steiner said:

> Among the Rosicrucians, along with the four Gospels, a fifth was taught. Through this spiritual gospel, the other four can be understood. It will be presented to part of humanity in the twentieth century, just like those [gospels] that were issued on the occasion of Christ's appearance 2,000 years ago. The adherents of the Rosicrucian movement, who will have a clear conscience, will understand the significance of this gospel for humanity.[13]

In Palermo, on Sicily, Rudolf Steiner indicated in this way that the Fifth Gospel already existed—it was taught in the esoteric Rosicrucian community. At the same time, he said that in the twentieth century, the Fifth Gospel will first be correctly unveiled or "presented" to part of humanity—a future promise. We do not know how Rudolf Steiner emphasized, accentuated, the next sentence. Did he say: *the adherents of the Rosicrucian movement*, who will have a clear conscience, will understand the significance of this gospel for humanity—or: the adherents of the Rosicrucian movement, *who will have a clear conscience*, will understand the significance of this gospel for humanity? Many years later, Ita Wegman wrote down in a notebook a statement that Steiner had made:

> Rosicrucianism must always be taught within Anthroposophy. Christian Rosenkreutz continually inspires one whom he has chosen; and we will never be able to maintain the Goetheanum unless a Rosicrucian stream, even if hidden, accompanies our Anthroposophical Movement.[14]

A remarkable statement. On one hand, Steiner identified the center of the Anthroposophical Society as being the Goetheanum, not the Rosicrucian stream. On the other hand, he said about the building: we will never be able to maintain it if a Rosicrucian stream does not remain connected with the Anthroposophical Movement. In Palermo, he said "the adherents of the Rosicrucian Movement, who will have a clear conscience, will understand the significance of the Fifth Gospel for humanity. Perhaps it can be understood in this way: the Rosicrucians who make the step to real spiritual science (who "will have a clear conscience") can recognize the significance, the relevance of the Fifth Gospel—neither all Rosicrucians, nor all people who are called Anthroposophists.

Be that as it may. Three years later, in summer 1913, in Munich, Rudolf Steiner quite unexpectedly announced lectures about the Fifth Gospel.[15] We do not know whether anyone hearing this announcement remembered the Palermo statement or was present in Sicily and might have understood the Munich announcement in its context. Today we are in possession of the complete lectures. At that time, however, different people heard the lectures in Palermo and Munich. Even if a few had heard Steiner in both places, would they have had the indication from Palermo, the future promise, in their consciousness, in their memory? Did they know that Steiner had announced something, and now, three years later, apparently decided to attempt the venture? Everything suggests that it was not easy for Steiner to make this decision; he had to wrestle with it—the decision to hold the lectures and to begin revealing the Fifth Gospel in a difficult, tense time. I think it belongs to our task today, also in the sense of the task of "filling the memory with Christ," that we consider in depth the events unfolding around Steiner; they are also actions of the world spirit. It is not simply a matter concerning the history of a society; or concerning an alleged "biographical" knowledge about Rudolf Steiner; rather, these events were expressions of the world spirit, breath of the world spirit. Steiner made the decision to speak about the Fifth Gospel in the face of the coming world war and many disastrous, demonic developments. Adolf Hitler had been in Munich since May, 1913. The war, fascism, the destruction of central Europe, anti-Christian nationalism, and racism came; and the Theosophical Society, which actually had been prepared to bring something else into civilization, had failed to a catastrophic extent.

Rudolf Steiner once called his having to live through these events a "martyrdom" about which he did not wish to speak further.[16] It was not only a matter of society history or even sect history; it was an aspect, a chapter of world history, which pained Steiner; but of course he spoke of it only in an indirect way. If the Theosophical Society had succeeded in preparing the Christ impulse in Central Europe; had enabled it to move into various fields, from education to social work, then everything could have been different. In the midst of this decay, knowing that people would endure unspeakable misery, visualizing their spiritual and physical catastrophes, Rudolf Steiner took a further step forward. Despite all the disasters, even in view of them, he regarded it to be necessary to prepare human souls to develop the forces of love and compassion in order to pave the way for Christ. At this time, it was announced that the course about the Fifth Gospel would be held in Kristiania (in Oslo), a place where Steiner could speak in a special way about anthroposophical Christology.

*

We know that Rudolf Steiner did not travel directly from Munich to Kristiania. Before going, he completed laying the foundation stone in Dornach, with a mantra that began with words about the domination of "evil." The mantra was part of the macrocosmic "Lord's Prayer" from the Fifth Gospel. Steiner spoke about the "cry for the spirit" in present civilization; about the longing for the spiritual, which was having difficulty finding its way. The Dornach building was to be a center of learning that would be an answer to this "cry" of distress. Spiritual necessity would lead to a civil catastrophe if answers to contemporary challenges were not found; if, in other words, the Christ impulse could not enter into all spheres of life, could not transform them. One can presume that Steiner anticipated living through the coming catastrophes; the war, as well as "euthanasia," fascism, and genetic engineering, which underlie the on-going developmental trend of materialism. He founded the Dornach institution in order to bring other, Christian, impulses into civilization. He said at the laying of the foundation stone:

> When we can hear humanity's longing call for the spirit, and we want to construct a real building from which the message of the spirit shall be increasingly proclaimed; when we feel this in the life of this world, then we have the right understanding this evening. Then we know—not in arrogance and not in over-estimating our efforts, but in humility, devotion, and willingness to sacrifice, we know in our persistent striving that we must be the pursuers of this spiritual work. This work has been realized in the West in the course of advancing human development, and it finally had to pass through the necessary opposing stream of Ahrimanic forces. Today humanity is at a point where souls must wither and become desolate if that cry of longing for the spiritual world is not heard. We feel, my dear sisters and brothers, these fears! It must be so, if

> we are to battle further in that great spiritual fight, a fight saturated with fire and love...[17]

With these words, and in this mood of soul, Steiner started for Kristiania, and thus he seemed "saturated with fire and love."

While laying the foundation stone of the "Johannes (John) Building" (later renamed, Goetheanum), Steiner had spoken about devotion and willingness to sacrifice, as well as about as shared feelings of fears ("Let us feel, let us feel these fears, my dear sisters and brothers.") He spoke about contemporizing and developing those forces related to forming the etheric body for the Christ being, about heart forces, about the essential person and feeling forces of joy and sorrow. The "Johannes Building" was not intended to be an introspective temple or a place for a small group's special attempts to satisfy its yearning for a worldview. The building was constructed, rather, as a place *for the world*—although this world scarcely sensed its necessity. Nevertheless, Steiner worked in view of human destiny, in the consciousness of it, and he jointly shared the responsibility for this destiny, even in all of its crises.

In the first seven years of anthroposophical life after 1902, Steiner had methodically built up anthroposophical work and brought it into the world. He had stimulated in a special way the forces of reverence and wonder about the spiritual content of the world, His writings, from *Theosophy* to *Occult Science;* his private and public lectures, and his esoteric lessons appealed to people's upward-looking devotional forces and activated them to participate in earthly-cosmic secrets. The gospel courses, the Christological writings, and especially the lectures about the Fifth Gospel worked in and upon the centerpoint of the heart, which is etheric-Christological, and deeply connected with the mystery of love. The final seven years of this methodically conducted work life, the seven years starting in 1917, were intended to appeal to the practical force of conscience, to the separate endeavors in the social sphere—on farms, in medical practices, in schools, for businesses. Thus, Steiner prepared the necessary sheaths three times for the Christ's second coming. However, the accounts from the Fifth Gospel belong to the etheric core: they are taken from this sphere and work on it as the *heart* of anthroposophical Christology. Therefore, they are indissolubly connected with the Dornach building in its etheric-Christological dimension. Steiner created this building out of his own etheric body. Ita Wegman, who knew this, wrote:

> His words proclaiming Anthroposophy built the Goetheanum etherically. Rudolf Steiner's condensed formulations and his own etheric body were united with the artwork, and were inseparably connected with him.[18]

The etheric body—and precisely the etheric body of a Christian initiate such as Rudolf Steiner—is a love body, a wisdom body, and a master builder. From this aspect of his being, the building arose and developed; and its central statue, its crowning, was the figure of Christ, the representative of humanity in the midst of opposing forces.

Steiner hastened to give the lectures from the Fifth Gospel, and he forged ahead with great intensity. One can sense that these lectures had to be begun prematurely; they should have been held a little later, inside the Goetheanum building itself. But Steiner had no choice; he had to begin, although the conditions were not favorable. He pleaded in Kristiania for the absolute protection of these lectures; that they be guarded as the "sole affair" of the Anthroposophical Society. He requested that people not spread the contents further, and that they not discuss them; rather, that they live in inner meditation with the them. The contents of the Fifth Gospel needed both the individual's inner sphere and the scope of a spiritual community. At the same time, Rudolf Steiner knew that such a community existed only conditionally, and was in no way complete.

*

Rudolf Steiner intended to make a written record of the Fifth Gospel, for a gospel is a written work, a readable text. He wrote much of it down, and read passages in various lectures.[19] The Fifth Gospel was intended to go into the world—but what was it that should go into the world? What was the content of the Fifth Gospel?

As early as 1910 in Palermo, Steiner said the Fifth Gospel is a "spiritual gospel" through which the four other gospels "first become understandable." According to him, the Fifth Gospel is about the figure of "Christ Jesus"; about the conscious comprehension of "Christ Jesus." In their gospels, Matthew, Mark, Luke, and John described Christ Jesus' path from birth or the Baptism in the Jordan until after Golgotha; until the resurrection, Ascension, and Pentecost. The Fifth Gospel, however, not only describes further details of these events, it also discloses in a fundamental way the prerequisites for the events, the anthroposophical-cosmological connections, along with preconditions for the central baptism process that Steiner described as the "centerpoint" of the Mystery of Golgotha.[20] Steiner's lectures from the Fifth Gospel sketch Christ Jesus's earthly biography as the three-year incarnation process of a divine being; an incarnation process that began with the Baptism, but did not end with the Baptism. Rather, three years passed before the Baptism was "completed."[21] The incarnation process of this divine being culminated on Golgotha, attaining there its goal and purpose: the complete entry of the Christ being into the reality of physical life, the unification with this mortal body. The three years were the necessary prerequisite and path—and the inner circle of apostles should have awakened to accompany and protect this process; but it failed to a large extent.[22] Then the Fifth Gospel describes the Christ being's transformation in the earth's atmosphere. Thus, it spans the entire framework within which the separate accounts of the four evangelists are assembled; it establishes the great cosmic anthropology of these three years up until and including the formation of the resurrection body.

In reading the chronicle of humanity's evolution, the cosmic memory of humanity's gaining consciousness, Steiner—and this still makes us breathless—described the Fifth Gospel events from the inner perspective of the apostles. One treads the "holy ground of human observation," Steiner said, when one comes close to these events and talks about them.[23] With what inner feeling, but also with what inner piety and humility, Steiner spoke in Kristiania! One could experience that he moved "on holy ground," with every fiber of his being. Thereby it should be considered that Steiner's description was not only from an internal perspective, not only from the confined experiential sphere of the inner community of the apostles, especially of Peter; his description was also, in large part, from the inner perspective of Jesus of Nazareth Himself. Steiner described the events, as well as the spiritual processes that Jesus of Nazareth had to go through as a prerequisite for the Baptism in the Jordan. From a tremendous closeness to Jesus, from an intimate connection with his existence and path, Steiner observed that the prerequisites included the mystery of the Nathan and Solomon Jesus children, the path of the youths after their union, and, finally, Jesus of Nazareth's receiving the Christ-Being at the Baptism.

*

Ever again, Steiner repeated his appeal to his listeners to study, to internalize these processes, so they might enter into the suffering of Jesus' soul—the suffering involved in humanity's spiritual destiny. For the Nathan Jesus was from the beginning, Steiner said, ingeniously and specially gifted in sharing the experiences of others in their joy and suffering. That was the truly special quality of this child. This soul, because of its special conditions of incarnation, based on its special type of being, lived completely with others. He directly identified and shared the joy and suffering of others, while radiating consolation and help. After his union with the Solomon being, mystery knowledge entered into the Nathan Jesus; and in ever increasing measure, the shared life and suffering of humanity's spiritual situation characterized his life. The scope of the task before him extended beyond individual destiny to the spiritual state of world culture, religion, and spirituality. The great suffering from the degeneration of the old mystery culture and the elite spirit of a contemporary order became a life drama for Jesus. He knew that it was absolutely necessary for spiritual impulses, spiritually created impulses for humanity, to bring ways of changing the misery. Existential suffering through sensing this necessity, along with the ultimate pain of the limitations of one's own being was, according to Steiner, the indispensable precondition for Jesus' receiving the Christ. This existential suffering made possible the event of the Baptism in the Jordan.

It is, in my opinion, important at this point to turn our gaze back to Rudolf Steiner and the beginning of the twentieth century, and then into the future. For by closer observation, we can see that Steiner's internal biography obviously was characterized by suffering from the spiritual "weeping," from his absolute consciousness of contemporary misery. This spiritual misery was also a poverty of ideas, which followed on the heels of the physical catastrophe of World War I. At the beginning of the twentieth century, two thousand years after the Jordan event, there was the next, heightened turning of the Christ Spirit toward the earth, not for a renewed incarnation but for the preparation and possibility of an appearance in the etheric realms. Steiner prepared people for this event; or rather, he brought them onto the path to help make the event possible. This preparation was accomplished through his spiritual-scientific Christological teaching, as well as through the spiritual steps he gave for inner individual development. Steiner's hope connected with his unveiling of the Fifth Gospel consisted—among other things—of enabling people to participate in Christ's destiny. More precisely, it consisted in encouraging the imitation of Christ; encouraging people in cooperatively creating

Christ's etheric body. In referring to Jesus of Nazareth and his painful experience of humanity's spiritual-cultural degeneration, Steiner said:

> When one directs a spiritual gaze to humanity's evolution, one learns to know a number of things about the pain and suffering in the world that people must endure. But one receives a tremendous impression from the soul that experienced the greatest pain out of pure sympathy with humanity; the most concentrated pain concerning the descent of humanity, concerning humanity's lost ability to receive what was prepared for it in the spiritual worlds.[24]

That is the actual drama of Jesus' suffering. In this drama, there should be someone to have compassion on people's life problems and crises; people should have the experience of receiving empathy, even in 1913. Steiner did not justify the appeal specifically; he only pointed to the significance of this spiritual process. He said that the Fifth Gospel is important in general; people will need it as a reference for strength and consolation in their future work. In the context of this consideration, however, we can sense that all this exists in connection with Christ's reappearance in the etheric; with its preparation, with its facilitation by the heart forces of the compassionate person. Thus, the great emphasis of the Fifth Gospel is certainly on passion; but it is passion for knowledge, which is dramatically different from worshiping the cross and adoring cloistered Christianity, Western institutional Christianity. Of course, Rudolf Steiner turned toward Golgotha, but in total harmony with the path of Christ Jesus. Understanding the Fifth Gospel makes possible a deeper understanding of Christ in an orientation toward the future.

> Little by little, it will be necessary for humanity to understand that, in reality, for earthly development to continue

> after Golgotha, this Christ being had to enter into the earth aura through pain. Humanity must feel its destiny connected with this Christ-pain, and the connection of humanity with this Christ-pain must become ever more concrete. Then one will understand how this pain has worked in a re-enlivening way for earth development since the Mystery of Golgotha.[25]

We must take a look at how unusual these statements by Rudolf Steiner are. It may seem that he simply assumes the old Christian-esoteric, monastic tradition, which is the connection of the individual with Jesus' pain. For Steiner, everything proceeds in the direction of the future out of "I" forces and world ties. The forces of pain are transformed and redeemed in the earth's aura, in the earth's circumference, now present in Christ's sphere—humankind's destiny is connected with this Christ pain; The resurrection forces, the "re-enlivening forces" seek to be effective in all areas of life on earth, in the midst of all its problems—which today are far from lessening.

One should, I think, also recognized that the sentences of Steiner last quoted were delivered on the eve of the greatest war that Central Europe and the earth had experienced up to that time. A few months later—and for many years—an enormous cloud of suffering surrounded many countries on the earth. But Christ worked in the surroundings. It is an earthly-cosmic situation and account: the pain, the aura of the earth, and the re-enlivening forces. One should not underestimate Steiner and his task; for him, it was a matter of the cosmos and earth, of their destiny, of humanity's destiny. Christ lives—and we live in a time where we may once again come to know this Christ reality in depth, to connect ourselves with its spirituality. Especially with this help, we can really get through what lies ahead, so that, in connection with resurrection forces, we can perform the work that must be accomplished for earth civilization.

*

In this regard, the esoteric community of the apostles can be a central theme for us. For people who will have to meet the events, the reality of the etheric Christ in the twentieth and twenty-first centuries, and beyond, it is the model and prototype of a spiritual community. Steiner once said that in the future, one will live with the etheric Christ in the earth's aura as the apostles lived with him in his time.[26] "So shall ye be my disciples," it was said on Maundy Thursday evening in the farewell speech,[27] with a view toward the distant future. It is a matter of human beings building an esoteric community; of their unified activity, their unified activity with Christ as the real nucleus of their community. It is a matter of community-building with the reappearing etheric Christ. We see Steiner as a teacher, but also as a preparer of this event. —Steiner, who himself went through much suffering, through spiritual shared suffering. We see the anthroposophical community; we see the people who gathered around Rudolf Steiner, who were instructed by him. They should have been prepared, so that the failure of Gethsemane and Golgotha—the apostles' sleep and their flight—would not have returned within the community. Andrei Bely immediately perceived this dimension of the Kristiania lectures, and wrote in desperation to Steiner: "We are sleeping apostles.[28] This deeply experienced, fully justified, and quite factually correct statement came from a Russian soul full of ardor. The lectures from the Fifth Gospel were not just interesting teaching subjects, but an existential challenge. Steiner said he was "responsible" for the lectures on the Fifth Gospel. He *had* to begin them, even though he could not continue to speak about this theme, and more or less had to break them off because of time constraints and because the lectures were not received with the necessary understanding.[29] Steiner was "responsible" for these lectures—they belonged to what he was responsible to bring to the spiritual community; to those Rosicrucians in Anthroposophy whom he hoped would be fully awake; he hoped would have a "clear consciousness." Steiner did not speak to them "about" Christ, rather, in a certain sense, he spoke out of himself in Christ's presence—as Sergei Prokofieff said in his words announcing this conference. We sense this quality in the lectures about or from the Fifth Gospel: they are not simply speaking "about" Christ, there is a deeply moving presence and Christ-reality in these lectures. Christ Jesus comes toward one, as a figure approaching—just as Steiner planned for the central Group statue in the first Goetheanum.[30] He said, "People must exchange the spirit of the 'merely intended' for the spirit of direct observation, directly empathizing with and beholding the spiritually alive Christ walking beside all human souls."[31] He spoke about all human souls—souls of every confession, every worldview, every stream, and every group. Christ is there; he is near. He comes ever closer. It is not a matter of knowing but of feeling, of a beholding.

Christ's life, according to Steiner, is increasingly "direct, personal experience."[32] One can see, in reviewing the twentieth century, that these experiences of direct beholding occurred especially in times of misery. Steiner also pointed to that early on: "...Christ will walk beside a person and be his counselor. That is not meant only as image. In reality, people will receive the advice they need from the living Christ, who is their counselor and friend; who speaks to human souls like a person who physically walks beside us."[33] Even in the basement of Block 11 at Auschwitz, the terrible death block, one of the darkest places of a demonic, completely abysmal site on earth, there was found a Christ figure carved in the stones of a cell wall, the last deed of a dying prisoner.[34]

*

The entire ethic of the Fifth Gospel is permeated with deep human modesty. Both opposing forces were at work: the ahrimanic suffocating power, the ahrimanic killing will, and the luciferic ecstatic power, the dizzy lightness of deception. In the

Nazi party during the years from 1933 to 1945, both powers worked in unison. In view of this coming time, Steiner held the healing lectures from the Fifth Gospel. He worked in advance for the far distant future. In one of the 1910 lectures about Christ's reappearing in the etheric, Steiner said unexpectedly, parenthetically, in a subordinate clause:

> Spiritual science will do everything in the coming centuries and millennia, so that people will have the opportunity to use incarnation in the right way....[35]

"Spiritual science will do everything in the coming centuries and millennia..." That is an objective statement. In 1913 and 1914, Steiner began to hold lectures on the Fifth Gospel in Central Europe; 12 years later he had to leave earth existence. In 1934, Ita Wegman experienced a near-death experience in connection with the etheric Christ being, and she experienced both together—Christ and Rudolf Steiner.[36] One can have the impression that Steiner held the Fifth Gospel lectures (for the sake of which, we are meeting here at Easter in the Goetheanum) not only for the people who were "accidently" gathered in Kristiania. Certainly he did speak to those people, and what they received depended to a great extent on their alertness and receptive capabilities. Yet he also spoke beyond them; he spoke for unborn souls, for the dead, for beings who stand above humanity, and perhaps also beneath.

We could ask where the people who joined the opposition to the Nazis, obtained the forces to do so. Some of them had exceptional powers—highly developed powers of moral conscience, a readiness for individual sacrifice and an affirmative attitude toward pain. Where did they obtain these forces?[37] Possibly this was part of their incarnation path, their foreknowledge, their pre-birth resolve. I suppose, Steiner's words in 1913 and 1914 could be effective in different ways and other places as a source of power and potential, more than we think in our often narrow (and only apparently) anthroposophical view. It is important we understand that the lectures from the Fifth Gospel and the themes of the etheric Christ-event, concern people's morality, not superficial spirituality and interesting viewpoints; rather, they concern human becoming in a very existential and moral sense. We know that Steiner once translated the three words "Thy kingdom come" as "Your kingdom extends into our deeds and into our moral conduct."[38] The coming kingdom, God's true coming realm is the sphere of His Son, originating in love. This realm gains importance, expands through human deeds and moral conduct, in the sense of building bodily sheaths and organs for the coming Christ, in the sense of humanity's capacity to work for the good.

I would like to close with Christ's words from Maundy Thursday evening. We know through John the evangelist, that at the end of the gathering, after the farewell speech, Christ turned spiritually to his Father and spoke the high priestly prayer. Friedrich Rittelmeyer has written some wonderful devotional studies on this prayer, and Steiner interpreted some passages from them. I want to read a few lines from Steiner's rendering because we are together this evening for this theme in the Goetheanum; and because these lines speak of the apostles and the reappearing Christ.

> They will live in the future by the fact
> That their soul's eye is prepared
> To behold Thee as the truly and only ground of worlds,
> And the creating Christ Jesus
> Whom Thou hast sent to them.[39]

The Mystery of the Resurrection in the Light of the Fifth Gospel

Sergei O. Prokofieff

"The Fifth Gospel is the anthroposophical gospel."
— Rudolf Steiner, October 3, 1913[40]

Dear Friends,

On this festive morning I would like to wish all of you Happy Easter. At this Easter time may light, love, and peace radiate in your entire life; those qualities we need, especially today, everywhere in the world.

It is no coincidence that this Easter conference of 2009 is devoted to the Fifth Gospel. Exactly 100 years ago, in the year 1909, two events took place that are connected with the contents of this conference. Later, in 1917, Rudolf Steiner pointed out that an initiate could have experienced the appearance of Christ in the etheric as early as 1909.[41] In an esoteric sense, this means that in 2009, already 100 years have passed since the beginning of this new epoch. For 100 years we have been living in the time of Christ's etheric reappearance. In autumn 1909, not far from here in Basel, Steiner spoke for the first time about the secret of the two Jesus children; the secret that also belongs to the Fifth Gospel, even though at that time Steiner did not yet use the term "Fifth Gospel."

At the laying of the foundation stone for the first Goetheanum, on September 20, 1913, Steiner spoke the Lord's Prayer for the first time, and mentioned that he would begin an account of the Fifth Gospel, specifically based on this prayer.[42] One year later, on September 19, 1914,[43] reviewing the laying of the foundation stone on its first anniversary, Steiner revealed something quite special. At the laying of the foundation stone a year earlier, he had been able to proclaim to humanity the words of the macrocosmic Lord's Prayer, which was central in the life of Jesus of Nazareth. And he had been able to speak this out of the direct inspiration of the entity who became the bearer of the Christ being on earth; out of the inspiration of the Nathan-Jesus, Jesus of Nazareth.

Why was it precisely this being who could give the account from the Fifth Gospel realm? Because he is the only one who had taken part at the time of Christ in all the events from beginning to end: Jesus of Nazareth was present for 33 years, during the entire occurrence. We can remember that Zarathustra, the Solomon-Jesus, was engaged in this incarnation initially for 12 years, then for 18 years; and Christ himself was connected with these events through the last 3 years. But there is only one being who participated in the *entire* path described in the Fifth Gospel, through the full 33 years: the being of the Nathan soul. Therefore, it is fully justified, and also logical, that in the spiritual world the initial inspiration for Steiner's accounts proceeds out of this being's domain, from the sphere of the Fifth Gospel.

In October 1913, directly after laying the foundation stone, Steiner spoke in Kristiania (Oslo) for the first time; and there he spoke the most directly and strongly about the theme of the Fifth Gospel.[44] There was an event preceding both this conference in Norway and the laying of the foundation stone in Dornach, surrounding the fourth Mystery Drama in Munich. Along with the performances of this drama, Steiner held a lecture cycle with the title "The Secrets of the Threshold." In a certain regard, the culmination of this cycle reveals the characterization of modern initiates who, when they want to come into connection with the true human "I,"—the highest spiritual aspect of the human ego—can experience something like a powerful leap over the world abyss. For here on the threshold to the true human "I," the initiates must leave everything behind that they have thought, felt, or carried out in their life with their will. They must actually become empty and stand before absolute nothingness while retaining consciousness. They must go through this nothingness, through this world abyss, into which they plunge—with the danger of not reaching the other side.[45] A shocking narration by Rudolf Steiner! He concludes by saying that when all prerequisites are fulfilled, the person receives something like a gift from the spiritual world; like the greatest gift from the other side of world existence, the *true "I."*

If a person reads this passage attentively, the question arises in the soul: from whom actually does an initiate receive the true "I" on the other side of the world abyss? One doesn't need to reflect for very long. Out of the complete flow of this cycle, an answer comes forth naturally: only from the one being who can grant a person the true "I," and that is the Christ being. An initiate who is accepted, receives from Christ's hands the true "I," and therefore the clearest, highest consciousness of the spiritual world. Only that initiate who has experienced the new baptism with the fire of the "I" and the spirit can research in the spiritual world as Steiner has demonstrated with the Fifth Gospel.

In one of his last accounts from the realm of the Fifth Gospel, he unveiled for us the manner in which this spiritual research comes about and forms the basis for delivering the Fifth Gospel.[46] There he related that in order to research the great connections of world development one must unite oneself with the world of the angels to such an extent that one experiences that "it is not I who am thinking, but the angel thinking in me." When one, by fully maintaining the "I," can experience being thought by an angel, then one is, according to Steiner, in a position to research the great connections in the spiritual world as they are represented from old Saturn to future Vulcan. If one wants to research shorter periods from the Akasha Chronicle, from upper Devachan, however, then one must enter into a still more intimate connection—with an archangelic being. Then one experiences oneself as though enveloped in the archangelic being, who carries one from one epoch to another. Thus, one can research the cultural epochs, for example, as well as the events on Atlantis, Lemuria, and so forth.

If a person wants to fathom individual concrete incidents that happened on the physical plane as they can be found, for example, in all their earthly details in the Fifth Gospel about the life of Jesus of Nazareth on earth, then as initiate one must go still one step further (we can also say one step higher)—into the area of the time spirits, the archai. Now a person must unite with the being of an archai—and here we can think particularly of Michael. Steiner offers a comparison in regard to the type of connection formed with an archai being. He says that one experiences feeling like a grain of wheat would feel when it is crushed between a person's teeth. The human soul being is consumed by an archai being. With this being, one comes into a connection with the highest spiritual communion. Only in this case, it is not in the way a person usually receives communion; but we ourselves become communion for an archai being. Why is this necessary? Because only here on earth can a person receive the true "I" from Christ's hand, and thereby recognize the being of the Mystery of Golgotha—precisely because this took place *on the earth*. Only a person on earth can receive such knowledge and approach the archai being. A tremendous perspective—a human being becomes communion for a hierarchical being! This condition—one could call it a *reverse communion*—becomes the condition for researching the life of Jesus of Nazareth on the physical plane.

I relate this in order to awaken in you a consciousness that we should in no way imagine such research as being simple or easy to attain. Steiner says that the researcher goes through great pain. Then something astonishing is possible. For united in consciousness with an archai, an initiated spiritual researcher can investigate events from the time of Christ in such detail that, for example, out of this research it emerges that the grave cloths, shrouds, and face cloths in which Christ was wrapped after his death after he was removed from the cross, lie there in every detail as is described in the John Gospel.[47] Steiner reported to us how surprised he was himself as he, through his communion with an archai being, a time spirit, came to this result out of the Akashic Record. Then, opening the John Gospel, Steiner saw that John had described the situation there exactly as he, Rudolf Steiner, had found it in his research before he consulted the Biblical account.[48]

*

If, with this as background, we turn to the accounts from the Fifth Gospel, it will at first surprise us that in Kristiania, Steiner began the actual account with the Whitsun event. In what follows he did not proceed chronologically, from the usual stream of time that flows from the past to the future, rather, he went backward in the stream of *spiritual time*. That is the stream in which all the hierarchies live and work; it flows from the future to the past, with the light of the future illuminating the past.

Out of this stream of time, Steiner began to speak about the Whitsun event, and with the light of this occurrence, he highlighted more and more the preceding happenings at the time of Christ: the 40 days of the dialogue between the Risen One and the apostles, the Mystery of Golgotha, and then the still earlier life of Jesus of Nazareth. In later lectures, Steiner converted—or transported—these events into the stream of normal time, so they can be understood by us earth-bound people. But there is a special significance that in Kristiania, he spoke out of the same spiritual stream of time in which he did the research.

What does it mean that the whole Fifth Gospel began with Whitsun, with the investigation of the Whitsun event? It is an allusion to the relationship Whitsun has to our present time, to every person in the present. For in our epoch we stand before a particular task: in the new initiation based on the anthroposophical training path, the spiritual student must come, through awakening capacities that slumber in every person, into a waking process in relation to the threshold, that is, in relation to the spiritual world. This waking process took place world-historically and archetypically in the Whitsun event; it was a waking of the apostles to an understanding of what they had previously experienced, but had not grasped at all. Therefore, the Whitsun occurrence is the most up-to-date event of the present and future. Humanity will be able to find its way in the future only when it is able to experience something that in the sense of modern initiation can be characterized as a renewed Whitsun;

that is, a Whitsun event for which the world-historical, cosmic archetype occurred at the time of Christ.

From this point of view, from the heights of the Whitsun event, so to speak, as modern people who are awakened in the consciousness soul for the reality of the spiritual world, we can look farther back to much greater occurrences, which are all grouped around the Mystery of Golgotha. The right path for the present does not lead directly to the Mystery of Golgotha; it leads first through the Whitsun event. First, the awakening to the spiritual sphere; and then from this sphere, seeking the connection with the central event of earthly and human development, with the Mystery of Golgotha. Today we must seek in a new and conscious way, which in earlier centuries was not yet possible in this form.

Now with two short examples I would like to clarify to what extent the events at the time of Christ are prototypes for what we can experience in our time, in relationship to the Christ being. First, I want to mention one event that lies outside the narrower area of the Fifth Gospel. Steiner often depicted the experience of Paul before the gates of Damascus; that is, the conversion of Saul to Paul out of a direct perception of Christ. In 1910, in the course of announcing the appearance of Christ in the etheric, Steiner never tired of repeating that this experience of Paul represents a prophecy for what will be an event for increasing numbers of people in the next 3,000 years: the new perception of Christ. For this perception, Paul's experience is like a world-historical prototype.

With still another example, now from the Fifth Gospel itself, I would like to point out this direct connection to the present. We know that as the most important result of the etheric reappearance of Christ, a metamorphosis of human conscience will occur. Conscience was, in earlier centuries a more or less inaudible voice. In the future, conscience will not only speak, but will unfold itself in a totally new world of imaginations. One can envision that this will appear all the more intensively when a person comes into a crisis situation, in a situation of unconsciousness, where one must exert all one's spiritual forces. One perhaps, nevertheless, could experience oneself as lost.

In such a situation, when during a quiet time, one seeks advice, it could happen that an experience arises of an imaginative sort of dream object, an imagination out of the future is shown, a deed that one will perform once in life. When one then further meditates on what this deed might signify in one's destiny, to this first image a second will be added, coming now not from the future, but from the past. In this second image, one would recognize something that perhaps years ago, decades ago, one carried out; a deed that needs karmic compensation. Steiner called this process the spiritual metamorphosis of conscience.[49] Then a person will experience how these two images move toward one another and penetrate each other. One will see how one task is brought from the past, and another from the future; and that these two tasks are connected with each other. And thus, one will be shown something that one has done wrong in the past; and now a compensation must be carried out in the future. And this will be the new voice of conscience having become *visible*. The person will recognize that this compensating act is of a special kind.

Increasingly, the meditating person will understand that this future deed not only balances mistakes from the past, but that it can also serve the advancement of all humanity. In this quality a person will understand today how Christ works as Master of Karma, which is that by balancing personal karma, people can serve not only themselves, but the ever greater well-being of humanity. With that metamorphosis of conscience, the karma balance will gradually become a force that promotes humanity's entire development, with the Christ as Master of Karma. Here we are concerned with a reality that has been experienced today by only a few people; but in the future, over the next 3,000 years, an increasing number of individuals will experience this.

Knowing what lies ahead and what people in the future will more and more frequently experience, when we look back now at the time of Christ in light of the Fifth Gospel, then we can see the awakening of the apostles at the Whitsun event as the archetype of all future events. Rudolf Steiner describes this most remarkably in his lectures about the Fifth Gospel: He says the apostles experienced an awakening out of the deepest sleep state. Their experience came first out of a crisis, out of a condition of full isolation and loneliness between Ascension and Whitsun, because the Christ, the dearest being, the one most important to them, had disappeared from their gaze. Out of this feeling of total unconsciousness, the apostles received their new consciousness on Whitsun day. With this, they could acquire memory images that showed them how before the time of their unconsciousness they had passed forty days with the Risen One, when he had spoken to them about the being of the Mystery of Golgotha and the secrets of spiritual worlds. They experienced these images, however, not in the sense of the past, but as a task for the future. From those images given at Whitsun, the apostles could ascertain that they had passed forty days on earth with a spiritual being, who (Steiner stressed continually) dwelt in time among them in a spiritual body. At that time, they did not know yet who this spiritual being really was. To be sure, they experienced the deepest heart connection; the deepest love for this being; but they could not recognize him during the forty days. Then the images that they had at first experienced, and which pointed them mightily toward the future, gradually joined other visions from a still earlier past: reflections from scenes that the apostles had experienced on earth before the Mystery of Golgotha in their physical-spiritual consciousness with Christ. There Christ had been present, he had been recognizable, but they had not yet been able to understand him in a deeper sense. Now they experienced how these two kinds of images, one from the future and the other out of the past, moved toward one another and penetrated each other. Out of this, they could understand the being whom they physically had accompanied in Palestine before the Mystery of Golgotha; the being with whom they had eaten at a table during the Last Supper. This being was the same who was shown to them through the images of the first kind. Now they knew that the suprasensory risen being they had met during this forty-day dialogue was the same being they had known from the time before the Mystery of Golgotha.[50]

Thus, the apostles experienced macrocosmically at the Whitsun event what ever more people will go through beginning in our time on the microcosmic level: the metamorphosis of conscience. In both cases, there occurs the awakening from a crisis situation; and in this awakening both types of images, from the past and from the future, are present. Then the images unite, clarifying one another, giving impulses for new activity, for the will. Out of this experience the apostles could, after Whitsun, take up the powerful force of the Christ impulse in their feeling and especially in their will, in order—as the Gospel relates—to carry this impulse to the end of the world.[51] However, Steiner said the apostles still had to wait a long time before complete understanding about the events of Christ would come to them; complete understanding came only in the spiritual world after their death.[52] Today, on the other hand, in the consciousness soul epoch, and with the help of Anthroposophy, this full understanding is possible on the earth, in clear "I" consciousness.

*

In the course of the Fifth Gospel, there is an account by Rudolf Steiner that throws quite a new light on the events at Palestine.[53] Steiner reports that the Baptism in the Jordan is comparable with human conception. The original text of the Luke Gospel also testifies that John the Baptist heard during the Baptism a heavenly voice that said: "This is my beloved son, today I have created him." This is how the original text reads.[54] Then, the life of Christ for three years on the earth is like an embryonic unfolding of his being. After that, the Mystery of Golgotha takes place—as the birth of the Christ being in the earth sphere. Then follow the forty days between the Mystery of Golgotha and the Ascension, which denote the actual life of Christ on earth with people, with the twelve apostles. We must, according to Steiner, compare the death of a human being with the resurrection following. After death, a person goes into the spiritual world and rises, after a time, into Devachan. Christ, however, did not leave the earth; he merely disappeared from the apostles' sight. They had to be tested before being illumined by the spirit, just as an examination always must take place on every true initiation path for human beings before the merciful attention of the spiritual world. Thus, we can say that between Ascension and Whitsun, Christ united himself with the earth to enter into the souls of the apostles at Whitsun, and then into the souls of other people; and in the future, through the mediation of the Holy Spirit into all people.

Why through the mediation of the Holy Spirit? Rudolf Steiner gives a shocking answer to this. He says that no human being can take Christ directly into the self without immediately withdrawing—because the cosmic Christ being is so powerful. Therefore, the Zarathustra "I" had to withdraw before the Baptism, because no earth "I" can endure the Christ-Being's direct presence. It is possible under only one condition: when Christ enters the human "I" through the mediation of the Holy Spirit.[55] Then the "I" not only is able to bear the Christ presence, but also to experience itself infinitely intensified and expanded. Steiner has shown us the concrete significance of this with his spiritual research.

If we summarize Christ's path on earth from this point of view, we can now ask: what is embryonic development? This is the condition in which the "I" has not yet united itself with its earthly physicality; rather, the sheaths, particularly the physical body, are formed from outside. Not until birth does the "I" slip into this body. In Christ's life, this happened at the Mystery of

Golgotha. Thereby Christ's physical body was transformed into the resurrection body or spirit body, in which He then lived on the earth and remained with the apostles during the forty days. But the apostles could not understand what he said to them; they were in a condition of detachment. Certainly they took into themselves what they heard, but were not yet able to make it fully conscious, to penetrate it cognitively.

What Christ said to the apostles during these forty days was not merely words; it was rather an active weaving of thoughts. This happened before the time in which the cosmic intelligence of Michael descended to earth, through which people would become thinking beings who could contemplate themselves.[56] If one had asked a person at the time of Christ where he obtained his thoughts, he would have answered: not from myself but from the sun. By "from the sun," the person would have meant from the all-encompassing sun being, which all mysteries considered as the leading being of earth development; from the being that later appeared as Christ on the earth. With each of Christ's words, the apostles absorbed living thoughts into themselves, just as people otherwise received them through Michael from the sun. Now, however, for the first time the apostles assimilated thoughts from the earth, for the spiritual sun itself walked among them. From this spiritual sun they directly received the living thoughts, the world thoughts, which could reveal to them knowledge of the spiritual world, as well as the spiritual aspect of the Mystery of Golgotha as an affair not only of humanity, but also of the gods.[57] Then suddenly everything became dark. These ten days after Ascension were for the apostles the most difficult time of their lives, a time when everything was taken away from them.

Before the Mystery of Golgotha, they accompanied Christ on the earth. They perceived Christ physically, but could not understand him. After the Mystery of Golgotha, during the forty days, they were able through the words of the Risen One to take up world thoughts into themselves, but were still unable to bring this world wisdom to full consciousness. At Ascension, they were suddenly fully abandoned by Christ—their sun had set. They stood in the darkness with only a faint echo of what they had received from Christ during the forty days. Even though they could not make what they had received conscious, they carried in themselves the inner force of what they had received earlier. This inner force, which was no longer perception, thought, or word, was now for them the only thing to which they could call on in order to withstand these ten days of the most difficult test between Ascension and Whitsun. They were entirely alone, dependent only on themselves to awaken to the full extent of the new spiritual consciousness on Whitsun morning.

As we summarize these mighty macrocosmic events, we can experience something from the Fifth Gospel that is deeply entrusted to all of us by Steiner's work. This is in an area, however, where at first perhaps one would hardly suspect a direct relation to the contents of the Fifth Gospel, which I have just sketched. When we turn our attention now to the theoretical knowledge base that is formed by the whole of Anthroposophy (that sounds somewhat dry here) and for which Steiner's early work stands—especially *Philosophy of Spiritual Activity*, which presumably deals only with philosophical questions—we realize with astonishment and great surprise that an existential connection to the contents of the Fifth Gospel can be discovered. What is going on here? We find in this book, among other things, the account of what the world of pure perception is. At first, we perceive everything without understanding it. Then, we are told what thinking is in itself, without any kind of perception. In this thinking we can experience a great deal; however, we have the feeling that one remains as though in a dream and does not penetrate to fully grasp reality. So in thinking, also, we are stuck with only part of reality. Then a third thing is described to us: the exceptional state, the breakthrough into the space of darkness, where everything is taken away from us, all perceptions as well as thoughts. Parenthetically, I would like to add here that the exceptional state is often understood as "reflecting on the thought content." However, this is not what is meant, for this would be ordinary memory. What must be achieved in the exceptional state is rather what we already know from meditation, where we repress all contents and concentrate only on the inner force that holds these concepts together. When we grasp *this force* in the exceptional state, then we have found the golden thread that can lead us on the wings of thinking into the spiritual world. This is where, according to Steiner, perception and thinking are no longer separate, but from the beginning reveal themselves to the observer in connection with one another.[58] Every spiritual perception carries world thoughts within it. Therefore, the modern path into the spiritual world leads through this exceptional state, whether it is on the path described in *Philosophy of Spiritual Activity* or through spiritual training and meditation.

We find the prototypes of these four steps (pure perception, pure thinking, exceptional state, and awakening to the spiritual) at the time of Christ; they are also described in *The Philosophy of Spiritual Activity* and *Truth and Science*. For the apostles before the Mystery of Golgotha, they had perceptions, powerful insights into the Christ being's effectiveness on earth, but—despite their desperate efforts—they could not understand these. Then, during the forty days, they also received cosmic thoughts, which really should have clarified everything for them. In this world of cosmic thoughts, however, they lived as though in a deep sleep, and consequently could not connect their consciousness with the previous perceptions. Then came the darkest time, the ten days in which they could rely only on the spiritual force within themselves, which they had received from the forty-day communion. Out of this force alone, they could overcome unconsciousness. Perhaps some of you remember that in the lecture "How Do I Find the Christ?"[59] Steiner alluded to unconsciousness and one's inner rising out of unconsciousness as the *present path* to Christ. For this relationship to Christ, we also have a model in the Fifth Gospel. The apostles retained *in their exceptional state,* as their final innermost connection with Christ, the spiritual power through which they had to overcome all of their unconsciousness, desolation, and loneliness. Not until their illumination with the light of the Whitsun event, did they receive at the same time, images of their living together with Christ Jesus. These images poured in from the spiritual world as perceptions and enlivened thoughts from the earlier forty-day dialogue with the Risen One. Then the apostles began to grasp the Mystery of Golgotha with present-day understanding, with actual cognition. This understanding, however, came from the spiritual side, from where memories came toward them as from the beginning, in perceptions permeated with world thoughts.

Thus, about Steiner's revealing the Fifth Gospel in the 1913 lectures, we can say that it was positioned not only at the chronological mid-point of Anthroposophy's development (between the years 1902 and 1924–25); but also that it forms the spiritual nucleus of the entire anthroposophical Christology. However, only when we build a bridge from the Fifth Gospel to Steiner's early work, to *The Philosophy of Spiritual Activity*, and understand that they are inseparably connected with one another, do we also discover something decisive in Steiner's biography. We find that like the one who wrote *The Philosophy of Spiritual Activity* and consequently continued on this path, we must come inevitably into the realm of the Fifth Gospel; for in reality, the seeds of the Fifth Gospel are already contained in *The Philosophy of Spiritual Activity.* Thus, the Fifth Gospel, the spiritual and chronological mid-point of Anthroposophy, is as well at its beginning, and is directly connected with Steiner's entire early philosophical work.

But we can go further. Let us look now at the fact that Jesus' early life history plays a very important role in the Fifth Gospel. Steiner spoke at great length about the youth of Jesus of Nazareth; about the long path that enabled him to receive the Christ being on earth at the Jordan Baptism. Why did Steiner speak so extensively about that? Naturally, one can think that the reason is obvious; the four gospels do not say anything about it, and Steiner wanted to fill the gap. Of course, that is right. But that explanation does not yet plumb the depths of this circumstance. To consider the issue more precisely, we must say that the basic gesture of the Fifth Gospel proceeds from Jesus to Christ. That is so because the being of Christ, his three-year life and suffering on earth, and the Mystery of Golgotha, will never be understood correctly until we fundamentally grasp the nature of the being of Jesus before the Baptism in the Jordan. For, as humanity, we are *all* on the "Jesus side"; that is, we are in the state before the Baptism in the Jordan. Like Jesus, we also must tread the path today "from Jesus to Christ." We must inwardly so transform ourselves that we can microcosmically also take up the Christ, as Jesus could macrocosmically take up the Christ at the Baptism in the Jordan. Therefore, for us today, the Fifth Gospel is a training book in the most modern sense. It is not merely the account of events 2,000 years ago, but a concrete guide to what we all essentially need as Christ-seeking people.

Today, one who in oneself wants to take up the Christ being in a conscious way needs two elements. One must create in oneself an inner likeness, so to say, of both Jesus-children. On the one hand, one needs full purity and an innocent childlike quality. That is, everyone who wants to take up Christ within must become like a child, just as the Nathan-Jesus archetypically experienced this childlike force. But that alone does not suffice in order to receive the Christ. To do that, we still need the second, quite polar side—the entire wisdom of a Zarathustra. At first this sounds like a contradiction. But we really must connect in ourselves, with the greatest simplicity and purity of the little child, the entire wisdom of which earth development is capable. For this, we need the models of the Nathan-Jesus and Solomon-Jesus entities equally. We require, along with the purity and childlikeness of the Nathan-Jesus, the entire wordly wisdom of Zarathustra, gathered through many incarnations and initiations.

In one place, Christ himself pointed almost imperceptibly to that. It is the place where he says to his disciples, "Be as wise as the serpent, and as harmless as the dove"—not naïve, but simple.[60] What are the connections? Only the forces of early childhood can take up the Christ in our souls. But these will be able to receive him only when the paradisiacal forces in us are permeated with the deepest wisdom we can acquire on earth. Only in the heart that is able to unite these two aspects, can there occur on the microcosmic level what is described to us by the Baptism in the Jordan: Christ's entry into the human being. For this to happen for a present-day person (and it is possible only in the light of the Whitsun event, through the mediation of the Holy Spirit), the Fifth Gospel must previously have become living in us; it must have become part of our life and being.

The Fifth Gospel is no mere historical account; it is not just a narration that introduces us to a new understanding of the events at the time of Christ and the Mystery of Golgotha. It is, rather, a concrete answer to the question of how a present-day person can receive the Christ being. How a person can become a Christ-bearer microcosmically; just as world-historically, macrocosmically, Jesus of Nazareth became the bearer of Christ in his soul, the true Christophorous. This happened through the archetypal connection of divine purity and the most wonderful and mature fruits of wisdom on the earth.

Previously we have seen that we cannot actually understand the Fifth Gospel correctly if we do not perceive the bridge, which has been described, between Steiner's early work and the Fifth Gospel. Likewise, we will not grasp the whole significance and singularity of the Fifth Gospel if we are unable to build a second bridge, which extends from the revelation of the Fifth Gospel in 1913 to the year 1923–24. The second bridge forms the connection from the Fifth Gospel to the culmination of Anthroposophy on the earth: the foundation of the new mysteries at the Christmas Conference. For only in seeing the central position of the Fifth Gospel between Steiner's early work and the foundation of the new mysteries at the end of his life, can we recognize the entire significance of the Fifth Gospel. Only in this way, can we grasp how the Fifth Gospel is essentially connected with the whole of Anthroposophy, and with us ourselves as Christ-seeking people.

In order to see this correctly, we must look at the Fifth Gospel through the lens of the events of Good Friday. Steiner continually pointed out, even outside his lectures on the Fifth Gospel, that in the moment on Golgotha when the blood flowed out of Christ's wounds, the entire aura of the earth was transformed.[61] We can ask ourselves, what is the relationship here? How are the facts of the flowing of Christ's blood and the earth's transformation connected with one another? Where is the concrete relationship? From other spiritual-scientific accounts by Steiner, we learn what happened with the blood of Christ; it went through a process of etherization. The transformation of the earth's aura began immediately in that moment when the blood left the body's wounds. If we think through this connection meditatively, we can say that right after this blood left the wounds, it etherized in the air—for air is the likeness of the earth's aura, the earth's astral aura. In this etherized condition, the blood joined directly with the earth's aura.

A perhaps somewhat prosaic example can clarify this. You perhaps can remember a chemistry class in school. A teacher shows you a container with a completely transparent fluid. In order to fascinate the students in the class a little, the teacher takes a single little white crumb and tosses it into the glass with the transparent solution. Suddenly, in an instant, the solution becomes golden yellow throughout. And so, also with potentization, a similar phenomenon occurs, in a somewhat different way. The more the substance is diluted, the greater the effectiveness becomes because ever higher spiritual forces work in it. Thus, only a small amount of Christ's etherized blood was needed to transform the entire earth's aura. This blood dissolved in the air as physical substance, and passed into the condition of etherization.

This theme cannot be further developed here; but later it was the Grail blood that appeared in this way. For it goes without saying that on Easter morning, Christ in his spiritual body, passing through the walls, did not bring to the imprisoned Joseph of Arimathea a physical vessel with physical substance, but a spiritual vessel with the substance of the etherized blood.[62] This blood became the nucleus of the Grail Mystery. Later, the supersensible vessel was delivered to the angels, who carried and cared for it in the spiritual world. After centuries, they entrusted it to Titurel for the founding of the Grail Mystery on earth.[63] In this way it continued. Most important to understand is that the holy blood dissolved from the beginning. Also the blood that flowed from the cross into the earth, Steiner says, went through a process of etherization as well,[64] so that by Easter Sunday none of the blood's physical substance remained. It all went into the spiritual aura of the earth.

In this connection, what the Fifth Gospel says about the destiny of the Christ body must be taken into consideration. Through the Christ being's three-year life in this body, it became so highly spiritualized that after removal from the cross and treatment with certain substances, it needed only a small shock in order to disintegrate into the finest dust. This dust was received by the earth through a cleft that formed following an earthquake, as the Matthew Gospel also indicates.[65] Thereafter, this substance dissolved completely; and through a type of special potentization, it was distributed over the whole earth, so that the earth could gradually become the body of Christ. The earth needed this impregnation, this potentization, this fine fermentation, this small amount of absolutely spiritualized substance in order to begin the process of spiritualization.

Thus, we have two mighty images: the transformation of the earth's aura through the etherized blood and the beginning of the earth's transformation through the spiritualized body. One almost wants to say that through the mediation of these special physical substances, which became so rarefied and spiritually influenced, every atom of earth's matter will be permeated by the Christ force by the end of earth development.[66] In order that this may eventually happen, the substance of the divine body had to be received by the earth. Therefore, on Easter Sunday, on the day of the resurrection, nothing physical existed anymore, neither the blood nor the body of Christ. The blood was taken up in the earth's aura and the body (with the remainder of the blood) was received by the earth, as a pledge that it can eventually become the new body of Christ.

Let us look now—at the present time, at the present day—at Easter Sunday. What happens on Easter morning? There appears the resurrection body—the fully transformed phantom, in Rudolf Steiner's terminology[67]—which, in accordance with its being, is connected with the body's dissolved substance in the earth, and therefore with the entire planet. This resurrection body is enclosed in the condensed etheric body,[68] which is connected with the etherized blood that has just transformed the whole earth's aura. Thus, in the resurrection, through his etheric body, Christ is connected with the transformed earth's aura because it received his etherized blood on Good Friday. Through his spirit-body, Christ came into relationship with the entire physical earth, which had taken in his body when it turned into dust. Both elements of this cosmic communion were necessary, so that through Christ's further activity, the earth—according a statement by Christian Morgenstern—would "eventually become sun."

Now, 2,000 years later, we have the new mysteries, which are intended to establish a basis for modern understanding of the resurrection event. Furthermore, they have the task of disclosing the path on which every person can unite consciously with the full reality of Ascension. This union occurs on the path of spiritual communion through the conscious connection of the spiritual student with the blood of Christ (that is, with his condensed etheric body); and with the body of the Risen One through the connection with the re-established phantom. This full reality of the Ascension, or actually the path to this reality, is the focal point of the founding the new mysteries. It was at the heart of the Christmas Conference, in what we all know as the Foundation Stone Meditation. This leads us to the full experience of Christ's resurrection body, and therefore to an intrinsic connection with the essence of the Mystery of Golgotha.[69]

If we look now more precisely at the Foundation Stone Meditation, we find described in its three microcosmic sections the being of the human body, the being of the most ideal body we can actually imagine on the earth, in which one can truly live, truly feel, and truly think. This unparalleled body, in which the most perfect soul lived at the time of Christ, is archetypically the body that was made available to Christ at the Baptism in the Jordan.

At the Christmas Conference on December 25, 1923, after Rudolf Steiner had read the first three sections, which are the microcosmic sections, of the Foundation Stone Meditation for the first time, he continued reading the fourth part, in which the connection of the perfect body of Jesus of Nazareth with the spiritual sun, with the Christ sun, is described. The union of the threefold physicality—the three systems of Jesus' physical body with the whole spirituality of the universe—occurred in the resurrection, as a result of this process. This is mentioned in the three macrocosmic sections of the Foundation Stone Meditation. This world spirituality encompasses everything: from the Holy Trinity and the nine hierarchies to the world of the elemental spirits. There lies the inner kernel of the resurrection mystery: the connection of Jesus' microcosmic physicality with the entire spirituality of the universe in light of the Christ sun.[70] The resurrection body came forth out of this connection. In it lies the key to the Mystery of Golgotha.

In the Foundation Stone Meditation, this key is presented to people as a meditative path to inwardly behold the Mystery of Golgotha. There the mystery of the resurrection body is concealed in spiritual communion. In the same way, Steiner led us at the Christmas Conference to establish a conscious relationship to the etherized blood as well as to the condensed etheric body of the Risen One. —For the etheric lives in rhythms, in continual movement, and is connected with the number seven. Thus, we find that Steiner adds to the contents of the Foundation Stone Meditation, its sevenfold rhythms as a revelation of the etheric. They are the mantric expression of the Risen One's etherized blood. In this way, the complete spiritual communion is given to humanity, and with it, the path that leads to the full reality of the resurrection.[71]

When we now ask about the origin of this path, or about the prerequisites for it, which the founder of the new mysteries at the Christmas Conference really made possible; it can be ascertained that they lie in the purview of the Fifth Gospel. For especially through the Fifth Gospel, we may learn about the destiny of Christ's blood and body on Good Friday; about the connection of the blood with the earth's aura, and the body with the earth itself, as a foundation for the resurrection on Easter morning and the prerequisite for founding the new mysteries in the twentieth century.[72] Thus, in a wonderful way, the Fifth Gospel is connected with Steiner's early work on the one hand; and on the other hand, with the foundation of the new mysteries at the Christmas Conference at the end of his life. It really is the epitome of Steiner's work and life—as his original task.

*

Now I want to close this account with a further aspect of this theme. The Fifth Gospel reports what suffering Jesus of Nazareth continually had to go through in his life; and how, starting with the Baptism in the Jordan, he became the bearer of all humanity's pain. With his exceptional capacity for sympathy, he did not have to travel very far at that time to experience humanity's entire suffering and misery. It was sufficient that he lived through only these three areas: degenerate Judaism, demonized paganism, and the spiritualized "I"ism of the Essenes, who were the most important initiation stream in the world at that time. Thereby, he encompassed the all cultural areas of the world at that time. Out of his contact with these spiritual streams, Jesus of Nazareth experienced the deepest pain, the worst suffering. We can well understand all that.

Today, as humanity on the earth, we are connected with one another quite differently from the past. We know immediately when an earthquake in Italy occurs, with many hundreds, or thousands, dead; we learn quickly about a tsunami in Asia or a person running amok in the USA or Germany. In that sense, we are a much more united humanity now than we were 2,000 years ago. Yet, it must be said, we are still far removed from actually experiencing humanity's intense suffering and misery, particularly all of its hopelessness and its cry for the spirit; we are farther from experiencing that than at the time of Jesus of Nazareth. Nevertheless, we certainly can gain a real idea of his suffering then.

Steiner reports in the Fifth Gospel that after the Baptism in the Jordan, Christ's suffering (which is unfathomable to us), was added to Jesus' great pain. About Christ's exceptional suffering in Jesus' physicality, Steiner reported that there is no human concept, no thoughts on the earth, with which we as human beings can approximately sense what occurred as Christ lived three years in Jesus' body.[73]

After these words, one might think that now Steiner, to clarify further, certainly will speak to us about Christ's passion: about the suffering of being taken prisoner, being crowned with thorns, the crucifixion and death on the cross. But Steiner doesn't utter a single word about all of that. In the lectures from the Fifth Gospel, he speaks about something quite different. For, what he says next is recorded only here in the Fifth Gospel, and cannot be learned anywhere else.

One must add that in the devastating times leading up to the destruction of the Roman Empire, there were thousands upon thousands of people who went through the terrible destiny of being taken prisoner and crucified. Around the year AD 70, an uprising against the Romans occurred in Judea. Many legions were sent from Rome to Palestine, and the uprising was brutally extinguished. Historians at that time report that thousands of people were nailed to crosses, which were lined up for miles. The crucified screamed for days, and the bodies were not removed from the crosses for a long time after their martyred deaths. In this cruel way, Roman soldiers tried to break the will of those rebelling against them.

All that was most inhuman and cruel, and through our imaginative power we can sympathize with the terrible destiny of these people. Steiner, however, particularly wanted to make known in the Fifth Gospel something we *do not even have the ability* to sympathize with, because we cannot really imagine it at all. On Golgotha, it was not simply the matter of crucifying the good, pious man from Nazareth (who had to suffer this horrific ordeal like hundreds and hundreds of other people before and after him) but of crucifying the *god being* in the human body.

Now, Steiner speaks out of the contents of the Fifth Gospel about what for us is the quite unimaginable suffering of this god being. He says this suffering did not begin with the passion. Rather, it began just after the baptism in the Jordan, with the first breath of this being on the earth; for Christ united himself with a human body, which, like every other physical body, was continually involved in the process of degeneration, of death. As normal people, we do not experience this process consciously. We come to the boundary of this area only at the moment of death; then, however, even before our souls can observe the body's degeneration processes, higher powers remove the soul from the physical body. On the other hand, the Christ-Being had to dwell in the body of Jesus, continually exposed to the process of dying. What it means to carry for three years, continual consciousness of death forces, and to fight with them in one's own body until the last fight with death itself at Gethsemane, Steiner tells us, no person can even approximately imagine *this* suffering, *this* pain.

To this ordeal was added yet a second, no less unimaginable source of pain: the pressing of his cosmic being, which is as immeasurably big as the whole universe, into this one point of a human body. What *that* signified, no human can understand at all. For this compression of the world-being into the little coffin-like space of a human body exceeds all that we can think and experience here on earth.

The great message of the Fifth Gospel requires that we look not only at the suffering of the man Jesus of Nazareth; but also for the first time, if only perhaps in a rudimentary way, that we seek to imagine what superhuman, unimaginable suffering *the Christ* went through in the body of Jesus. Steiner adds in one place: if a human soul (and I think this relates also to initiates' souls) would try to remain conscious in such a body as that in which Christ lived three years on earth, the soul would have to leave immediately because no soul could stay in a body that "is on the verge of becoming a corpse."[74]

Dear friends, what has become of this infinitely unimaginable suffering of Christ? Only the Fifth Gospel reports about it: Out of this suffering, all-prevailing, all-encompassing cosmic *love* is born on earth. Superhuman suffering and pain went through a mighty metamorphosis, bringing about omnipotent cosmic love, which entered earth development through the Mystery of Golgotha to fructify the apostles' souls on Whitsun day and bring them to full awakening.[75] Since then, this infinite cosmic love is connected with the earth for the entire future, so that every person who seeks Christ can be fructified by it.

Here we find the decisive relationship of the Fifth Gospel to the new mysteries. For at their center is not only the Foundation Stone Meditation as an artistic creation, but a really new creation of the spirit. By "new creation," I mean Steiner's creating the foundation stone of the Anthroposophical Society at the Christmas Conference; this imaginative foundation stone was woven together out of the purest love substance.[76] Steiner formed this suprasensory foundation stone, and provided it with a thought aura, so that we all can come into a conscious relationship with the *entity* of love. When we ask about the origin of this love substance, then in light of the Fifth Gospel, we must answer: this foundation stone was formed out of all-encompassing cosmic love, which was born on earth for all people, through the Mystery of Golgotha at the moment of the death on the cross. This cosmic love was then bound with Steiner's human love, and fashioned into the foundation stone of the new mysteries *and* simultaneously the foundation of the Anthroposophical Society. Thus, the new mysteries and their foundation at the Christmas Conference, considered in the light of the Fifth Gospel, have a direct relationship to the Mystery of Golgotha.

Therefore, at the end of his life, in pointing to this secret, Steiner could write the following words: "The event of Golgotha is a free cosmic deed that derived from cosmic love and can be grasped only through human love."[77]

These are a few perspectives of the Fifth Gospel that I wanted to share with you on this Easter morning.

4.
The Christmas Conference and the Founding of the New Mysteries

Preface by Sergei O. Prokofieff

PETER SELG

1923, The Year of Destiny—Rudolf Steiner's Path to the Christmas Conference

SERGEI O. PROKOFIEFF

The Nature of the Christmas Conference and Its Sources of Inspiration

Appendix

First Class Admissions by Rudolf Steiner (with facsimiles)

Rudolf Steiner (1861–1925)

Preface

The Christmas Conference 1923/1924 was, without a doubt, not only the high point of the history of the Anthroposophical Society, but also of the whole Anthroposophical Movement. In Rudolf Steiner's life, this event marked the culmination of his earthly activity and revealed his mission as a great Christian initiate of the present time. The laying of the Foundation Stone on December 25, 1923, during which the words of the Foundation Stone Meditation were spoken for the first time, was the center-point of the Christmas Conference, its esoteric heart. From then on, all activities in the Anthroposophical Movement should be imbued with the new esoteric quality, even right into its social forms.

Rudolf Steiner began three initiatives out of the impulse of the Christmas Conference: designing the outer form of the second Goetheanum, the Karma lectures, and establishing the School for Spiritual Science as the Michael School on earth. Behind these and many other initiatives that emerged during or after the Christmas Conference stood the never-before-existant revelation of the new Christian mysteries, which bear the seed for the further evolution of humanity.

The year leading up to the Christmas Conference was possibly the most difficult in Rudolf Steiner's life; against the background of the crisis of the Anthroposophical Society he had to make a powerful step into the future. Because of the importance of this time, as well as the tremendous resolve of Rudolf Steiner, this book begins with an examination of the difficult, fateful year of 1923, at the beginning of which stood—like a warning sign for the whole twentieth century—the burning of the first Goetheanum. This lecture will illuminate the underlying motives in Rudolf Steiner's work and the history of the Anthroposophical Society in such a way that the Christmas Conference that ensued at the end of the year can be comprehended and appreciated in the right way. In this sense, the lecture is inseparably connected with the events and the whole tragedy of the year 1923.

Only against the background mentioned in the first lecture does the examination of the Christian foundations of the Christmas Conference, to which the second lecture is dedicated, receive its deeper meaning.

SERGEI O. PROKOFIEFF

Goetheanum, Dornach
January 2011

1923, The Year of Destiny

Rudolf Steiner's Path to the Christmas Conference

PETER SELG

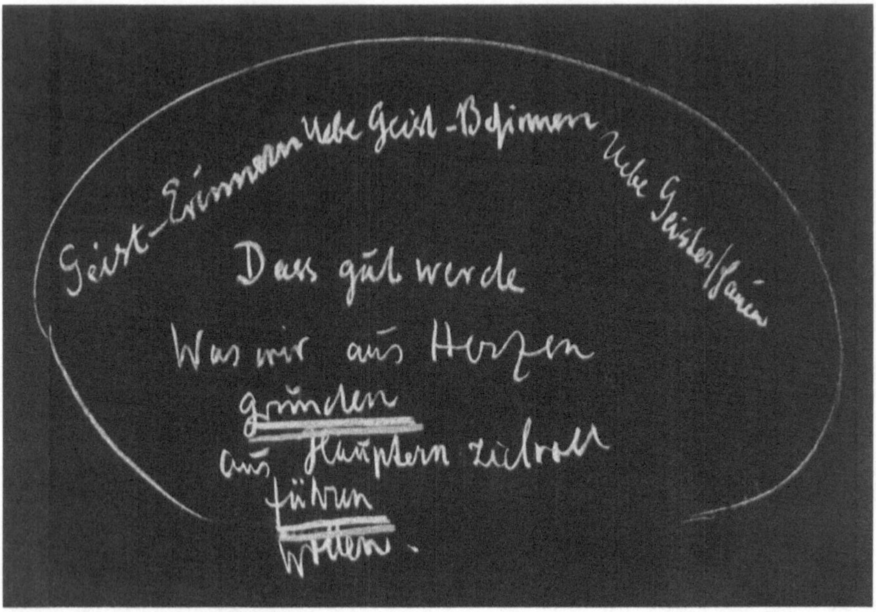

The Sunday-rhythm of the Foundation Stone mantric verse
given by Rudolf Steiner on December 30, 1923

THE YEAR THAT ENDED with the Christmas Conference of the General Anthroposophical society and the new founding of the School for Spiritual Science in Dornach, was the same that began with the burning and destruction of the first Goetheanum, a catastrophe of the greatest magnitude. The New Year's Eve of 1922/23 brought the extinction of a building that was to form a "site of love";[1] an entity whose substance was love and sacrifice; and whose task was "to lead human souls together harmoniously on the Earth," as Steiner emphasized shortly after the beginning of World War I.[2] At the beginning of 1923, of everything that had been built through intensive work by people from seven nations, for ten years, only a heap of rubble remained.

With the arson attack, the Anthroposophical Society lost not only its home and center, but also the possibility to work publicly for modern spiritual science, which Rudolf Steiner had planned for the Goetheanum from the beginning. From the Goetheanum, Anthroposophy—as contemporary mystery knowledge—was to move into the world and to impart an impulse for scientific renewal in the various areas of life in the spirit of esoteric Christianity and in Michaelic form.[3] The first Goetheanum, according to Steiner, was meant to prove "that Anthroposophy has nothing sectarian in nature; that it encompasses the great tasks of our present time, which consist of focusing the raying of a new spiritual light that has become accessible to humanity again and imprinting it in human cultural and civilization resources."[4] With the destruction by fire, a singular building was demolished, along with a manifestation of Anthroposophy and its decisive assistance for our civilization in the trials and crises of the twentieth century: "Only with the Goetheanum, I would say, was there the real possibility to draw Anthroposophy out of a sectarian existence and give it relevance, which according to the nature of the matter always has had to be mentioned since its inception."[5]

The attack on the Goetheanum did not come as a surprise to Rudolf Steiner. For years, he had emphasized in private lectures how critical the situation in Central Europe was at the beginning of the 1920s, and how hard-fought the anthroposophical impulse really was. The historical lessons of World War I were not remembered; to the contrary, since 1918, the situation in Germany had become ever more difficult. "Human beings are preparing themselves for the next world war. Culture will be further destroyed," Steiner declared as early as December 1920 in Dornach.[6] The intensifying nationalism in Germany and Central Europe; the imminent collapse of the unstable post-war democracy; and the economic crisis in the midst of many unresolved policies gave a sense of how dangerous the political situation would be in the next years, although the last world catastrophe had only just ended. Steiner had already spoken emphatically about a next "world war," and since December 1920 he repeatedly pointed out to the members of the Anthroposophical Society that opponents surrounded the building impulse in Dornach. In April 1921, he said:

> For a long time I have continually had to say that what approaches as opposing forces will be ever more intense; and today that has already happened. It is also not possible to say today that this opposition has reached its culmination. This opposition has by far not reached its culmination.... The powers that want to acquire forces rising from the spiritual world to the vitality of their own soul are weak. The world has taken on an Ahrimanic character.... Humanity is strongly possessed by evil forces, by love for evil. Those who today cannot account for this love for evil, with this ever-growing love for evil in the fight against anthroposophical spiritual science, will not be able to develop a feeling, a knowledge in themselves about what opposing forces and powers still can emerge.... They assume they can undermine the soil within us. We must

> work on ourselves as much as possible; and if the soil should be undermined and we fall into a crack, then our work must have been such that it still finds its spiritual path through the world. For what emerges there is the last tremor of a declining world; but it can still, when it is the last tremor, flail about like a raving mad person. One can lose one's life through this raving mad flailing about; therefore, one must know at least out of what impulses the raving mad flailing happens.[7]

Less than two years later, on January 1, 1923, the Goetheanum was a ruin. "Evil forces continued possessing people"; this principle was to unfold its real impact a decade later when all of civilization was affected.

The Historical Year of Destiny

The year 1923, which had begun with the destruction of the Goetheanum and ended with Rudolf Steiner's decision to hold the Christmas Conference of the General Anthroposophical Society and to establish the Goetheanum anew, was also an epochal crisis year in Germany and Central Europe. "One may assume that our century is one of authority, rights, and fascism," confidently announced Benito Mussolini, who was about to succeed in becoming dictator in Italy.[8] His colleagues Primo de Rivero in Spain and Stalin in Russia were also confident of this. An international arms race was ignited in great style under the leadership of the anti-communist United States, and the situation in Germany became strained throughout the year, with consequences for the entire European community of states. "The key to the future of democracy in Europe was—as it was through the whole century—Germany," wrote English historian Mark Mazower in his study evaluating the century.[9] Because of the "reparation payments" required by Article 231 of the Versailles Agreement as the "sole war debt," the economy of

Germany staggered for a long time. Its national debt, resulting from "costs due to the consequences of war," left little leeway for additional expenditures. In January 1923, barely four years after the war ended, Belgian and French troops occupied the Ruhr area, seized its coal, and took over the control of German financial concerns. There came dramatic reactions, with a mass expulsion of people, as well as displays of refusals and passive resistance. The health of the local population, as well as in other regions of Germany, deteriorated rapidly because of malnutrition and medical shortages. Inflation galloped nationwide, and many companies—among them anthroposophical institutions—had all but collapsed. German emigration rate and suicide numbers climbed, and at the end of the year the United States stopped all immigration from Germany.

In view of "an army of millions of disappointed and impoverished people,"[10] the German political landscape became impressively even more radical in the course of the year. In January, the Nazi Party held its big convention in Munich, and in February began to distribute its agitating daily newsletter "Völkische Beobachter." In late autumn there were uprisings and putsch attempts from the left and right in Hamburg, Küstrin, the Rhineland, Saxony, and Spandau. On November 8 and 9, Adolph Hitler tried to come to power for the first time in Munich, but was not then successful. Gustav Stresemann resigned as Reich Chancellor, defeated and disheartened. "We live in the midst of feverish conditions.... Need drives people to extremes."[11] At the end of 1923, in his luxurious Landsberg prison, courted by numerous visitors and supported by sympathies from wide sectors of the population, Adolph Hitler continued writing his book *Mein Kampf*. In contrast, Rudolf Steiner arranged to give up his Berlin apartment on Motzstrasse, and he transferred all anthroposophical books from Marie Steiner's publishing company to Switzerland. "When this gentleman comes to power, my foot can never touch German soil again."[12] At that time he gave Anna Samweber, a co-worker from Berlin, a message for the future times of need to take back to

Berlin friends. He never returned to the city. He did not witness on earth its transformation to national-socialistic domination and a center of war, or the inferno of 1945.

To Berlin Friends

The human being sees
With the eye created by the universe;
What he sees tethers him
To world joy and world pain;
He is bound to all
That is there as well as
To all that plunges him
Into the dark regions of the abyss.

The human being looks
With the eye conferred by the spirit;
What he looks at connects him
To spirit hopes and sustaining force;
It unites him with all
That is rooted in eternity
And bears fruit in eternity.

But the human being can behold
Only when he feels the inner eye
As part of the God-spirit,
Because activities of the gods weave
On the stage of the soul
In the physical human temple.

Humanity is oblivious
To the inner being of God,
But we want to receive it
In the clear light of consciousness,
And then carry over rubble and ashes

The gods' flame into human hearts.
If lightning tries to destroy
Our sense organs;
We erect soul temples
Out of iron-strong
Knowledge weaving light.
Destruction of the external
Shall be the dawning
Of the inner most part of the soul.

Suffering presses upon us
Through material power forces;
Hope illuminates
Even when darkness surrounds us;
And it will one day
Penetrate our memory,
When after the darkness
We may live again in the light.
We do not want luminosity
To be lacking in the future
Because we now in affliction
Have not planted it in our souls.[13]

The Norwegian committee could not find a suitable Nobel Peace Prize winner in 1923, and refrained from making an award. At the end of the Christmas Conference Rudolf Steiner said: "When one looks at the world today and one sees that there has been present for years such an extraordinary amount of destruction and such forces at work, one can guess the depths into which Western civilization is being steered."[14] Eight weeks earlier, in October 1923 after a lecture in the carpentry shop, a guard asked Steiner whether cyanide gas would be used in the next war. Steiner replied in the negative, but said that "other terrible things" were being prepared. Then George Groot wanted to know whether this was being done from America. "No, in Germany."[15]

The Crisis in the Anthroposophical Society

"For our time, our present time—please take these words very seriously—our present time is one of great decision. Many tremendous arrangements are being made for people at present," Steiner told members of the Anthroposophical Society in 1923.[16] He repeatedly urged them to consider the "prosperity of the anthroposophical matter" as a concern of present-day civilization."[17] The center in Dornach had been built starting in 1913, and continuing during the difficult years after World War I. It had been built with extraordinary energy, vigor, and great sacrifice on the part of many individuals, and it had absorbed a lot of resources. But it did not come to completion with enlightened activity in the way envisioned by Steiner. In the years before the fire, Steiner had regularly indicated not only the full force of Anthroposophy's enemy (especially from right-wing nationalist and white-collar circles), but also the need to protect Anthroposophy and its Dornach building with a strong and concentrated effort. A few weeks before the arson and destruction, he said in The Hague:

> It would, of course, be highly desirable that the center in Dornach not fall victim, but that it would find friends who could provide help.... At the moment when the Dornach center collapses, everything will be destroyed; and I just wish this would come to consciousness, because it has to a great extent vanished from awareness. This is actually—I must say—a very serious concern for me: an overwhelming burden.[18]

After the fire, Rudolf Steiner constantly made it clear to the responsible members of the Anthroposophical Society (especially within the largest national association in Germany) that a reconstruction of the Goetheanum was only reasonable and justified, provided there was a consolidation, that is an awakening to their responsibilities toward the Anthroposophical Society. He never considered the Dornach building as an insider undertaking or as an "internal temple," but rather as functioning for the School for Spiritual Science, handling tasks for civilization in difficult circumstances and, contributing to the project initiative. "The idea of a School for Spiritual Science is the necessary consequence resulting from the delivery of spiritual knowledge, which in our time has become respected," Steiner wrote in a newsletter in autumn 1911.[19] Members of the Anthroposophical Society responded to the destruction of their beloved Goetheanum by fire with utmost dismay, grief, and bewildered despair. Steiner did not have much to say about the pain that struck him with full force, but said consistently beginning in early 1923, "Out of the pain we need to find the strength to work more intensely and energetically on our goals, which are so well founded on the history of human evolution."[20] The Central European and world-historical situation was critical—and the time for spreading humanistic initiatives was fading. The Anthroposophical Society was weak, and hardly an effective instrument for disseminating Steiner's future intentions.

After the catastrophe had happened, Steiner did not say much more about Anthroposophy's opponents and the forces that had destroyed the First Goetheanum. He presumed they were known, and devoted himself to future issues and tasks connected with the anthroposophical community. "The main thing is that the Anthroposophical Society understands what its duties are."[21] In the course of 1923, with compelling emphasis, he broached the subject of the deficits and weaknesses under which he had suffered for years; and which were also partly responsible for the lack of protection (based on inadequate awareness and neglected work) of the now destroyed building. With the ruin of the Goetheanum, the Anthroposophical Society was perched on the rim of the abyss; its existence after the loss of the Dornach center was highly tenuous, the Dornach ruins being a symbol of its own internal state. Steiner spoke about a real "self-reflection," which had to occur in the shortest time possible in order to anticipate and counteract the rapid collapse of the Anthroposophical Society. According to Steiner, Anthroposophy, as such, could neither be destroyed nor eradicated from the world. Nevertheless, the failure and possible end of the Anthroposophical Society would be fatal, because it was the task of this society to engage effectively in spreading modern spiritual science in present-day civilization. A decline of the Anthroposophical Society would decidedly delay the civilizing effect of Anthroposophy "A tremendous momentum ... would be lost for the development of humanity."[22]

Against this background, Rudolf Steiner's speeches and contributions to the emergency meetings of the Anthroposophical Society after the Dornach fire became very concrete *memories* of the basic tasks and work required of that community, which had been founded at the end of 1912 in Cologne. From the point of view of Anthroposophical Society members, according to Steiner, it was necessary in the long run to work so that people could catch "fire" for the Anthroposophy approaching them through the Society. Anthroposophy as such has an inner "clout" ("Thus, we need not worry about the impact of Anthroposophy, my dear friends"[23]). The question was, however, how the society founded for Anthroposophy could now achieve the strength and effectiveness it had lacked in recent years. The Anthroposophical Society should be, according to Steiner, a factor in contemporary conflicts, something "that has a say in current affairs."[24] This would be successful only if members have sufficient consciousness of present problems and a specific subject matter to represent, with which they identify themselves actively and bravely in contemporary discussions. It should be "so that it [Anthroposophy] is presented positively in the world, and people finally know what the Anthroposophical Society works for."[25]

Steiner expected keen interest in the world from the anthroposophical community, a primary problem- and task-awareness instead of internal complacency, discussions, and pretensions. It is of paramount importance, neither to rise haughtily and arrogantly over the world, nor to stand apart from it passively and anxiously, but to learn the real needs of people at present and to cooperate in finding solutions for identified problems. "What good is it if we tell people again and again that we are not a cult, if we behave as though we are a cult?"[26] The technological consequences of materialism, as well as its repercussions for humanity and nature, had since the nineteenth century already created huge problems that had to be processed in detail and penetrated in order that effective future impulses could be developed. "The misery that can be seen today within this civilization should be an invitation to adopt a spiritual human and world view. We can do only this if we have an eye open for all that is going on in the world."[27] In this light Steiner prepared and established[28] the Dornach School for Spiritual Science. Beyond his own activity, however, there was little demonstrable success coming from Dornach that made any impression on the world. According to Steiner during the crisis of 1923, one could not generate the "pretense" of having a "School for Spiritual Science" in Dornach and then not perform the scientific work. On the one hand, he spoke of a "crying shame";[29] but, more positively, he said that in the future, specific spiritual tasks connected with the Anthroposophical Society and the Goetheanum must be addressed to make public what had been achieved internally. "All these things must be placed before the whole world." It must come about "that even opponents know something is there; that they have high respect for what is being accomplished in the Anthroposophical Society."[30] Steiner knew there were highly talented and industrious people in the Anthroposophical Society, who had acted devotedly in this matter during the past few years. He knew, too, that their work was largely ignored or rejected by company representatives and national leaders; this rejection had resulted in their work not being published or noticed by the public. However, it was the task of the Anthroposophical Society leadership to persist, not in self-satisfaction and complacency; but to publicize achievements arising from its own ranks. "Yes, it is an asset to appreciate things, to form an opinion about what exists in the Society, that is what matters; not to accept everything with an overwhelming lethargy, not to take things for granted."[31]

In addition, Steiner expected that the Anthroposophical Society would be prepared in the future to take real responsibility for planning and implementing start-up projects that proceeded from its own members out of an anthroposophical impulse. Waldorf schools, anthroposophical medicine, and anthroposophical pharmaceutical companies needed the support of a powerful and responsible Anthroposophical Society that would stand up for them in an efficient way; not "representatives" privileged to sit on "curule chairs."[32] In 1923, all anthroposophical institutions needed effective assistance and active support in order to survive and continue maintaining the place they had achieved in civilization and with the public. Steiner wanted and expected from the Society a firm commitment—in a bold and direct way—to the cause of Anthroposophy, and thus also to anthroposophical institutions. "It is a question of having so much internal security for Anthroposophy that no matter what one's position is in life one can represent what is anthroposophical."[33] "What is needed for this is courage, courage, and more courage."[34] Although he had a cosmopolitan approach and world interest, Steiner by no means associated with the tendency for diplomatic compromise, or acceptance of popular thought forms and catchphrases. Rather, he demonstrated the ability to address the problems and needs of the time from basic principles—from the spiritual center—to answer out of Anthroposophy. "For the propagation, for the right conveyance of Anthroposophy in the world, we can do nothing better than to become more and more aware of the meaningful impulse Anthroposophy should provide for the further progress of civilization."[35] In February 1923, Steiner said in a Stuttgart crisis meeting that he sometimes had the impression "that all feeling for what really should be presented with Anthroposophy is lost."[36]

Nevertheless, Steiner worked onward, and hoped for a rebirth of the community. He knew that the Anthroposophical Society existing at the beginning of 1923 had not become a reality yet; it had so far not assumed a task "for which outside people can have some respect ... no positive task resulting from a concrete volitional resolution."[37] He characterized the Society as a downright "specter" and called it "a very ahrimanic product"; ... "The Anthroposophical Society is totally riddled with ahrimanic forces."[38] However, he opted for a general awakening and existential rethinking in contemporary terms, as well as an orientation to internal tasks for the given situation. The awareness of this need existed among some individuals. On February 25, 1923, in a speech in Stuttgart about the situation of the Anthroposophical Society, Eugene Kolisko said: "With no internal unity, we face a world of enemies; the members do not even know how strong that world is, and how it works toward bringing the whole Anthroposophical Movement to an end. We must be clear; the less something is done for the society, the more a vacuum will form inside; that vacuum will allow the opposition outside to be strengthened and expanded."[39]

*

In the course of 1923, Steiner organizationally inspired and personally promoted the creation of autonomous national societies within the Anthroposophical Society. Especially because of the situation in Germany, which no longer could play a leadership role as in the past, Steiner emphasized the task as being to "constitute the whole society according to the spirit of the times in an accountable way."[40] With his support, national anthroposophical societies were founded in Switzerland (April 1923), Norway (May 1923), England (September 1923), Austria (September 1923), and Holland (November 1923). Beyond that, societies were also constituted in France and Sweden. In May, Steiner spoke in Oslo about his intention for the individual national societies to take a further step (still adhering to the basic principles, and maintaining their national independence) of joining together with neutral Switzerland. "One can say that the Anthroposophical Society's international life and weaving will flourish best when national societies founded in the individual language areas become affiliated with Dornach to form an international Anthroposophical World Society."[41] The acceptance of new members into the various national societies should occur within the countries, with membership cards being sent from the association's headquarters in Dornach. The secretaries-general of the various countries should be prominent personalities, people "who are known" and who are able to represent Anthroposophy substantially and effectively in their country. Steiner indicated how he imagined the mentality and personality profile of such "secretaries-general" by expressing clear personal preferences in individual countries. For example, in Holland Willem Zeylmans van Emmichoven almost archetypically embodied in his spiritual and intellectual qualities and skills the type of secretary-general desired by Rudolf Steiner.[42]

Through most of the year 1923, it remained unknown how Rudolf Steiner would finally decide in regard to the future of the Anthroposophical Society. In the German center there was little positive movement. "For the [German] society, I really have to say I would prefer not having anything more to do with it. Everything its directors do, disgusts me," Steiner wrote to Edith Maryon in Dornach on March 25, 1923, after countless meetings.[43] His call for establishing national societies worldwide laid an essential building block for the future, especially in view of the contemporary situation, and the threat of Germany's decline, which was already in the initial phase. Germany was the country in which Anthroposophy started, and in which there were still by far the most members and working establishments. In a way, Steiner was preparing for something that would survive the coming fall "into the gloomy regions of the abyss"; that is, German fascism and the night of the "Dark Continent";[44] preparing in order to be present and visible in an important hour sometime in the future.

> But one thing should not come about, because that would be the most terrible thing: that when the world cries out—and that is what it will do in a relatively short time—cries out for the resurrection of Central European spiritual life as its own salvation, there would be no people in Central Europe who could be at the right spiritual place, because they cannot understand this appeal.
>
> If someone can say the world outside of Central Europe is waiting today for spirituality, then it would be fatal to find out that Central European humanity is not waiting for this spirituality. That would be a great loss for the whole world. That would be one of the worst disasters the earth could experience, when the appeal is made to Central Europe—no matter how it looks on the outside—when the appeal is issued: We need this spiritual life—and in Europe one would heedlessly pass by this appeal, because this Central European spiritual life cannot be appreciated. Let us remember today the fact that it might just be the mission of the Central European people in the near future to understand, out of the essence of the Central European spirituality, what the world of Central Europe will want to receive; it would be terrible if there was nobody in Central Europe who would have an understanding of what should be done.[45]

Spiritual Preparation for the Christmas Conference

Anthroposophists' "self-reflection," in the sense of deepening their knowledge of self and purpose ("which happens in a person's inner core"[46]) was also one of Rudolf Steiner's important lecture themes during 1923. He spoke one year after the Goetheanum burned, not about knowledge of karma in the narrow and specific sense; but, rather, in an introductory way, giving a basic orientation about the destiny of people coming to

Anthroposophy, and about the nature of Anthroposophy itself. The correct interpretation of the word "anthroposophy" is not "wisdom of the human being," but "awareness of one's humanity"; that is, directing the transformed will, experiencing knowledge, witnessing the destiny of time to that point, giving the soul a conscious direction—a Sophia."[47]

In 1923, Steiner spoke to members for the first time about the fact that it is not only possible, but also absolutely necessary, to feel Anthroposophy as a living being "who walks invisibly among us, and at the same time to whom one feels responsible."[48] This sense of responsibility toward Anthroposophy includes the connection of one's being with it; the entry into, and honoring of, a real relationship of destiny that leads to true self-knowledge. "And we are then aware of how something from Anthroposophy knocks on the door of our heart and says, 'Let me in, for I am yourself, I am your true human nature.'"[49] If the anthroposophist treads this path, Anthroposophy begins "pulsing" in the heart; one can feel it in the central organ, the destiny organ of earthly existence. In 1923, Steiner also unfolded the essence of Anthroposophy in its cosmic greatness, as modern mystery knowledge, which brings humanity into a real relationship with the spiritual universe; that is, in reality it guides us in this cosmos. "Anthroposophy is a path of knowledge that guides the spiritual in the human being to the suprasensory in the universe," Steiner wrote in 1924, in the first "Guiding Principle" of the General Anthroposophical Society.[50] In 1923, however, he began by first letting the cosmic imagination of this "spiritual in the universe" become an individual experience. Undoubtedly, connected with this, Steiner attempted to assess, within the tragic and dangerous situation in Central Europe, the prerequisites for Michaelic activity in a community for the future. Michael, he once said, could be the genius of civilization's development—so long as people succeed in finding the connection to the seasons in the spiritual sense.[51] In the middle of his cosmic-imaginative lectures of 1923, Steiner developed the Michael theme further;

he spoke for the first time, starting with the 1923 Easter festival, about the possibility of a future Michael festival. People should develop "spiritual fire"—but not a physical conflagration—in the future. He said that the Michael thought in people at this time was too weak to be effective for civilization, and here key changes were possible and necessary. Steiner gave people courage to follow their own ideas and spiritual initiatives, and to hold fast to them even in difficult times.

> The self, soaring to realize that one can be just as engaged by thoughts about the spiritual as by anything in the physical world: that is Michael power! To have confidence in the idea of the spiritual (if one has the ability to absorb it), you must relinquish yourself to the spiritual; make yourself an instrument of its guidance. A first failure comes—don't be concerned! A second failure occurs—never mind! And if there are hundreds of failures—it doesn't matter! No failure is ever absolute in obtaining the truth of a spiritual impulse, where its activity is penetrated and grasped internally. Only then, one has faith in oneself—the right confidence in a spiritual impulse that one has conceived at a particular time—and one says to oneself: I've had failures hundreds of times, but this can at most prove to me that in this incarnation the conditions for implementing this impulse are not available to me. That this impulse is correct, I can see through its particular character. If, after the hundredth incarnation, the forces for realizing that impulse do not accrue to me; still, nothing can convince me of the penetrating power or non-penetrating power of a spiritual impulse, other than its own nature. If you imagine this thinking occurring in a person's mind, as great trust developed for all that is spiritual; if you think that one can hold firmly to something one sees, can think of it as a spiritual victory; can hold so firmly that one still does not let go when the outer world is very much against

> it; if you can imagine this, then you have an idea of what the Michael power, the Michael entity actually wants from people. Only then do you have an intuition of what great confidence in the mind is. One may defer any spiritual impulse, even for the whole incarnation; but once the impulse is grasped, one must never waver, but cherish and care for it in the soul; in this way alone, one can conserve it for the following incarnations. When in this way, trust for the spirit establishes such a soul constitution that a person comes to experience the spiritual as real as the ground beneath our feet (of which we know that if it were not there, we would not be able to stand on our feet), then we have a realization of what Michael really wants from us.[52]

In the midst of the political destruction of the year 1923 and in view of continuing instability in the Anthroposophical Society, Steiner tried in this way to strengthen the spiritual incarnations and future impulses in the hearts of individual anthroposophists and in the anthroposophical community as a whole. He began with the seed of what he would do extensively in his 1924 karma lectures (and within the newly founded "esoteric school of the Goetheanum"). That was to remind the souls of anthroposophists about the Michael School, which they had experienced prenatally in their hearts. Michaelites should find each other again, and cooperate in the mutual work of the Anthroposophical Society, in awakening to their associated tasks. In this connection, Steiner also gave courses on the ancient Ephesian, Hibernian, Eleusinian, Kabirian, and Rosicrucian mysteries, which he held in December 1923. Description of the ancient mysteries was part of the courses for the Michael School; Steiner also included a complete description of how Christ's deed harmonized and fulfilled the mysteries, and of Christianity's orientation for the future. Anthroposophists should remember the mysteries, and awaken for their mutual tasks in the age of Michael. "You, spirit-knowledge student / heed Michael's wise beckoning / receive the world-will-love-logos / effective in the lofty goals of the soul."[53]

The successful awakening of the higher self to its soul and spirit with the help of Anthroposophy, should occur in the depths and existential dimension of destiny, in the human individuality's basic being. Steiner spoke of this awakening in February 1923 in Stuttgart, as a pre-condition for a social culture of the Anthroposophical Society. Real social understanding should arise as the first stage of karmic knowledge; in this way the Anthroposophical Society would be able to unite everything that is segregated.

Awakening to Destiny

Ita Wegman wrote about Steiner's inner mood in the middle of 1923, in a lecture manuscript: "Rudolf Steiner was always looking for solutions; for what a change (in the Anthroposophical Society) could bring about. He was very sad. Courses were held in 1923, in Penmaenmawr and Ilkley. It seemed to me as though, from that moment on, Rudolf Steiner envisioned a solution. He spoke about how the scorching fire that destroyed the old Goetheanum had revealed such powerful secrets that only now was the bigger picture gradually becoming clear to him. Mystery knowledge has now become free, and this mystery knowledge, which was guarded in the various previous mysteries, should now become the educational material of Anthroposophy. The society must, however, be reorganized. Here Rudolf Steiner spoke no more about the society's ... being inspired; rather, he spoke about a new organization. Dr. Steiner spoke these words after the trip to England. A great activity developed in Rudolf Steiner's nature. It was as if he could not quickly and thoroughly enough approach the changes."[54]

According to Ita Wegman, Steiner penetrated only gradually the spiritual experiences he had during the burning of the Goetheanum. He spoke about them at the beginning of

December 1923, in a lecture in Dornach[55] Wegman reported that in the summer of 1923, his visions became successively clear in their overall connections. That clarity went hand in hand with Steiner's decision to make the old mysteries (which to a certain extent had been freed by the fire) the content of his coming lectures and to provide the Anthroposophical Society with a new organization. Ita Wegman's memories in this regard are no doubt significant; they indicate that Steiner first decided in, or after, Ilkley and Penmaenmawr to take the mysteries a step into the future. He decided, according to Wegman, out of an inner situation that had previously been marked with deep "sorrow;" but then he experienced an important, indeed crucial, change. The fact that she was involved in this change, Wegman mentioned in no lecture, but wrote about it only in her notebook:

> Destiny awakening
>
> Penmaenmawr karma
> Fully disclosed,
> Understanding on my part
> For the soul element.
> He said
> The spiritual world was jubilant.
> The next step
> In the physical world was
> For the Dr.
> To connect it
> With the society.
> This should produce
> A flowering.
> Esoteric and even more
> And more esoteric
> Mystery renewal,
> Revelation of
> All karma.[56]

Ita Wegman's understanding for the "fully revealed" karma and the joy of the spiritual world concerning this successful inner step, was a prerequisite for Steiner's will impulse in regard to the Anthroposophical Society. On the morning after the night of the fire at the Goetheanum, as Rudolf Steiner investigated the fire, Ita Wegman was standing next to him. This was, after considerable preparation, the beginning of a close esoteric student/teacher relationship and cooperation, which grew to great intensity in 1923–24.[57] There are many indications that the successful esoteric student/teacher relationship and the karmic awakening of the individuality of Ita Wegman (which was not interacting with Rudolf Steiner for the first time), was the indispensable prerequisite for what happened in the following months, which they culminated in the Christmas Conference. "An ancient karma existing between him and me was renewed."[58] On the basis of this activity, Rudolf Steiner could proceed. Ita Wegman was also the one who asked him (in or after Penmaenmawr) about the possibility of founding the new mysteries in concrete terms.[59] "Only because this question was asked, was it possible to establish the Michael School on earth. In this school, lies the core of what is possible for the future." While on his sickbed, Steiner said these words to Ludwig Polzer-Hoditz about the "esoteric school of the Goetheanum."[60] Steiner planned to organize the school into three classes. Steiner had intensely accompanied Ita Wegman's inner path after the fire, and especially after Penmaenmawr. Their esoteric cooperation had great importance for the further success of his work, and for the Christmas meeting. These things were known extensively only in 2009, upon release of Ita Wegman's esoteric estate, sixty-six years after her death.[61] "Be complementary to him with understanding / Succeed in his spiritual task / Of which an image is presented / In his earthly accomplishment / We need his broad spiritual path / He needs your companionship."[62] "Preparing for the Christmas Conference with her no doubt inspired him the most, if not exclusively," Elisabeth Vreede wrote in her memoirs about Rudolf Steiner and Ita Wegman.[63]

*

In November and early December of 1923, it was by no means clear whether the reorganization of the Anthroposophical Society would succeed at Christmas; the whole project was a risk, and remained a risk. The prerequisite self-knowledge for the society that Steiner had described in detail, especially in Stuttgart, had hardly been achieved; the expected transformation had not taken place. Willem Zeylmans van Emmichoven reported about Rudolf Steiner's speaking on November 17 to a small group in Den Haag, saying that he was uncertain "whether it was possible at all to continue with the society." Zeylmans continued in his writing:

> He complained that nobody seemed to understand what he wanted; and that it might be necessary to continue working with only a very few people, within a small circle. This made an almost painful impression on the few people present at this conversation. One experienced, without being able to understand all the details, that there had come a point in the spiritual development of humanity, where previous forms of community were no longer able to bear spiritual content; a point at which only a completely new impulse could enable going further.[64]

Nevertheless, Rudolf Steiner decided to retain the Anthroposophical Society, and to give it a new shape. He wrote on December 1 to Marie Steiner that for the society, he set his "last hopes on the Christmas meeting."[65]

A little over three weeks later, Rudolf Steiner completed giving the new form for the Anthroposophical Society and personally assumed its chair. He formed around himself an "initiative-board," whose members directed the departments of the newly founded school, and with whom he wanted to work esoterically: "*It must be an initiative-board; it must grasp the tasks that have been placed before the Anthroposophical Movement by the spiritual world; must accept these, must direct them in the world...*"[66] "A stronger momentum is needed than was available previously, if the spirit, whom people need, is to take up residence."[67]

The previously formed national societies joined with the General Anthroposophical Society. Together, based on gradually implemented knowledge of destiny, and in a cosmopolitan Michaelic orientation, the societies once again attempted everything possible to bring a powerful, historical interactive impulse from the esoteric center of Anthroposophy to a threatened world; to bring a "curative" effect on twentieth century civilization. Thus, Steiner, together with his masters and "Christ-Michael,"continued into the future despite all obstacles, historical conflicts, and disasters.

The Nature of the Christmas Conference and Its Sources of Inspiration

Sergei O. Prokofieff

"Quietly, and in a way that is not as deafening as in the old mysteries, students of the *new mysteries* are able to access spiritual wisdom, which brings tidings necessary to them about eternal human nature and the world."

— Rudolf Steiner[68]

"A person who is sincere regarding the spiritual world looks at a human will that most certainly is born according to the *new mysteries*; spirituality reappears among humanity in the light of *new mysteries* in which people find the spirit in a more knowledgeable, enlightened way than in the old mysteries, and in which they can be led in a more developed, complete way to the spiritual, divine world, and thereby to the source of humanity."

— Rudolf Steiner[69]

"In earlier times, a person who had accomplished such an esoteric deed might have had to pay for it with sudden death. Now such things are possible *with the Christ force*; and because in its present condition humanity needs it, one must have the confidence and courage to do such phenomenal things."

— Rudolf Steiner to Ita Wegman, 1924[70]

Dear Friends,

Let us turn our thoughts to the esoteric meaning of the Christmas Conference as the founding of the new mysteries.[71] In doing so, we should direct our gaze especially to the eternal character of this event. Regarding the esoteric nature of this conference, it must not be considered only as something historical; we must also regard it as an immense task, or even a whole complex of tasks, placed before us for the future. We have the challenge to continue working on these tasks, based on our close connection with Rudolf Steiner and his loftiest mystery deed.

I would like to approach the Christmas Conference directly through a statement Steiner made on February 6, 1924, in Stuttgart, as he reported about this conference to a large anthroposophical community. Not long before, he had encountered both positive and painfully negative experiences connected with these people and this place. Now he made this succinct, yet staggering statement: "The crux of the matter is that this Christmas Conference is either nothing, or it is everything, for what concerns Anthroposophy" (GA 260a).

In observing Steiner's own life between the Christmas Conference and his death on March 30, 1925, one notes that he exemplified with steadfast loyalty and endurance (almost until his last breath, one could say), what it really means when one takes literally the thought just quoted, that this Christmas Conference is indeed "everything" for a person.

A concrete example illustrates this. Until three days before his death, Steiner alone signed all the pink cards of new members entering the Anthroposophical Society. He also read all applications for acceptance into the School for Spiritual Science, and evaluated and decided upon them, in most cases positively. Often he wrote across the entire paper only a single word: "Yes," and punctuated it with an exclamation point. Sometimes there followed a short commentary, or only his signature.[72] Thus, he reserved for himself, as first chairman of the society and spiritual leader of the School for Spiritual Science, the decision about admissions into both institutions.

From this example, one can clearly see that until the end of his life, Steiner considered the School for Spiritual Science and admission into it a very serious matter; and he approached it realistically; he also wrote and spoke about it that way in many essays and lectures. This is a fact that proves conclusively, even in the face of adverse rumors and assumptions, that for Steiner (even after February 8, 1925),[73] the School for Spiritual Science and the Society—and therefore naturally also the Christmas Conference—were still completely valid realities. Could a person imagine that Steiner would be serious about the society and the School for Spiritual Science, and yet question the spiritual source from which both emanate esoterically? From the beginning, these three belong inseparably together. If one would doubt the Christmas Conference, one would also question the Anthroposophical Society, as well as the School for Spiritual Science, which spring from it.

Until his last breath, Rudolf Steiner wanted to serve this higher reality of the Christmas Conference and to develop the further initiatives arising from it. That precisely is the sense of what he said at the Stuttgart lecture: "The Christmas Conference is real only through what will be made out of it in the future.... Whether the Christmas Conference will be effective for life depends upon whether it will be continued.... We have, of course, completed it; however, this Christmas Conference should never be ended, but always carried forward in the life of the Anthroposophical Society" (Ibid.).

With unswerving purpose, Steiner continued everything he announced at the Christmas Conference. The best example is the First Class review lessons, which he began in September 1924, and had to interrupt because of his illness. When one considers the first review lesson, which begins with a direct reference to the Christmas Conference, one realizes that it if it had been up to Rudolf Steiner, this series would not have ended with the contents of the eighth lesson. There is no doubt that if he had had the physical energy, he would have brought this series to completion. Also, he constantly carried on writing the chapters for his *Autobiography*, all the "Michael Letters," and the "Leading Thoughts" through all the months of 1924 and the few months of 1925 that were still left before the end of his life. And he did it, to be sure, entirely in the spirit of the Christmas Conference.

While on his sick bed, Steiner told Marie Steiner that she should wait with publishing the first part of the "Last Address," because he wanted to add a second section.[74] From this information, it follows that he still hoped the higher powers of destiny would allow him to hold more karma lectures. "The Last Address" demonstrates that he wanted to pursue more karma lectures, albeit in a quite different form.[75]

Steiner's inherent attitude, unmistakably orienting his whole activity to grow consequently out of the Christmas Conference, was immediately adopted by all the executive committee members, as his closest colleagues and students in the esoteric leadership. Although after his death, great problems eventually arose in their circle, these problems came about, in a deeper sense, from the divergent karmic streams of these five important personalities. With this in mind, one can be all the more impressed that each of them was steadfastly loyal, nevertheless, to the original impulse of the Christmas Conference. This steadfast loyalty remained intact until the end of their lives.[76]

Today it is especially moving to read how these five executive committee members, despite the schism that developed among them, nevertheless could agree to formulate the management board's first collective statement after Rudolf Steiner's death. That statement began with a reference to the spirit of the Christmas Conference and reached a culmination with a mutual commitment of loyalty to their teacher. This executive committee, holding itself together as though with the last ounce of strength, hoped that Steiner might continue to work spiritually through them in directing the Anthroposophical Society. Even today, there is no justifiable reason to doubt the sincerity of their statement in the least. The executive committee memorandum of May 3, 1925,[77] begins with the statement: "The guidance of the Anthroposophical Society shall be conducted further in the same manner Rudolf Steiner specified at the Christmas Conference." Therefore, "the executive committee appointed by him [Rudolf Steiner] considers its duty to remain in its functions, and to continue to work in Rudolf Steiner's spirit, who persists as leader *in its center.*"[78]

Although the cohesion of the executive committee could no longer remain intact, it is still of great importance that after Rudolf Steiner's death the committee at least tried to perpetuate its intercommunity in his spirit. The executive committee sought to achieve this intercommunity by developing the resolute will to remain true to Rudolf Steiner and to keep working out of the impulses coming from the Christmas Conference; these were the two basic pillars of the committee's esoteric existence. When one envisions more precisely what is meant here, one is even more strongly touched, despite the first conflict in the society (in 1935) with all of its destructive consequences; and the second conflict (in the 1940s), with its no less devastating effects. It is moving to see that the three main proponents of these conflicts each announced clearly and unmistakably at the end of their lives, that they remained loyal, in one form or another, to the original Christmas Conference impulse.

In a 1946 letter, Marie Steiner explained again her efforts to incorporate the Estate Association into the School for Spiritual Science as one of her sections; on this occasion she wrote about "reconstructing the (Anthroposophical) Society by returning to the original principles outlined by Dr. Steiner at the Christmas Conference."[79] She wrote that letter to voice her conviction regarding the leadership and necessary advanced training in the

School for Spiritual Science. "Now only a *council* consisting of the section leaders can take over the task of directing a School for Spiritual Science, and of forming the new sections foreseen by Dr. Steiner." (ibid.; italics M. Steiner) If one reads this letter, one can understand that the inner connection with the Society and the School still really lived energetically in her.

In the year of her death (1948), Marie Steiner responded to Ehrenfried Pfeiffer's wonderful characterization of the esoteric nature of the Christmas Conference; for Pfeiffer, the question of Rudolf Steiner's spirit continuing to work through the Anthroposophical Society was a focal point, full of appreciation and enthusiasm.[80] The true esoteric impulse of the Christmas Conference still lived in Marie Steiner vividly, so many years afterward.

Furthermore, one can recall that one year before the catastrophe of 1935,[81] Ita Wegman experienced a life-threatening illness. During this illness, on the threshold to the spiritual world, she had an important suprasensory meeting with the Christ and with Rudolf Steiner's spiritual being, who sent her back to earth—even though at this time she really wanted only to die—because her task was not yet completed. And what was this new task, which filled the rest of her life, along with her medical activity? The task was further work with the First Class of the School for Spiritual Science. After her return from the threshold of the spiritual world, the most important concern in the remaining years of her life was to renew the work of the School. She did this by conveying the unmitigated liveliness, timeliness, and effectiveness of the class lessons to her friends, and to all members who wanted to receive it from her. This was the task beyond life and death that she had received directly from the Christ and Rudolf Steiner, and to which she remained steadfastly loyal until her last breath.[82]

Albert Steffen also set an example through his unshakeable loyalty to the Christmas Conference impulse over many decades and in numerous ordeals, until the end of his life. Despite many disappointments and conflict situations, he always tried to lead the society in the sense and out of the spirit of the Christmas Conference, many moments of resignation and doubt notwithstanding. In reflecting on this life one can only ask, from where, out of what higher source could Albert Steffen, this very sensitive and often indecisive man, draw the unshakeable inner power that kept him steadfast his whole life long, in all these storms? Was it not his true relationship to the spiritual world? He was among the minority of Rudolf Steiner's students who had their own spiritual experiences; out of those experiences, did he at once recognize the whole *spiritual* importance of the Christmas Conference? Perhaps then, he worked further only out of this impulse. This is a riddle that is reserved for future researchers of his biography.[83]

One could also consider the visit of Willem Zeylmans van Emmichoven to Albert Steffen at the beginning of the 1960s. Zeylmans had been the general secretary of the Dutch National Society from the beginning. Now in the 1960s, he wanted the Dutch National Society to reestablish relations with the Goetheanum in Dornach. (Later, the English National Society also followed this example.) He succinctly summarized the reason why he and the Dutch members had decided to take this step after so many years: "Because we want to."[84] This will impulse derived from the deepest essence of the Christmas Conference, and was immediately recognized as such by Albert Steffen. Therefore, he accepted Zeylmans' offer without attaching to it any conditions, or recalling what had happened many years before, during the catastrophe in 1935.

Albert Steffen received this message with great joy and genuine gratitude, and acted in conversation with Zeylmans in such a way that a type of "occult love" could be perceived now by the people who had earlier been actively involved in the expulsions. This true brotherly love, as a new and future basis for the further cooperation of these two very different individualities, resulted from their mutual steadfast loyalty to the Christmas Conference.

If one seeks for the source of this loyalty, which these very fundamentally different men (they were almost polar opposites) carried within themselves, one finds the source without doubt in the inner relationship to Steiner as their spiritual leader. "For the love of Rudolf Steiner," Willem Zeylmans later said to his closest friends. He indicated that "in a spiritual experience he had witnessed Rudolf Steiner as still being connected with the fate of the Anthroposophical Society."[85] This was the beginning of atonement for the injustice that had happened; the door was once again open for all members to restore the good karma of the Anthroposophical Society, in the sense of the original Christmas Conference impulse. Albert Steffen perceived this also.

Marie Steiner's answer to Ehrenfried Pfeiffer's letter (mentioned earlier) testifies that she also felt this way. Above all, she really lived according to the exemplary conduct of her teacher. She loyally carried further what she had received spiritually from Steiner, and she wanted to continue following the path prescribed by him, according to her energy and abilities. Because of the fact that she never left this path (although she was initially isolated), we owe it to her today that the Anthroposophical Society still exists in the world as a unity, despite all its differences of opinion and inner tensions. It is no longer a splintered society; rather, it is a society that knows the necessity of safeguarding its unity, despite all external and internal obstacles. This unity is safeguarded in the spirit of the Christmas Conference, which was established by Rudolf Steiner 85 years ago for the far-distant future. This unity reveals its members' loyalty to the original impulse of the Anthroposophical Society.

Something quite singular is connected with the Christmas Conference; in reflecting about it, Steiner continually said he did not know what would be the consequences of his deed. How can such a thing be possible? We can understand this in its deepest sense if we envision that whenever there is a real creation out of nothing; that is, when deeds are achieved out of people's highest moral intuition, no one can know in advance what consequences such deeds will have for the world. In the sense of *The Philosophy of Spiritual Activity* these deeds are accomplished out of pure "love for the objective." (GA 4, Chapter IX). In this case, the deed was accomplished out of the spiritual leader's sacrificial love for his students who were gathered on the earth in the Anthroposophical Society. In a description of the protagonists in the fourth mystery drama, Steiner writes about the spiritual leader: "In *The Soul's Awakening*, Benedictus is no longer to be thought of as simply standing above his students; rather, his own soul's destiny is interwoven in the soul experiences of his students" (GA 14).

What Steiner expressed prophetically in that statement, actually took place at the Christmas Conference: he voluntarily connected his own karma with that of his students. The same evidence of this karmic background of the Christmas Conference has remained preserved for us by two totally different people. These are Marie Steiner and Ita Wegman, who both regarded Steiner's sacrificial deed in the light of his being a follower of Christ; and in light of his full connection with the karma of the Anthroposophical Society, which means with the karma of all his students.

Less than one month after Rudolf Steiner's death, in her essay "In Remembrance of the Christmas Conference," Ita Wegman wrote: "Rudolf Steiner received the karma of the Anthroposophical Society into his own destiny. It was an unprecedented risk; as it was happening, one could almost experience and feel the whole cosmos trembling."[86] A little more than a month later, she once again addressed this theme. "Something unheard of happened there.... The master connected his destiny with the Anthroposophical Society. The sacrifice was carried out, purposefully and consciously.... In the same way the Christ being united himself with the earth for the well-being of humanity, so Rudolf Steiner identified himself with the Anthroposophical Society. It was a Christ deed."[87]

In 1942, at the end of her long life, Marie Steiner also wrote about this in her first "Appeal for Accord" to the members.

"In view of this sacrifice and this death [Rudolf Steiner's], in which we certainly are all guilty together, as individuals and as a society—for he took *our* karma upon himself—can we not forget, reconcile, and open our doors wide to seekers?"[88] One year later, she expressed the same thoughts again, this time more generally. "As is emphasized so often by trustworthy sources, to this activity [by Rudolf Steiner] belongs the Anthroposophical Society, whose karma he took upon himself twenty years ago at the Christmas Conference."[89]

Rudolf Steiner finally decided in the last moment (possibly right after his trip to Holland in November, 1923) out of pure sacrifice, to enact this deed, which was consummated at the Christmas Conference. The deed was of such a kind that nobody, neither on earth nor in heaven, could know in advance what its consequences would be, because through it something completely new entered into the development of humanity.

Here there is nothing less than a new creation, which at that time did not occur from above to below, but from below to above, through the free deed of a human being. We can truly say this Christmas Conference was the concrete, practical realization, and concurrently the highest culmination, of what Steiner had established a few decades before in his book *The Philosophy of Spiritual Activity*, where he described the free deeds of human beings. Thus, there resides in the Christmas Conference, especially because Steiner did not know the consequences of his deed, a real fulfillment of what is presented in *The Philosophy of Spiritual Activity*. At the same time, it is the highest sacrifice, brought by a person out of full freedom, as the basis for a true creation out of nothing. This is how one can summarize the essence of Steiner's deed at the Christmas Conference.

With this creation out of nothing, we enter directly into the divine realm of the new mysteries. It is quite interesting that Rudolf Steiner, perhaps because of his great modesty, spoke mostly about a *renewal* of the mysteries, and not about their *founding*. But on two occasions he did point directly to the *new* mysteries: the latter occasion was in Dornach in the Apocalypse cycle for the priests of the Christian Community, September 1924.[90] Four months before that on May 26, 1924, in Paris he mentioned this theme quite unexpectedly at the end of his last public lecture, which was titled "How Does One Attain Knowledge of the Supersensible World?" Here he stated with great energy that only the new mysteries can rescue humanity, because only they open an appropriate path for present-day people to the spiritual world, where the being of humanity originated and can be found.[91]

Also, we know the astonishing statement Steiner made during the Christmas Conference in this regard, showing a direct relationship between the Christmas Conference and the Mystery of Golgotha, which finds a kind of renewal in the new mysteries. The obscure statement expressed at the end of the Christmas Conference indicates this is the "beginning of a world-turning point" in humanity's evolution (GA 260, 1.1.1924).[92]

With this statement, Steiner pointed to the direct connection of the Christmas Conference with the Mystery of Golgotha, in which humanity is not only given new information and revelations; but also those in its center receive a new creation, in bringing into being what can be characterized as the resurrection body of Christ. "For what is important is not what Christ Jesus taught, but what he gave to humanity. His resurrection is the birth of a new member of human nature: an incorruptible body" (GA 131, 10.11.1911).

If we understand the Mystery of Golgotha correctly in this sense, we can also recognize its connection with the new mysteries. Then we are not surprised that where there is a real relationship to the Mystery of Golgotha—as in the founding of the new mysteries at the Christmas Conference—it is not primarily a matter of wisdom but of a new creation (this was imparted in the evening lectures.)[93] Just as Christ, with the resurrection at the Mystery of Golgotha, macrocosmically introduced a new creation into the evolution of the whole world and humanity;

so does the founding of the new mysteries at the Christmas Conference out of the same source, establish now, microcosmically, a new creation into humanity's evolution, through the free creative deed of a *human being*.

Whoever wants to build upon the Mystery of Golgotha does it not by proclaiming a new wisdom, but by initiating a new creation. Thus, we find in the heart of the Christmas Conference as its esoteric kernel what has been created through a free spirit. This is a double creation by Rudolf Steiner: the suprasensory Foundation Stone and the Foundation Stone Meditation, which expresses the being of the suprasensory Foundation Stone in mantric form. Although the two are, of course, deeply connected with one another, they are at the same time two totally different things.

This suprasensory Foundation Stone—Rudolf Steiner also called it a "dodecahedral imaginative love image" (GA 260, 12.25.1924)—which he created as a real spiritual being in the suprasensory world bordering the earth, is a new creation, and it is consequently encased in the mantric words of the Foundation Stone Meditation. Like a cloak, like a veil, the words of the Foundation Stone Meditation surround this Foundation Stone that is preserved and cared for in our hearts. Planted in the soil of our hearts, the words reveal to us the full reality connected with the Foundation Stone to which it will lead.

Thus, these two are closely related, and thereby form the true kernel of the new mysteries. They are especially connected with two spiritual beings who preside over these mysteries, and who participated from the suprasensory world in the founding of the mysteries during the Christmas Conference. Steiner names these two beings in the *Leading Thoughts* and the *Michael Letters*, their description culminating in the fact that he joins their holy names together and places them before us as one being—Michael-Christ. In this sense, there is an existential connection between the inner composition of the Foundation Stone, the Foundation Stone Meditation, and these two beings: with

Michael as the cosmic countenance of Christ and with Christ himself. This reference, although only sketchy, will now be followed further.

When we examine the subject matter of the Christmas Conference from the remaining stenographic notes, it occurs to us that the conference had a three-part course of events. Every evening, Steiner provided the necessary nourishment for the attendees' thought forces in his lecture series *World History and the Mysteries in the Light of Anthroposophy* (GA 233). Every morning in a esoteric-ritual session, he spoke directly to the heart of every person as though the heart had become a new organ of knowledge.[94] And third, there were discussions lasting for hours about the statutes of the newly established General Anthroposophical Society in which the will of those present at this new founding was directly addressed,[95] the will to work together and mutually shape the social life. Reading the statute discussions, one experiences the wonderfully friendly and loving gesture of Rudolf Steiner, who apparently wanted all his students (who were at the same time his friends) to express themselves there freely. One is constantly surprised at how patiently and generously Steiner behaved, even treating muddle-headed, inappropriate comments freely and lovingly. Implicitly, he wanted all those present to participate in this process of mutual deliberation because it was a matter of forming a community will or will impulse out of which the new society would emerge as a karmic community of the future.

The three major results of the Christmas Conference for the further development of the Anthroposophical Society and Movement also correspond to the mentioned three-part division of this conference. Steiner later continued the theme of the evening lectures, in his great karma writings of 1924. The actual esoteric event of the conference was performed every morning throughout the days of the conference, first as laying the Foundation Stone, and then as delivering and considering the Foundation Stone Meditation rhythms corresponding to the days of the week. This work achieved its further development and culmination in the founding of the School for Spiritual Science, which Rudolf Steiner also called the Michael-School. The results of the daily statute discussions were decided on, only after reading them three times so they could later be entered into the commercial registry.[96] This action served to make the society legally and publicly visible; and it corresponded (in a certain sense) to the second Goetheanum, which was built later, and also promotes the Anthroposophical Society's visibility in the outer world.

From a more esoteric point of view, one can also understand the three influences of the Christmas Conference in the following way. Rudolf Steiner's indications about the karma of the Anthroposophical Society culminated in the karma lectures. Central here is the description of the suprasensory Michael-School in the Sun sphere, where Michael himself instructed the human souls connected with him about Anthroposophy. This suprasensory school, as Rudolf Steiner described many times in the karma lectures, represents a high ideal that ever since rests in the depths of every anthroposophist's soul. In order to transform this ideal into a living reality, the way to its fulfillment must be found on earth. And that is precisely what happens in the esoteric lessons of the First Class, which originate directly from the suprasensory Michael-School, and therefore can lead to its culmination.

Because the Michael-School took place in the spiritual world, that is, on the other side of the threshold, the path to it must also lead beyond that boundary. Therefore, questions about the threshold, and consciously going beyond it, are among the major concerns of Michaelic esoteric knowledge at the present time. Its significance and timeliness can be better understood when a person considers that one of Steiner's most important research discoveries was that humanity as a whole had unconsciously crossed over the threshold to the spiritual world in the second half of the nineteenth century.[97] It follows that a decisive step toward the future must be taken to raise this new condition out of unconscious darkness to full daylight consciousness. If this is not done, humanity will encounter increasing difficulties and ever more catastrophes, which result from an unconscious relationship to the threshold.

This problem can, however, be eliminated only on an esoteric path, within the First Class, whose mantric contents lead to crossing the threshold in full consciousness.[98] One can get a clearer idea of the solution to this problem by studying, in an artistic sense, the transition from the first to the second Goetheanum. The development of the first building can be traced very well on the basis of its models, which still exist. The building actually consists of an inner space in which spiritual forces are active from the center toward the periphery, and on that directional path the forces create all the internal forms of the building.[99]

In contrast to this, the second Goetheanum emerged through forces that are active in the opposite direction, from the periphery to the center. This can be examined quite wonderfully in the model made by Rudolf Steiner. Between the two buildings was the burning of the first Goetheanum, whereby it was transformed from an earthly to a heavenly, peripheral being (more details follow); and since then, its forces also work in the second direction described, from the periphery to the center. The second building has come about out of this effect.

If one considers this metamorphosis even more closely, one sees that it relates principally to a full transformation of the inner forces, which began to flow into it from outside, from the world periphery. A similar metamorphosis, a type of eversion of the inner forces coming from outside, is experienced by the human soul when it consciously crosses over the threshold to the spiritual world. What one previously experienced inwardly as soul content changes at the threshold into objective forms in the spiritual world surrounding one. Thus, one can recognize in the forms and architectural thoughts of the second Goetheanum, especially in comparison to the first, the guardian of the threshold. Thereby, one is prepared to cross over consciously at sometime time in one's own biography.[100]

If one looks at the entire form of the Christmas Conference in its threefold nature, one is at first astonished about the fact that the name Michael is not mentioned during the entire conference, except in a single short statement during an evening lecture, in which it is only pointed out that we live today in a Michael-Epoch that began in 1879, and that since that time "a new calling from the spiritual heights to humanity [has come about]."[101]

On January 13, 1924, exactly 12 days after the Christmas Conference ended, two things happened. For the first time, the Foundation Stone Meditation was published in the *Mitteilungsblatt*; and on the same evening, Rudolf Steiner gave a lecture in which a totally surprising picture of Michael appears. Michael is described as a waiting, reticent spirit, who gives no directives, inspirations, or impulses in our time; he waits to see what people do out of what has been given to them as spiritual knowledge (GA 233a). The reason for Michael's special behavior toward people lies in the fact that he is the only one of the archangels who completely respects humanity's freedom. Therefore, he does not concern himself with moving us to action, but only with the resulting consequences. "This rests on the fact that Michael actually has the most to do with what human beings create out of the spiritual. He lives in the results of what is created by people. The other spirits live more with the causes; Michael lives more with the consequences. The other spirits inspire people to action. Michael is the real *spiritual hero of freedom*" (GA 233a, 1.13.1924).

At the end of the lecture Rudolf Steiner gives a gripping imagination. The souls of people stand before Michael with the consequences of their free deeds, either in full consciousness as initiates, or only after death, or (for all people) every night in sleep. They appear before Michael, and he judges their deeds not in words, but only with his glance and gestures, which announce whether he considers these deeds justified in light of universal guidance. If the deeds are justified, Michael accepts them into his spiritual realm, where human deeds become cosmic deeds. Steiner describes it in this way: "When a person out of freedom, impelled by reading the astral light, does a deed consciously or unconsciously, then Michael carries what is an earthly human deed into the cosmos so that it will become a cosmic deed" (ibid.).

When one reads today what was stated exactly twelve days after the Christmas Conference, then one will realize (sooner or later, as though struck by lightning) that what Steiner presents here in a quite impersonal, objective form, really has an autobiographical character. No one else could be imagined in this position, other than Rudolf Steiner himself. With his highest creation, the Foundation Stone of Love, Steiner now stepped before Michael, anticipating how the spiritual world would judge his free creative deed, and receiving the answer from Michael's strict gaze. "That is right, that is justified before the guidance of the cosmos" (ibid.). Then Steiner saw that in the light of universal guidance, this new creation was received by Michael into his spiritual realm where the free creative human deed becomes a cosmic deed.

That is the reason why, during a night trip from Dornach to Stuttgart, Steiner could say conclusively to Guenther Wachsmuth and Ernst Lehrs, "With the Christmas Conference, Anthroposophy has been transformed from a former earthly affair to a cosmic affair."[103] And for which "cosmic affair" will the Foundation Stone form the basis now? To what does this suprasensory Love Stone point as a cosmic fact?

The answer had long since been provided by Steiner, specifically at the end of his book *An Outline of Occult Science,* where he wrote about the future Cosmos of Love, which appears at the end of the Apocalypse as the New Jerusalem, and has emerged out of white magic.[104] Through pure, white magic, the Foundation Stone of Love was created by Steiner in the spiritual world bordering the earth. It is the true Foundation Stone for the New Jerusalem, the future Cosmos of Love.

Steiner describes in the same book how it was possible for him to achieve this new creation. "From the Earth condition on, the 'Wisdom of the Outer World'[105] will become inner wisdom in human beings. And when it is internalized there, it will become the seed of *Love*. Wisdom is the prerequisite for Love; Love is the result of wisdom born again in the 'I'" (GA 13, italics Rudolf Steiner). Out of his individual, free "I" that had internalized the complete wisdom of the world (this is what an initiate can read today in the astral light), Steiner created at the Christmas Conference, with white magic, the Foundation Stone of Love, following solely in his activity the "comprehensive archetype of love" (ibid.), which appeared on the earth at the Mystery of Golgotha.

The Foundation Stone was created by Steiner, not out of earthly substances, which are subject to the boundaries of space and time, but out of the spiritual substance of pure love in the spiritual world bordering the Earth. Therefore, since the beginning, the Foundation Stone has been fully independent of all earthly space and time relationships. It is also independent today, after eighty-five years; so it is up-to-date, real, and present in the spiritual world, as it was then, at the moment of its creation. Thus, there is still the possibility to plant it in our hearts freely, as the spiritual foundation of the Anthroposophical Society, as the inner source of all anthroposophical life.

Out of the highest forces of the spiritual world imaginable to human beings, out of the forces of the divine Trinity itself, Steiner put together this most important creation of his life—as a free human deed. During the esoteric activity of laying the Foundation Stone on December 25, 1923, he said, "Out of these three forces: out of the divine Holy Spirit; out of the peripheral Christ-Force; out of the Father might that stream out of the depths, we want at this moment to form in our souls the dodecahedral Foundation Stone, which we take into the depths of our hearts, so that it can be a strong symbol in the mighty foundation of our souls, and so that we can stand on this firm

Foundation Stone as we participate in future Anthroposophical Society activity" (GA 260).

Thus, the foundation of the General Anthroposophical Society at the Christmas Conference is concerned with a mystery deed of the first degree. According to its nature, it truly belongs to the realm of eternity, beyond all limitations of space and time. And then what happens with this Foundation Stone? We have already seen that after Steiner had created it, it did not remain one moment with him. From that moment on, as soon as the creation process was completed, the Foundation Stone belonged to the world. It belonged especially to those who were gathered together at the founding of the new human community; but it also belongs to all the following generations of anthroposophists; all who participate in the life of the Anthroposophical Society and who want to work for its future prosperity. This is why the Foundation Stone was passed on to us by our spiritual leader.

How was this event consummated in reality? How was it possible that the Foundation Stone became, on the one hand, the basis of a new spiritual reality, a future cosmos, in Michael's realm; and on the other hand, at the same time bore the possibility of being entrusted to every human heart? This was possible only through a process Steiner describes in various connections as a definite reality for the spiritual world. This process involves a spiritual multiplication, in which something is propagated through higher powers; it is made accessible from one source to many people who strive for it and are prepared to fulfill the necessary inner conditions. We find the prototype of this process in what happened at the Mystery of Golgotha with Christ's resurrected body.

What happened at that time on the macrocosmic level can now be repeated by a Christian initiate on a microcosmic level. Thus, Steiner speaks in the lecture cycle *From Jesus to Christ* about this secret. "We must imagine what has arisen out of the grave (on Golgotha) as increasing, multiplying in number to the same extent as the ovum reproduces in the physical body" (GA 131, 10.11.1911). The apostle Paul, especially through his Damascus experience, knew the secret that Christ's "spirit body," which had appeared to him, "propagates like a seed and passes over to all people" (op. cit., 10.12.1911).[106] The Foundation Stone of the Christmas Conference is part of the same stream—on a microcosmic level.

From this point of view, it is impressive to observe with what foresight Steiner gradually prepared his students for the new mysteries, for the suprasensory reality of the Foundation Stone, nine years before the Christmas Conference. On September 20, 1914, on the first anniversary of laying the Foundation Stone of the first Goetheanum, he pointed out at the end of his address: "Let us become conscious that when we learn to speak correctly about Christ, we learn to speak correctly about the history of humanity. Christ does not belong to only one folk group; Christ belongs to everybody. Christ did not speak only to those connected with one folk stream: You are my brother. He spoke to those connected with all humanity. We then find the path to each human being, to the peace-chorus of all the higher hierarchies, and to Christ. That, my dear friends, must also be a foundation stone we want to lay in our hearts, on which we want to build the invisible building for which the visible building is the external symbol."[107]

With these words, the modern "path to Christ" is brought into direct connection with the suprasensory Foundation Stone. All individuals can voluntarily place this Stone in their hearts;[108] and on it a spiritual temple, rather than a material building will be erected, for which everything "visible" is only an "external symbol." When one encounters such a statement in Steiner's work, one is especially amazed how consistently he advanced certain basic tenets of the Anthroposophical Movement, and gradually expanded what he had established earlier.[109]

The next step on this path occurs exactly two years later. On September 20, 1916, the third anniversary of laying the first

Goetheanum's foundation stone, Steiner made this statement in Dornach: "In many of our souls lives honest, true willing. And this honest, true willing, when it remains true to itself, will add understanding to the honesty of the will. And then in all our souls will be formed the other foundation stone, which brings, *replicated many times*,[110] what is spiritual into the world, which erects itself in our ideas above the physical foundation stone that we devotedly entrusted to the earth three years ago here on this hill."[111]

From these preliminary steps to the later creation of the suprasensory Foundation Stone, it is clear that Steiner wanted to connect the actual founding of the new mysteries with the esoteric opening (or initiation) of the first Goetheanum,[112] which probably should have occurred in 1923 at the twenty-first anniversary (1902-1923) of Anthroposophy's public appearance.[113] After developing for three seven-year periods to that point, Anthroposophy had achieved its "I" stage, which corresponded to its maturity and full manifestation on earth.[114]

Seven years before the Christmas Conference, Steiner spoke about a suprasensory Foundation Stone, which was not yet there, but "will be able to form" in our hearts sometime in the future. Replicated in the spiritual world, it would be placed in every human heart that is seeking it as a higher spiritual reality. When one reads such remarks now, one has a wonderful feeling about how consistently Rudolf Steiner arranged his own deeds in the greater universal context. And precisely this awareness of universal context must be considered at every step of a new creation, so that deeds completed in the sense of *The Philosophy of Spiritual Activity* really produce goodness in the world. Thus, we read in Chapter 9 of that book: "I do not cognitively examine whether my actions are good or bad; I perform them because I *love* them. They are 'good' if my love-filled intuition has the right relationship to experience intuitively the universal context, 'bad' if that is not the case" (GA 4, italics Rudolf Steiner).[115]

Quite in this sense, the Foundation Stone was placed in the

greatest possible "universal context," namely, in the spiritual stream that emanates directly out of the Mystery of Golgotha, and since then penetrates the whole earth evolution. It is a fact that such a deed as Rudolf Steiner's during the Christmas Conference is possible only out of "love-filled intuition." This is because "the event of Golgotha is a free cosmic deed, which originates in universal love and can be comprehended only through human love" (GA 26, "Leading Thought" 143).

With the quotation from *The Philosophy of Spiritual Activity*, the bridge was also built to the Foundation Stone Meditation and the words contained therein. "What is good is...." Every human deed is really good only when it is placed in the universal context of the "Christ-Sun," whose light can be found in the spiritual part of the Earth since the Mystery of Golgotha.

The Foundation Stone also has this deep connection to the Christ being and his deed on Golgotha. Steiner said during its creation that now the warmth and the light of the Foundation Stone are strengthened by the Christ-Being's source of warmth and light, which stream to us out of the Mystery of Golgotha. It now becomes quite clear how real and consequential the connection to the appearance of Christ at the Mystery of Golgotha is made by creating the Foundation Stone. All that happened at the Christmas Conference was carried out by Steiner only in the light of the Christ-Sun, which can warm and illumine our hearts and heads at all times, when we need it, in order to carry its impulse consciously and bravely into the world.

The previously considered motif of the spiritual building that will be erected on the suprasensory Foundation Stone, which must find fruitful ground and the possibility for growth in people's hearts, was taken up again on the last day of the Christmas Conference. "We have laid the Foundation Stone here. On this Foundation Stone the building will be erected, whose individual stones are the work performed in all our groups by individuals outside in the wide world" (GA 260, 1.1.1924). In the same connection, Steiner had spoken immediately before about the "physical Goetheanum" to be built in the near future, which will be "only the external symbol for our spiritual Goetheanum" (ibid.).

It is the "spiritual Goetheanum" or the "Good Spirit of the Goetheanum" about which Steiner spoke after the conclusion of the Christmas Conference in his response to Louis Werbeck's words of appreciation. Everything "happening here [at the Christmas Conference] occurred fully responsibly in looking up to the Spirit who is, and will be, the Spirit of the Goetheanum."[115] The whole Christmas Conference was penetrated by this Spirit.[116] And only through the participation of this Spirit during the entire event, was it possible for Steiner to work and speak at this conference as he did. "In His name I have allowed myself to say many things these days that could not have been so assertive, had it not been for respecting the Spirit of the Goetheanum, spoken to the good Spirit of the Goetheanum." (ibid.)

Three examples will clarify what Rudolf Steiner was allowed to express during the Christmas Conference through this Spirit of the Goetheanum. In his commentary about the first rhythm of the Foundation Stone Meditation,[117] he indicates it is a "message coming from the universal Word" (See GA 260, 12.16.1923).Then, on Sunday morning, in the commentary to the fifth rhythm, he points out that everything happening at the Christmas Conference occurred out of the Spirit who had gone through the Mystery of Golgotha at the Turning Point of Time. One feels how cautious Steiner is being at this point. The holy name is mentioned only in the mantra, and yet it is quite clear who Steiner means when he speaks in connection with all the events at the Christmas Conference about "what really appeared at the Turning Point of Time, and in whose spirit we want to work and strive further" (GA 260, 12.30.1923). It is the direct presence of Christ himself. Therefore, it is immediately understandable why in this place the holy name is not uttered directly; it is for the same reason that the name of Michael hardly appears during the Christmas Conference. For when such lofty beings *are directly present*, their names may not be spoken except in mantric words because the power that is connected with them can have an overwhelming effect on those present. In such essential details, one feels even more strongly how Michael-Christ[118] was really present at the founding of the new mysteries. Truly: nothing or everything!

Out of awareness of this spiritual situation, one can also understand the third example, which has already been mentioned. We find it in the key words for the whole Christmas Conference: "Beginning of the Universal Turning Point in Time" (GA 260a, 1.1.1924).[135] which achieves its full reality based only on the spiritual presence of *Michael* and *Christ*.

By following further in this direction, one can discover ever deeper relationships between the mystery deed of the laying of the Foundation Stone and the present effects of the Being of Christ. Thus, one can ask why the three components of the Foundation Stone created by Steiner are correspondingly paired, that is, cosmic and human at the same time: *universal-human* love, *universal-human* imagination, *universal-human* illuminated thought.

If one considers that the further goal of the Foundation Stone was, and is, to be planted in the depths of the human heart, then it is understandable that through its dual nature, it connects the two streams of the etherized blood. That is, on the one hand the human etherized blood stream that ascends continually from the heart to the head; and on the other hand, the macrocosmic stream of Christ's etherized blood. After the Mystery of Golgotha, this stream was first discovered by the true Rosicrucians, and then researched by Steiner anew. These two streams ascend in the human being parallel to one another, from below to above. The task is to connect these two streams with each other. According to Steiner, that connection leads to consciously perceiving Christ in the etheric.[119] For this reason, the Foundation Stone in its macrocosmic-microcosmic form, is laid in human hearts at the source of both streams, so that its microcosmic part has a natural connection to the human stream of the etherized blood, and the macrocosmic part is connected to the stream of the etherized Christ blood. Inasmuch as the Foundation Stone, despite its dual nature, forms a *unity*, it has the capability of uniting the two streams. Therefore, it becomes the portal for experiencing the etheric Christ. Expressed in other terms, it becomes the new organ of perception in our hearts, enabling us to experience the full reality of the resurrection.

The Foundation Stone Meditation is also constructed in this manner. Its three first parts consist also of microcosmic and macrocosmic sections,[120] which are then summarized and united in the fourth part. In the light of the Christ-Sun, the human being is connected with the cosmos for the entire future of Earth development. We can make this connection by contemplating the Foundation Stone Meditation so that it embraces the spiritual power of the Foundation Stone in our hearts and transforms it into an ever more effective organ of perception for the etheric Christ.

At this point, one could introduce still more examples in which the multifaceted relationship appears between the Foundation Stone and what Steiner represented in many lectures as the basis of anthroposophical Christology. I would like to limit my remarks here to the social aspect of the Foundation Stone, that is, its community-building quality.

First, it must be strongly emphasized that only on a strictly individual path of developing the consciousness soul can one plant the Foundation Stone in one's own heart. It is a very personal event, which proceeds from, and is rooted in, a cognitive process. No other person can accomplish, or even demonstrate, this intimate and individual deed for us; it must occur first through ourselves. However, when this Foundation Stone has once been planted in the depths of our hearts, it is there not only for ourselves. According to its innermost nature, it is not created for individuals, but for a human community. Therefore, it is a great error to say, "Surely, I feel the Foundation Stone in my heart, but I am not interested in the Anthroposophical Society nor in working at building its community. I feel quite comfortable being alone with this Foundation Stone." If one hears something of this sort, then one must realize that such an attitude contradicts the deepest nature of the Foundation Stone. The person concerned has not comprehended its basic underlying principles; and in dealing with the Foundation Stone has not yet achieved the full reality for which it was, and still is, connected from the beginning. In this case, one finds oneself somewhere in the middle of the path, and erroneously considers what is only a part of the process to be the complete process.

When the whole process is carried to its conclusion, one knows *out of one's own experience* that this individually planted Foundation Stone in one's individual heart is not there only for oneself, not only for one's own development, not even for a small, limited group of people, but for the world community of Michael students and for the world community of the Anthroposophical Society that Rudolf Steiner founded at the Christmas Conference. Therefore, one can measure one's concrete relationship to the Foundation Stone by one's own striving and wanting to work on the tasks and goals of this world community, despite its many imperfections and all the difficulties in its conflict-ridden history. The full reality of the Foundation Stone appears only in the unfolding of the social impulse. And then it really becomes a solid foundation for the future of humanity.

The following scripture reference clarifies concretely what this means. With the creation of the Foundation Stone, something is given to a person that realizes its full value only in the sense of Christ's words that Steiner often quoted in his lectures. It is the statement, "My realm is not of this world" (John 18:36). Commenting on these words, Steiner says, "The realm of Christ Jesus is not of this world; but it must work into this world, and human souls must be tools of this realm, which is not of this world" (GA 175, 2.6.1917). How can we better understand Rudolf Steiner's comment? What did Christ do after he spoke these words at the Turning Point of Time? He brought his divine realm to the earth, which is ruled over by the unjustified prince of this world: Ahriman. And since Golgotha, Christ lets all people of goodwill participate in this realm, so they can cooperate in its further unfolding.

With the help of Steiner's commentary, we can understand the situation of the Anthroposophical Society's esoteric founding during the Christmas Conference in the light of Christ's statement. At the founding, by creating the special form of the Foundation Stone to underlie the higher reality of the Anthroposophical Society, Steiner fulfilled for our present time the words of Christ quoted earlier. That is, Steiner inaugurated a new community-building principle, which from our time on and into the most distant future, as long as it is Christian in the esoteric sense, will be the only Christian principle of true community. In other words, this refers to a society or human community that does not close itself off from the outer world, does not erect something like a cloister or ashram, but stands fully and completely in the middle of present-day civilization with all its manifold problems—this civilization in which the unjustified prince of the world also rules.

This means that such a human community must accomplish its task in Ahriman's domain with real Michaelic courage. How can such a community remain intact in this Ahrimanic world without "being shot full of holes"[121] (to use Steiner's words from a period preceding the Christmas Conference in reference to the Anthroposophical Society), without in time totally falling prey to him? That is possible only when, even though exposed to all the problems of the contemporary world, a community can stand in the midst of the ruling Ahrimanic powers; can stand mutually on something steadfast that is not of this world, but that originates from the realm of Christ. And this "something" is the Foundation Stone, this mysterious, "imaginative love object" (GA 260,

12.25.1923), which one can neither see with the eyes nor grasp with the hands. One may not, at first, know what it really is.

To come even closer to its suprasensory reality, one must remember what Rudolf Steiner said only three months before the Christmas Conference, on September 28, 1923, the evening before a Michaelmas Festival, in a lecture in Vienna. There he asked his anthroposophical audience the question: What does Michael *expect* from people today? "We have a feeling in our souls of what Michael really wants from us when our trust in the higher world develops the soul condition of experiencing this spiritual reality to be as real as the ground under our feet; of knowing that if the spiritual were not there, we could not take a step with our feet" (GA 233). It is very moving to note that at Michaelmas, 1923, in Vienna, Steiner reveals what Michael wants from us, in order to accomplish it himself three months later, by giving us something purely spiritual on which we can stand as firmly as on physical ground.

Here is our most current test as individual members, as well as for the entire Anthroposophical Society: Are we connected to such an extent with Michaelic thought, and through it with Michaelic will[122] that we understand the Foundation Stone in its full suprasensory reality (Michaelic thought), and can also experience it (Michaelic will)? Can we stand on it steadfastly with our entire activity, both individually and at the same time as a community of Michaelites? Do we know well that this Foundation Stone stems from the realm of Christ, and is unassailable by all the evil powers of this world?

This opens a totally new perspective of community-building in the purely Christian sense that will remain applicable not only for centuries, but for millennia. We as the Anthroposophical Society are called upon in all modesty, and in consciousness of our deficiencies, nevertheless to build the first community of this kind. We are to be a model for all later communities that one day will emerge everywhere in humanity in the original Christian sense.

*

Steiner spoke not only of the Michael Being and Christ during the Christmas Conference, but he also spoke of a third being. Steiner focused on a third being who is connected in a special way with the whole movement, and also with the Anthroposophical Society from the beginning. Therefore, it is significant to note the first time he spoke about this suprasensory being. This was in February 1913 on the occasion of the first general meeting of the newly founded Anthroposophical Society, after its detachment from the Theosophical Society. At that time, the detachment was experienced as necessarily becoming free, as from a tight and constraining corset. From that time on, the field was open for further development. After the independent Anthroposophical Society was founded on December 28, 1912, in Cologne, its first general meeting was held in February 1913. On this occasion, Steiner spoke on February 3 in Berlin for the first time about the *Being Anthroposophia.*[123] At the end of the lecture, after he had sketched the course of this suprasensory being through all of western spiritual history, he spoke this name. Now Steiner spoke no longer as usual about Anthroposophy, but about *Anthroposophia* as a real being in the spiritual world. For in reality, Anthroposophy is not a teaching; it is in the suprasensory world a mighty being, who bears the name "Anthroposophia." And this being then connected itself with the first *free* formation of community based on Anthroposophy. Steiner said at this first general meeting of the Anthroposophical Society, "What we receive through Anthroposophy is *our own being*.... For it is the nature of Anthroposophy that its own being consists in what the human being is; and that is the nature of its effectiveness, that one receives what oneself is in Anthroposophy and must place it before oneself because one must exercise self-knowledge" (ibid.).[124]

Then nearly ten years passed. In summer of 1923, in the middle of this tragic year, which Peter Selg discusses, Steiner spoke for the second time about this being. Steiner was then in Dornach, and spoke in the lecture cycle that bears a significant name: *The Anthroposophical Movement* (GA 258). And there, where it concerns the history of the Anthroposophical Society's community-building out of the Anthroposophical Movement, he spoke about Anthroposophy as an "invisible person" to whom we have "the greatest responsibility imaginable" and "whom one must question about one's individual activities in life" (GA 258, 6.16.1923).

Steiner returned to this theme yet another time, at a social event on the occasion of founding the Dutch National Society in November 1923. In moving words, he characterized this being not only as a suprasensory being, but also on an even deeper level, as a "universal living being" who stands in front of the door to the human heart, knocks, and says, "Let me in, for I am you yourself; I am your true humanity!"[125]

Then this being appeared at the Christmas Conference, and Steiner presented all anthroposophists with a double task. First, he said one must achieve "the experience of Anthroposophia in one's heart" (GA 260, 12.2.5.1923). Only after we experience this in the right way, are we ripe for the second task. Now we may work further in the Anthroposophical Society, so that a true human community emerges *for Anthroposophia*. This is the powerful, ground-breaking task going into the future—to build a community for a suprasensory being.

This, then, was the esoteric task of the Christmas Conference, which retains its validity not only for that time, but also for now, and into the future of the Anthroposophical Society. When the Foundation Stone had been laid, Steiner said: "My dear friends, listen to it (what the elemental spirits call to human beings in the Foundation Stone Meditation)[126] resounding in your own hearts (where the being Anthroposophia is present); then you will found a true society of human beings for Anthroposophia" (ibid.).

*

Michael, the Spirit of the Age; the being Anthroposophia, who connects us today with the all-encompassing cosmic spheres of the divine Sophia; and Christ are the three beings who form the spiritual source of Anthroposophy and are an intrinsic part of the new mysteries. This source is evidenced by the three elements of the Foundation Stone that connect us with these three spiritual beings.

The substance of universal human love establishes our connection with Christ. This is in the sense of the statement by Steiner (mentioned earlier) that the Mystery of Golgotha can be understood as the greatest deed of love only through the purest human love. Thus, the ascent of human love to universal love is a modern path to Christ.

The second path, from human imagination to universal imagination, leads us directly into the cosmic sphere of the divine Sophia[127]—which Luther renders in German as [28] this "taskmaster" of God, or in the Russian translation, "artist on God's throne"—who as the divine Sophia adorns the entire cosmos with beauty and is revealed in every creative human imagination.

Let us turn our gaze now to the third path, which leads from human thoughts to Michael's cosmic thoughts; on this path we currently can fulfill our task to Michael. This is the task of transforming human intelligence, which once belonged to Michael and his cosmic realm;[129] transforming intelligence through Anthroposophy, so that it finds new access to the universal intelligence of the hierarchies in Michael's realm. Steiner points this out in the following wonderful imagination. "Knowledge in anthroposophical spiritual science, which spiritualizes spatial judgment, works from below to above, reaching hands out from below to above in order to grasp the outstretched hands of Michael. This is how the bridge can be created between human beings and the gods" (GA 219, 12.17.1922).

Those are the paths to these three beings as the spiritual initiators of the new mysteries: to the Christ-Being, to the being of Sophia through Anthroposophia as her intermediary, and to the being of Michael. And they all are mantled in the Foundation Stone, so that through it, in our hearts, we can find new access to these three beings in the spiritual world. We live in a time in which cooperation with them should begin within the new mysteries, for the well-being of humanity.

Finally, we must look from the Foundation Stone to the spiritual Foundation Stone Meditation enveloping it, to this wonderful mantric word-picture that summarizes the entirety of Anthroposophy. In this meditation, Anthroposophy appears after its twenty-one-year development (from 1902[130] to 1923[131]) as though curled up in a seed. After the Christmas Conference, Anthroposophy could begin to unfold anew its developmental spiral, in the wonderful eurythmic movement of contracting and expanding, in order to reach ever higher and more illuminated evolution. Even though this unfolding lasted only a few months, nevertheless, it was powerfully and unmistakably present.

What is the Foundation Stone Meditation's main message? As extensively explained earlier, it bears the secret of the resurrection, which means the secret of the new creation lying hidden in Christ's resurrected body.[132] That is the deepest aspect, or even highest aspect of this invocation. This invocation alone forms the basis for the new mysteries. Because the invocation is in the form of a meditation, it is at the same time a path to grasp internally, in a conscious and free way, the full reality of the resurrection, so that human beings gradually acquire the likeness of the resurrected body.

As we increasingly understand what Steiner created with this meditation, we can gradually realize that a new epoch in the development of Christianity as a whole is involved. Steiner once characterized this epoch by indicating that in our time Christianity has reached the fourth, the "I" stage in its development.

"Christianity has become 'I'."[133] In this short statement, Steiner points to a momentous fact. Christianity passed through its first phase, the physical stage, at the Mystery of Golgotha. From then until the tenth century it passed through the etheric stage; later came the astral stage; now, with the appearance of Anthroposophy, Christianity has reached in our time the fourth stage, the "I" stage. Christianity will unfold the full effectiveness of its "I" force in the new mysteries, which were founded in the light of, and out of the source of the "second Michael revelation" by Steiner at the Christmas Conference.

In the course of his lectures, Steiner refers twice, quite clearly, to this "second Michael revelation." First, in a 1913 lecture, he spoke in more detail than ever before about the suprasensory Mystery of Golgotha as the spiritual starting point for the etheric appearance of Christ. Then he brought this event into direct connection with the present Michael epoch. "And although in all of humanity we are only a small society, which strives to understand this new truth about the Mystery of Golgotha [its recurrence in the spiritual world]; to grasp this new Michael revelation, we nevertheless build up a new force. This force does not in the least depend on our belief in this revelation, but alone on the revelation itself, on the truth itself" (GA 152, 5.2.1913). Directly after the words quoted, Rudolf Steiner describes this *new Michael revelation* also as Christ's current revelation to humanity of the present: "From now on there is a new revelation of Christ" (ibid.)· Michael appears in the spiritual world, not only as the cosmic countenance of Christ, but also as his disciple in humanity ("He, the Christ disciple"[134]), of which Christ himself testifies by saying "I will always speak to you through my Day Spirit[135] when you seek the path to me" (GA 194, 11.22.1919).[164]

For the second time, and in still more detail, Rudolf Steiner speaks six and a half years later in Dornach about Michael's second revelation. Now, however, he points directly to the real consequences of the Mystery of Golgotha for our time. "Human flesh must once again become thoroughly spiritualized so that it will be able to live in the realm of the Word and observe the divine secrets. The Word becoming flesh is the first Michael revelation; the flesh becoming spirit must be the second Michael revelation" (ibid.).

Out of this statement emerges the idea that the archetype for this second Michael revelation must be sought in the Mystery of Golgotha. This must be achieved today, but with a new spiritual consciousness, which is the result of the second suprasensory Mystery of Golgotha, on whose foundation and out of whose source Steiner has developed the conclusive Anthroposophy. For this Anthroposophy has emerged, both in its entirety, and in all its details, from this new Christ consciousness.[166] In this sense Steiner says about Christ: "One could say that humanity experienced the resurrection of his body at that time (at the Turning Point of Time); humanity will experience the resurrection of his consciousness from the twentieth century on. ... And the mediator, the messenger [for this] is Michael, who is now Christ's delegate" (GA 152, 5.2.1913).

Thus, as "Christ's delegate" Michael leads us today to a new understanding of the great Mystery of Golgotha by fanning the flames of the new Christ consciousness in human souls. This new understanding is the direct result of the second, suprasensory Mystery of Golgotha. Steiner testifies about this by saying: "When it is possible in the twentieth century for souls to develop an understanding of the Mystery of Golgotha, then from this event [the second, suprasensory Mystery of Golgotha] there also comes the possibility for beginning a new understanding of Christ in the sense world" (op. cit., 5.20.1913). This "new understanding" for Christ through Michael's mediation is not, however, merely theoretical; rather, it brings human beings into a direct relationship with the living, present-day Christ. Steiner continues, "Therefore, Christ is also united even more intimately with all that is the destiny of human beings on earth" (ibid.).

In the sense of the second Michael revelation, the time has already begun in which individuals must find a direct and conscious access to Christ's resurrected body, in order to take into themselves its archetype, and thus follow the path leading to humanity's becoming the Word. In Anthroposophy, that path is provided, especially in meditative work with the Foundation

Stone Meditation, which for present-day human beings opens the path into the resurrection sphere of the living Christ, whose cosmic-human reality lies at the center of the new Christian mysteries.[137]

Even though initially, this explanation gives us only a little glimpse into the depths of the new mysteries, it is sufficient to let us recognize the steadfast endeavor with which Steiner strove until the last day of his life to truly anchor the Christmas Conference impulse on Earth. Above all, he strove to anchor that impulse in human hearts and in the common will of Anthroposophical Society members, so they could carry these impulses with faithful loyalty and inner courage further in the world. At the Christmas Conference, Steiner connected that with spiritually laying the Foundation Stone for the Anthroposophical Society by stating: "And we must lay today's Foundation Stone in the right ground; the right ground being our hearts in their harmonic interaction and in their goodwill penetrated by love, together carrying anthroposophical will through the world" (GA 260, 12.25.1923).

Out of the mystery dimension of the Christmas Conference and its connection with the esoteric history of Christianity, one can gradually come to understand the entire meaning and spiritual significance of what Rudolf Seiner cryptically described as a "promise" he gave the spiritual world at the Christmas Conference; and which, according to him, he must fulfill wholeheartedly. He talked about this promise only once during the introduction to the karma lectures in Arnheim: "In a sense, there is a promise to the spiritual world. This promise will be fulfilled steadfastly, and in the future one will find things happen as they were promised to the spiritual world" (GA 240, 7.18.1924).

We all know this promise was connected with a great tragedy in Rudolf Steiner's life to which we should not close our eyes, because it cannot be separated from the subsequent history of our movement and society. In order to fulfill this lofty promise; to remain unconditionally true to it (even though it has become clear that his students did not carry out the conditions for it sufficiently), Rudolf Steiner had to leave the earthly world.

Thus, he went away from us prematurely, for only in this way could he completely redeem his promise to the higher worlds. The immeasurable tragedy of our movement and society is that Steiner was not able to fulfill his task on earth.[138] Yet it follows that in the spiritual world he has by no means given up what he inaugurated on earth as the culmination of his life mission, that is, the esoteric impulse of the Christmas Conference. "For such a thing as our Christmas Conference, one is not dependent on what happens within the earthly realm" (GA 260a, 1.18.1924). Therefore, Rudolf Steiner crossed over the threshold of death in order to work further on building the new mysteries in the spiritual world.

From what has been said, it is clear that it does not depend on Steiner, but *only on us*, the members of the Anthroposophical Society, whether Rudolf Steiner can work further through us and the society.

In 1948, thirteen years after the society's first great conflict, and in the midst of the second conflict, Ehrenfried Pfeiffer wrote from the United States to Marie Steiner, quite in the spirit of the Christmas Conference, concerning this matter. "It was the greatest deed of Steiner's that during the Christmas Conference he identified himself with the society. In this way, the society became *his body*; it could be for Steiner in the spiritual world a spiritual body on earth. Only when we place Steiner's sacrifice, this mystery deed, continually before our souls, can he work through us and the society, and use it as a physical instrument. There is no substitute for it; the best we can give is to aspire to be the limbs and organs of this spiritual life on earth. Then we can participate in Steiner's spiritual being."[139] Two weeks later, from Beatenberg, Marie Steiner answered this profoundly true description of the Christmas Conference in its esoteric relationship to Steiner's individuality. "You have described Rudolf Steiner's mystery deed marvelously."[140] She wrote this short sentence in the year of her departure from earth (December 27, 1948), summing up her long life in the service of Anthroposophy and Rudolf Steiner.

Shortly thereafter, Ehrenfried Pfeiffer (probably encouraged by Marie Steiner's favorable reaction) wrote also to the board, which at that time, in addition to Marie Steiner, consisted only of Albert Steffen and Guenther Wachsmuth. "The Christmas Conference of 1923 was the crowning point in the life work of Rudolf Steiner, our honorable teacher and spiritual leader. By founding the society anew as an esoteric institution, Steiner connected himself with the society. As the spirit being Anthroposophia, it became the body, the carrier of *his* being. This is a goal. This goal can be realized only when all members share in its implementation in community, to the extent that they become the limbs and organs of this spirit body on Earth."[141] There exists no doubt that Ehrenfried Pfeiffer, as well as Marie Steiner, who received this communication so positively, were fully convinced in 1948 that the spiritual connection with Steiner was still possible, if only members of the Anthroposophical Society really wanted it; and if out of the common will they allowed a real community of true Steiner students to continue on earth. "If this community of all those who want to follow Rudolf Steiner really would exist on earth, then Steiner could also work *today* as leader and chairperson" (ibid.). In this sense, and in clear understanding of this fact, it appeared to Ehrenfried Pfeiffer that a further step was possible, which he called "a will decision to which all (members[142]) can profess themselves out of freedom. The will decision is to maintain the *spirit body* of the society, and to make possible that Steiner's leadership spirit and Anthroposophy can be realized within it. This is Steiner's divine and esoteric legacy, which we want to uphold" (ibid.; italics by E. Pfeiffer).

Is that what *we* want? For the Anthroposophical Society today, that is still the main question regarding its esoteric existence, which depends on maintaining the spiritual relationship to Steiner by sincerely cultivating the Christmas Conference impulse among its members. According to him, "everything depends on humanity's finding the possibility of concerning themselves energetically with this Christmas Conference, really taking up its content" (GA 260a, 1.18.1924).

We must ask ourselves: What do we have in common with Steiner today in the sense of inwardly continuing the new mysteries, when we are here on the physical plane and Steiner is in the spiritual world? First, we have in common Anthroposophy, with which he still remains connected. Then also quite concretely, we have in common what we can share with him: the relationship to the Foundation Stone of Love, which is spiritual. The Foundation Stone is always accessible, not only to us, but also to all spiritual beings. As his original creation, Steiner also lives with it in the spiritual world.

In this new millennium, the Foundation Stone can also be placed in the depths of every anthroposophist's heart, so that along with much else that has already been mentioned here, it can be a foundation for our relationship to Steiner and for Steiner's relationship to every one of us. For the true relationship to this great Christian master in the spiritual world occurs not only through thoughts and feelings, but above, all through the strongest commonality with him in conceptualizations and will intentions. As we know from the Foundation Stone Meditation, human beings live in the spiritual world in the element of will as their life element.[143]

This means that when we seek Rudolf Steiner today in the spiritual world and hope to find him there, we can meet him only where our will intentions flow together with his own. These intentions can best be united where we have something that, on the one hand, belongs to the spiritual world and that, on the other hand, at the same time is a full reality in the hearts and souls of human beings who are incarnated here today on the earth, and who *want* to connect themselves with one another so that "we can stand on this firm Foundation Stone in furthering the activities of the Anthroposophical Society" (GA 260, 12.25.1923).

In this sense, we must strive (just as Steiner remained loyal to the reality of the Christmas Conference until the end, and in so doing presented to us a tremendous model pointing the way to the future), out of ourselves we must strive to follow this model faithfully and devotedly *together*. Such togetherness was not attained by Steiner's closest students and collaborators at that time. In spite of all the conflicts and human tragedies in our society, each one of those early members, no longer united with the others, had to go on further. Yet, as we have already seen, each one remained steadfastly true in their deepest will intentions until the end. One may assume that despite all the earthly rifts and limitations, after their death they now once again belong to Steiner's closest suprasensory circle. One may assume they gather around the suprasensory Foundation Stone of Love from the Christmas Conference to better understand it, and then to work further together on bringing the Foundation Stone to fruition in their next earth life.

The after-death destiny of Christ's closest apostles can serve as an archetype of this work. Steiner stated in a lecture that they were able to understand the full cosmic and telluric dimensions of the Mystery of Golgotha only in the spiritual world. In this regard, Steiner literally said: "The strange fact is that until the third century after that event, Christ's contemporaries, whose love for him had prepared them for a life in Christ after death, were not able to grasp the full significance of the Mystery of Golgotha by means of their own human powers. Those who had lived in communion with Christ as his disciples and apostles died and lived on in the spiritual world, and during life in the spiritual world their powers increased, just as they do on Earth. Immediately after death, we are not as advanced in understanding as we are 200 years later. It was not until the second century AD—toward the beginning of the third—that Christ's companions had advanced to the stage in the spiritual world between death and rebirth where they were able by developing their own powers, to understand what they had experienced (as the

Mystery of Golgotha) on the earth two to three hundred years before (GA 182, 10.16.1918).

Only through their love for Christ could the apostles really grasp the nature of the Mystery of Golgotha after they died. Solely through love for Steiner can our relationship to the Foundation Stone remain intact, also beyond death. Thus, the esoteric path we must tread to achieve the spiritual reality of the Anthroposophical Society remains intact for us today. However, we must recognize our real relationship to Steiner, and the new mysteries as the crowning deed of his entire work, to realize the divine duty to achieve *together* what was not yet fully possible for earlier generations of anthroposophists. That is, to become a real association of members established on the Foundation Stone of Love, which we voluntarily plant into the depths of our hearts as followers of the great model—Rudolf Steiner.

*

I want to close this theme with a double image; although it is taken from the Gospel, it still has a direct relationship to the present. In the Gospel of St. John, the most profound of the gospels, Christ's momentous message in his farewell address sounds like a validation of Anthroposophy. After making many attempts to instill in the apostles (who could not grasp it yet) the nature of the coming Mystery of Golgotha, He makes one last effort to do so. He speaks about the coming of the Spirit of Truth (the Paraclete) as a promise to reveal to people the deepest secrets of the Mystery of Golgotha.[144]

In this context, Christ's words resound decisively: "I call you friends; for unto you I *have made known all things* that I have heard from my Father" (John 15:15). It is understanding alone that transforms a person from being a servant of God to being His *friend* and free collaborator.

When, as already mentioned, Steiner points out that even the apostles could not really grasp the full cosmic-earthly dimension of the Mystery of Golgotha immediately, but only later in the spiritual world after their death; then from this parallel occurrence, we recognize the entire significance of Anthroposophy. Today, out of the source of the Eternal Spirit, Anthroposophy characterizes Christ as the Spirit of Truth, proclaiming true knowledge, and making the Mystery of Golgotha understandable to human beings as the central event in the evolution of humanity and the world.

Today on earth, Anthroposophy is the modern revelation of this Spirit of Truth sent by Christ. In this case, we need not be surprised that at the Christmas Conference after the Foundation Stone was laid, the Spirit of Truth appeared from this source; this Paraclete (advocate, helper) promised by Christ, and revealed in the illuminated thought aura of the dodecahedral Foundation Stone of Love.

Steiner bore witness to this reality in the following words, and turning directly to all the anthroposophists present at the Christmas Conference, at the same time he assigned another task: "Carry the Spirit that rules in the thought-light shining around the dodecahedral Love Stone out into the world where it will shine and provide warmth for the advancement of human souls, for the progress of the world" (GA 260, 12.25.1923).

When Steiner went to Stuttgart (where a large anthroposophical group lived and worked, second only to that in Dornach) for the first time after the Christmas Conference, he indicated what was most important about the conference. "We want to work together with the Spirit connected with the Christmas Conference so the active impulse of this event will never end among anthroposophists; that through this anthroposophical striving, the Dornach conference will increasingly unfold its real significance; that this Dornach conference will never cease, through what anthroposophists make of it everywhere in the world; that the Spirit whom we tried to summon there, that this Spirit will always be there through the goodwill, through the devotion, through the penetrating understanding of the membership for Anthroposophy and anthroposophical life" (GA 260a, 2.6.1924).

It is this Spirit that brings to present-day humanity the true knowledge of the Mystery of Golgotha—that is, especially, the knowledge of the resurrected body—whose being (we have already seen) came to new manifestation in the Foundation Stone Meditation for the first time in humanity's history for the awakened human "I" consciousness. At the same time, this Spirit opens the modern path to co-experience the full reality of the resurrection in light of the second Michael revelation.

Out of this emerge the important tasks of Anthroposophy at the present time. These tasks lead to understanding the Mystery of Golgotha as the central event in our Earth evolution in its universal dimension; understanding in a modern and free way in our epoch of the consciousness soul. That we really can do this today is because of Rudolf Steiner's inaugural deed. The founding of Anthroposophy and its culmination at the Christmas Conference are deeds Steiner performed out of the Spirit of Truth; out of the Spirit of Higher Knowledge pre-announced by Christ. On this path, we can gradually begin to be transformed from servants of God and the law to friends of Christ. We learn not only to understand through Anthroposophy what happened at the Turning Point of Time; but also we learn through Anthroposophy to experience the grace to know what are the guidelines of evolution that emanate from Christ. These are guidelines specifically for the *present time*, so that we become his free collaborators now and in the future.

If we truly comprehend in this way such an unparalleled "validation" of Anthroposophy, then we also know that right at the Turning Point of Time, it was a matter of understanding the Mystery of Golgotha, whereby one becomes a friend of God. With this as background, and with this role model in our hearts, we can now once again turn to the being of the new mysteries. We can remember (as Steiner continually emphasized when reflecting on the Christmas Conference), how crucial it is that the membership really understand what this conference is in its true nature. According to Steiner, "the success of what should now succeed ... [depends on] an understanding being awakened in the broadest circles of anthroposophists for what was desired through the Christmas Conference" (GA 260a, 6.7.1924).[145]

If we are able to accept this clear challenge from Steiner with sufficient seriousness, and to keep in mind the archetype mentioned earlier, then we can find our task in it (perhaps as a debt of gratitude toward Rudolf Steiner). We can finally understand this deed of his, and then take the first steps for its accomplishment. There is no benefit in arguing about inadequate concepts like "succeed" or "fail;" we must try to realize the founding of the new mysteries in their entire scope. Thereby, loyalty to this deed, which Steiner, along with his closest collaborators rendered through their entire lives and certainly after their death, can become a shining *leitmotif* on this path. Only when we learn to understand this highest master-deed of Steiner—considering all that we have spoken of here—will we in our time, be true friends of Rudolf Steiner, in the sense of the words of Christ.

Appendix

The School for Spiritual Science Admissions by Rudolf Steiner in the Last Months of His Life

(*with facsimiles*)

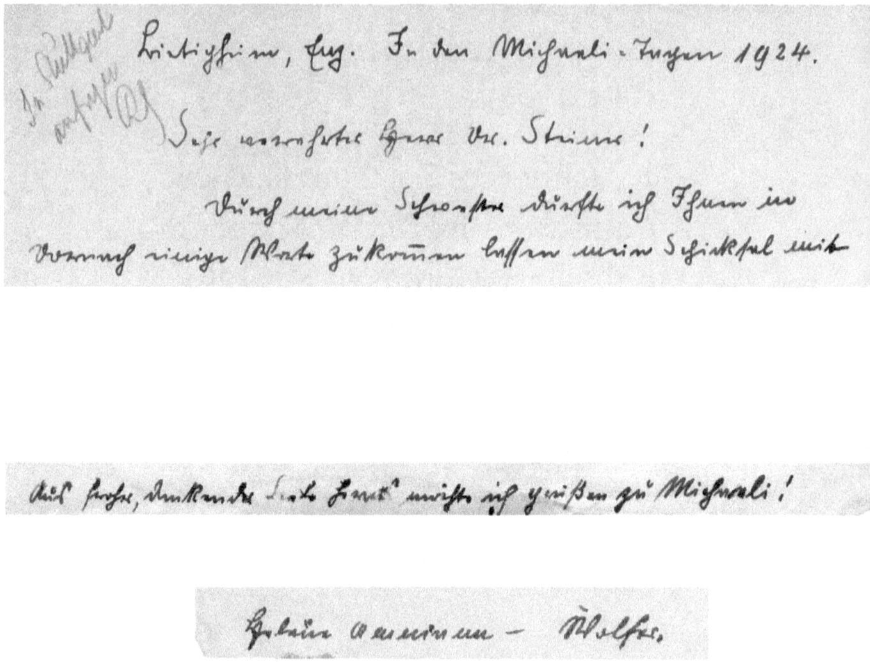

Lichtigheim, Aarg. In den Michaeli-Tagen 1924.

Sehr verehrter Herr Dr. Steiner!

Durch meinen Schwager durfte ich Ihnen im Vorjahr einige Blätter zukommen lassen mein Schicksal mit

Auch frohe, dankende Seele Herz möchte ich grüßen zu Michaeli!

Helene Ammann - Wolfer.

Bietigheim, Enz. Michaelmas 1924

Dear honorable Dr. Steiner!

Through my sister I send this message to you in Dornach ...

With happy, thankful soul I greet you today at Michaelmas!

Helene Amman-Wolfer

Only the beginning and end of the application are reproduced here.

Above left on the page, Rudolf Steiner noted in handwriting with pencil:

"Inquire in Stuttgart—RS"

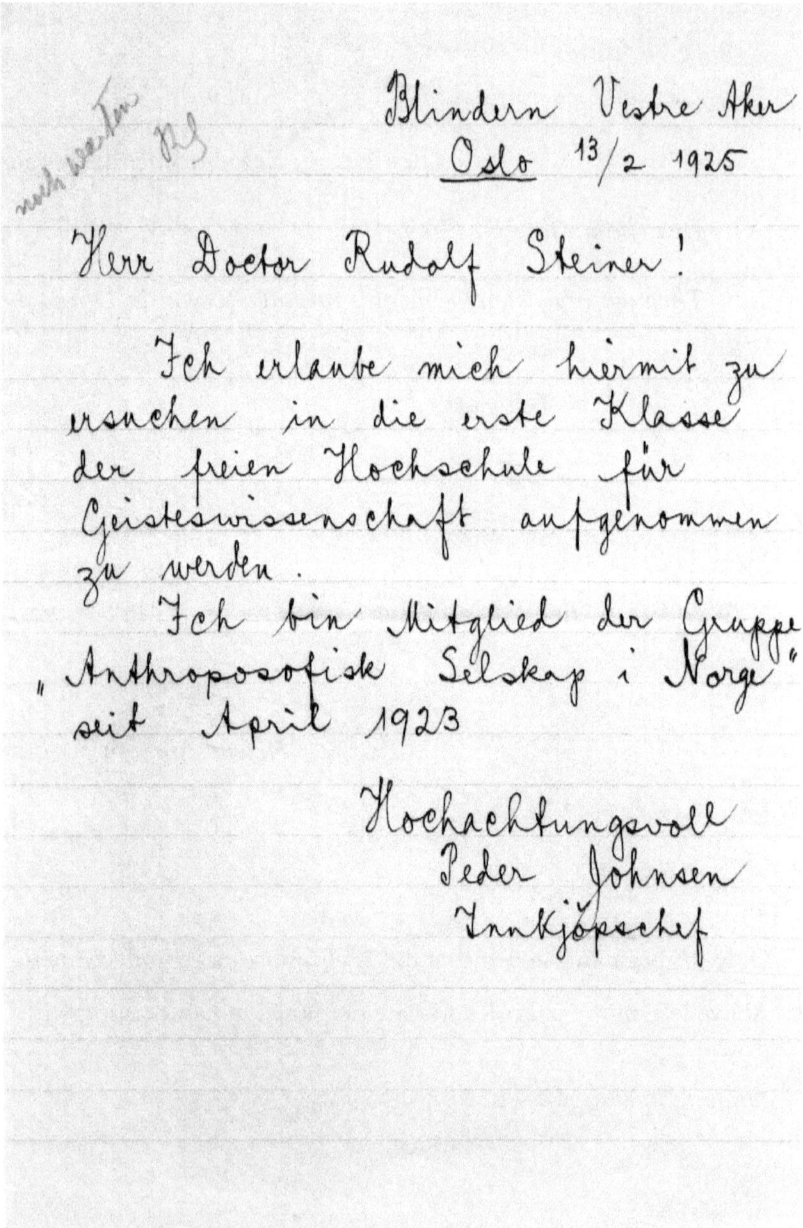

noch warten RS

Blindern Vestre Aker
Oslo 13/2 1925

Herr Doctor Rudolf Steiner!

Ich erlaube mich hiermit zu ersuchen in die erste Klasse der freien Hochschule für Geisteswissenschaft aufgenommen zu werden.

Ich bin Mitglied der Gruppe „Anthroposofisk Selskap i Norge“ seit April 1923

Hochachtungsvoll
Peder Johnsen
Innkjöpschef

Blindern Vestre Aker
Oslo 2/13 1925

Doctor Rudolf Steiner!

Herewith I would like to apply for admission to the First Class of the School for Spiritual Science.

I have been member of the group "Anthroposofisk Selskap/Norge" since April 1923.

Yours respectfully,
Peder Johnsen
Innkjöschef

Above right on the page, Rudolf Steiner noted in handwriting with pencil:

"*Wait awhile — RS*"

The reason for this is probably that on February 13, 1925, the conditions determined by Rudolf Steiner of two-year membership in the Society before acceptance into the First Class was not yet fulfilled.

den 18. Februar 1925.

Sehr geehrter Herr Johnsen,

Auf Ihren Antrag um Aufnahme in die erste Klasse der Hochschule lässt Ihnen Herr Dr. Steiner sagen, dass Sie damit noch eine Zeit lang sich gedulden möchten.

Mit freundlichem Gruss

February 18, 1925

Dear honorable Mr. Johnsen,

Concerning your application for admission to the First Class of the School for Spiritual Science, Dr. Steiner has asked me to tell you that you will have to be patient for a little while longer.

Most sincerely,

The copy of the reply letter to Mr. Johnsen preserved in the Goetheanum Archive.

The original of the answer sent was signed by the secretary, Mrs. Mariann Metzener-Day, who at that time was responsible for the School for Spiritual Science correspondence.

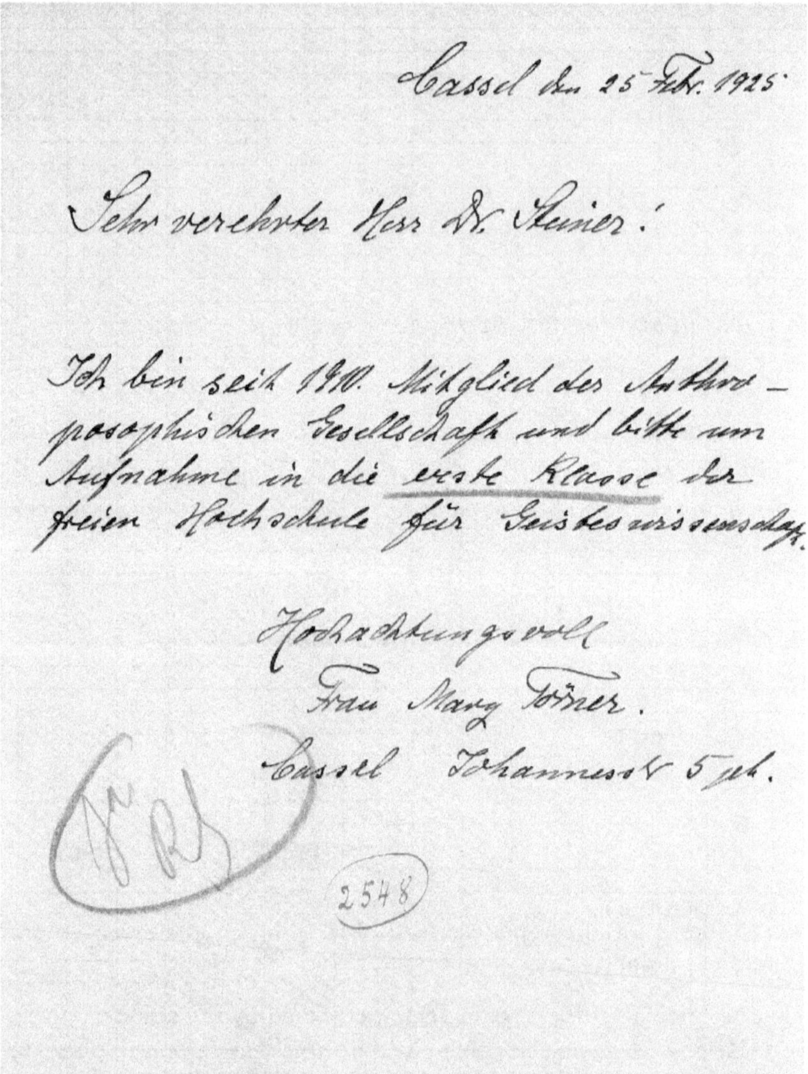

Cassel den 25 Febr. 1925

Sehr verehrter Herr Dr. Steiner!

Ich bin seit 1910 Mitglied der Anthroposophischen Gesellschaft und bitte um
Aufnahme in die erste Klasse der
freien Hochschule für Geisteswissenschaft.

Hochachtungsvoll
Frau Mary Törner.
Cassel Johannesstr 5 pt.

2548

Kassel, February 25, 1925

Dear honorable Dr. Steiner!

I have been member of the Anthroposophical Society since 1910 and request admission to the First Class of the School for Spiritual Science.

Yours respectfully,
Mrs. Mary Torner
Kassel, Johannesstr. 5 geh.

Below left on the page, Rudolf Steiner noted in handwriting with pencil:

"Yes—RS"

Below that, added later, the number of the blue membership card.

In the register, the date of delivery is March 25, 1925.
That is the day on which Rudolf Steiner signed this blue card.

Rudolf Steiner himself signed the pink cards for admission to the Anthroposophical Society as well as the blue cards for admission to the School for Spiritual Science. As the first chairman and spiritual leader of the Michael School, he bore full responsibility for both institutions. Only based on his signature did the respective person become a member of the General Anthroposophical Society and the School for Spiritual Science.

In the Acceptance List from the year 1925 preserved in the Goetheanum Archive it can be seen that even in the last days of his life Rudolf Steiner signed the blue cards for admission into the First Class of the School for Spiritual Science.

Here are some examples:

March 14, 1925: 5 admissions.

March 15, 1925: 3 admissions.

March 17, 1925: 2 admissions.

March 18, 1925: 1 admission.

March 25, 1925: 8 admissions.

March 26, 1925: 1 admission.

And the last admissions occurred only one-and-a-half days before he left the earth's plane:

March 28, 1925: 13 admissions through Rudolf Steiner's signature on blue cards.

Notes

1.

The Christology of the Book *An Outline of Occult Science*

1 GA 112, 6.30.1909.
2 Rudolf Steiner Archives, Dornach.
3 Ibid. note page no. 1561.
4 GA 13, p. 25.
5 Ibid.
6 Ibid., p. 28.
7 Ibid.
8 Ibid., p. 28f.
9 Ibid., p. 30.
10 Ibid., p. 31.
11 Ibid., p. 31f.
12 Rudolf Steiner Archives, Dornach.
13 GA 13, p. 144.
14 Ibid., p. 148.
15 Cf. GA 89, p. 230ff.
16 GA 89, p. 107.
17 GA 264, p. 65.
18 For the universal content of the old concept of "occult science" compare among others GA 52, GA 56, GA 95, and GA 97. Rudolf Steiner spoke about the "present spiritual science or occult science" on October 14, 1909, in Berlin in his lecture "The Mission of Spiritual Science in the Past and Present" (GA 58, p. 37).
19 GA 89, p. 315.
20 Ibid.
20 Ibid.
21 Cf. for this, Rudolf Steiner: *Lesen in der Akasha-Chronik. Ausgewählte Texte*. Ed. Andreas Neider. Dornach 2008.
22 GA 262, p. 90f.
23 GA 89, p. 315.

24 Cf. Peter Selg: *Elisabeth Vreede. 1879–1943*. Arlesheim 2009, p. 29.

25 GA 89, p. 315.

26 GA 11, p. 232.

27 GA 28, p. 26.

28 Cf. for details on this: Peter Selg: *Rudolf Steiner und Felix Koguzki. Der Beitrag des Kräutersammlers zur Anthroposophie*. Arlesheim 2009.

29 GA 262, p. 16.

30 Cf., among others, GA 89, p. 302.

31 GA 233a, p. 24.

32 Rudolf Steiner: *Selbstzeugnisse. Autobiographische Dokumente*. Dornach 2007, p. 47.

33 "The first time that I became acquainted with the Theosophical Movement this book made no impression on me. I was happy not to have read this book before I had an opinion from my own soul life. For its content was repulsive to me, and the antipathy against this way of representing the suprasensory would have prevented me in the beginning from advancing further on the path prescribed" (GA 28, p. 137).

34 GA 62, p. 197.

35 Ibid.

36 GA 262, p. 87.

37 GA 28, p. 413.

38 Marie Steiner: *Die Anthroposophie Rudolf Steiners. Gesammelte Schriften I*. Dornach 1967, p. 117.

39 Cf. C. G. Harrison: *Das Transzendentale Weltall.* Stuttgart 1990 (reprint), p. 71ff. In English: *The Transcendental Universe.* Great Barrington, MA: Lindisfarne Books 1993.

40 Ibid., p. 105.

41 Ibid., p. 22. According to Harrison, the "great materialism of the first half of the nineteenth century" had to be overcome before an occult theory could be communicated (ibid., p. 26). Harrison described—as later, Rudolf Steiner also did—1840 as a crisis and climax year of materialistic development, and he also knew the significance of the year 1879 (ibid., p. 80). For the development of esoteric occultism with

a Rosicrucian character, and for the partial publication of *Occult Science*, compare Rudolf Steiner's groundbreaking presentation in the "Documents of Barr," GA 262, p. 23ff.

42 "Nobody who passed the guardian could ever be tempted to reveal the secret of the threshold, because only an idiot would saw off the branch on which he sits. Regarding the knowledge that belongs to the region of the other side, there exist differences of opinion as to what extent it is sensible to publish it. It obviously would be a responsibility to inform the world about many things, if we could be sure the details would not be misused. It would be useful for everybody to know certain facts related to human procreation. Many unpleasant things springing from lack of knowledge about causes of illness could easily be averted, and poor health could be remedied without resorting to pharmacies. Much time and effort could be spared if the relationship of harmonious etheric vibrations were known, and if our skillful mechanics were in the position to serve "fine natural forces." The difficulty is that none of these things can be revealed out of themselves. The secret of birth and death is a key to the gates of an invisible world inhabited by the most lethal enemies of humanity; dangerous in terms of sympathy existing between the lower and higher natures, and forming a fateful bond of attraction that is ruinous in its effects for humanity. In a similar way, we cannot distinguish between knowledge about how to heal illnesses, and how to cause them; and it is a serious question whether, on the whole, distributing this knowledge would be a blessing or a curse for society as it is now composed" (Harrison, p. 24f).

43 Ibid., p. 35.

44 Ibid., p. 36.

45 Ibid., p. 17.

46 Ibid., p. 87.

47 GA 89, p. 88.

48 Regarding the problem—according to Rudolf Steiner—of the "European occultists [...] who are close to the leading Christian party," criticize Blavatsky and Sinnett, and reject the thoughts of reincarnation; cf. indications in GA 254, p. 70ff.

49 GA 54, p. 135.
50 Cf. for this, Andreas Neider in: Rudolf Steiner: *Lesen in der Akasha-Chronik. Ausgewählte Texte*, p. 21ff.
51 Cf. for this, among others, GA 254, p. 70ff.
52 GA 129, p. 241.
53 GA 243, p. 185ff.
54 GA 26, p. 14.
55 GA 219, p. 129f.
56 GA 82, p. 171.
57 Cf. Peter Selg: *Elisabeth Vreede. 1879–1943*, p. 70.
58 GA 221, p. 58f.
59 Ibid.
60 Ibid.
61 GA 262, p. 26.
62 GA 175, p. 30.
63 GA 266, volume III, p. 328.
64 GA 152, p. 116.
65 Ibid.
66 Ibid., p. 116f.
67 GA 162, p. 198.
68 "Thoughts are in it [*An Outline of Occult Science*], but they are not customary thoughts. They are thoughts that are active creatively in the outer world. One can live in these thoughts when one is on the other side of the threshold that leads to the spiritual world. A person can live in these thoughts that are active in the world. It is the first thing one finds when one enters the suprasensory world" (GA 211, p. 34).
69 GA 268, p. 313.
70 GA 13, p. 415f.
71 GA 13, p. 15.
72 Cf. GA 149, p. 47.
73 GA 123, p. 19.
74 Ibid., p. 9.
75 GA 13, p. 392.
76 Ibid., p. 149.
77 GA 132, p. 24.—Rudolf Steiner also emphasized this in an observation in a lecture to his theosophical readers, in which

he spoke in an exemplary way about the description of the Sun condition in *Occult Science*: "[...] It is of course arduous—as you see from the difficulty in understanding just this chapter of my *Occult Science*—it is difficult to describe this old Sun condition. There I have made the scenes more obvious to people by relating them, so to say, to the nature aspect. In the time when *Occult Science* was being written there would have been little understanding to be found in the Theosophical Movement if I had alluded to more moral aspects that were also experienced in observing the old Sun period" (GA 137, p. 189).

78 GA 233a, p. 13.

79 Rudolf Steiner said in the above-mentioned lecture cycle that his book *An Outline of Occult Science* "had to remain in a certain sense in the area of maya" (GA 132, p. 50). "Naturally, a person does not present an incorrect account, but, in a certain sense, one that is pictorially engulfed in maya, illusion. The reader must first work through the illusion in order to gradually penetrate to the truth of the matter" (ibid., p. 24).

80 GA 13, p. 21.

81 GA 127, p. 83.

82 GA 184, p. 130.

83 GA 149, p. 31.

84 GA 221, p. 141f.

85 GA 233a, p. 139.

86 GA 192, p. 371f.

87 Ibid.

88 GA 181, p. 425; emphasis by author.

89 "If a person goes so far as it was necessary for me to go in my *Occult Science* to describe a real cosmology, a science of world becoming and world evolution in individual concrete forms, then usually today the enlightened person ceases when faced with the discussion. That anyone in our time could be able (out of whatever grounds of knowledge) to say something about the spiritual origin of the world, about spiritual effective forces in world evolution, about the possibility that world evolution could return again to a spiritual form of being after it has passed through its sensory-physical phase—as with the

concrete descriptions that appear for example in my *Occult Science*—will be more or less be perceived by "enlightened" people so that they will not have anything more to do with one who claims to know these things. Then it is probably thought that when a person volunteers to give details about such things, he is basically close to losing his mind. At least one cannot compromise by admitting oneself into the discussion of such details" (GA 83, p. 135f).

90 GA 212, p. 158.

91 Cited according to Michael Bauer: *Christian Morgensterns Leben und Werk*. Munich 1933, p. 95f.

92 Christian Morgenstern: *Werke und Briefe*. Stuttgart edition (SE). Stuttgart 1987ff. Volume v, p. 311.

93 Ibid., p. 467.

94 Cited according to Michael Bauer: *Christian Morgensterns Leben und Werk*. p. 299.

95 Cf., for this in detail, Peter Selg: *Christian Morgenstern. Sein Weg mit Rudolf Steiner*. Stuttgart 2008, p. 78-144.

96 Lecture of 4.15.1909 (unpublished). Cf. ibid., p. 78.

97 Christian Morgenstern: *Werke und Briefe*. SE, volume II, p. 215.

98 Ibid., p. 229.

99 Ibid., p. 247.

100 GA 162, p. 198.

101 GA 155, p. 166.

102 Lecture in the Goetheanum on April 27, 2008, on the occasion of the conference "The Christian Foundations of *An Outline of Occult Science*." Some supplementary themes were incorporated in the text on hand from the lecture the author held on November 22, 2009, in Munich.

103 *An Outline of Occult Science*, from the preface of January 10, 1925.

104 See GA 110.

105 GA 132.

106 Lecture of 10.31.1911.

107 A eurythmy performance directed by Lili Reinitzer, expressing the Saturn stage of evolution preceeded the lecture.

108 GA 13, p. 27.

109 GA 4.
110 GA 130, 11.18.1911.
111 Matthew 27:46. Rudolf Steiner testified to the reality of this word from the cross in the lectures of September 12, 1910 (GA 123) and September 23, 1912 (GA 139). This does not, however, contradict the fact that in the spiritual world these words can be heard as the new enlightened message of the imminent ascension: "My God, my God, how you have glorified me!" (GA 97, December 2, 1906).
112 Matthew 27:40.
113 Matthew 27:49.
114 Therefore, Rudolf Steiner says that in the Mystery of Golgotha, Christ has "redeemed humanity ... with human forces" (GA 109, April 11, 1909).
115 GA 132, 10.31.1911.
116 GA 105, 8.14.1908.
117 See GA 148, 10.3.1913.
118 GA 202.
119 GA 233a, 1.4.1924.
120 GA 271.
121 GA 105, 8.14.1908.
122 See GA 189, 2.16.1919.
123 See GA 189, 2.16.1919.
124 GA 131, 10.12.1911. In the lecture of November 22, 1919 (GA 194), Rudolf Steiner speaks about a present second Michael revelation, which states that in the future "human flesh ... [must] be spiritualized again so that it is capable of living in the realm of the word." The archetype for this is found in Christ Jesus' resurrection.
125 See more detail for this in Sergei O. Prokofieff: *The Mystery of the Resurrection in the Light of Anthroposophy*, chapter II, "Easter, Ascension, and Whitsun in the Light of Anthroposophy." Forest Row, U.K.: Temple Lodge 2010.
126 GA 202, 12.18.1920.
127 See Sergei O. Prokofieff, *What Is Anthroposophy?* Forest Row, U.K.: Temple Lodge 2006.
128 GA 175, 2.6.1917.

2.
The First Goetheanum and Its Christological Foundations

1 Christian Morgenstern: letter to Friedrich Kayssler, 2.27.1914, unpublished. Cf. Peter Selg: *Christian Morgenstern. Sein Weg mit Rudolf Steiner*. Stuttgart 2008, p. 289.
2 Alla Selawry: *Ehrenfried Pfeiffer: Pionier spiritueller Forschung und Praxis*. Dornach 1987, p. 27f. In English: *Erenfried Pfeiffer: Pioneer of Spiritual Research*. Mercury Press, Spring Valley, NY.
3 Ita Wegman: "Das alte und das neue Goetheanum." In: *Nachrichtenblatt*, 5.3.1925.
4 GA 261, p. 240.
5 GA 268, p. 345.
6 GA 153, p. 182.
7 GA 260, p. 287.
8 GA 261, p. 301.
9 GA 262, p. 125.
10 GA 284.
11 GA 96, p. 320.
12 GA 260, p. 280f.
13 Marie Steiner-von Sivers: "Rudolf Steiner und die Künste." In: *Erinnerungen von Marie Steiner: Aufsätze und Gedichte*. Volume II, p. 14.
14 Rudolf Steiner: "Der Baugedanke des Goetheanum." Lecture in Bern, June 29, 1921. In: *Das Goetheanum als Gesamtkunstwerk*. Dornach 1986, p. 58.
15 GA 36, p. 315.
16 Cited in Christoph Lindenberg: *Rudolf Steiner: Eine Biographie. Band 1. 1861–1914*. Stuttgart 1997, p. 531.
17 Ibid., p. 534.
18 Ibid.
19 GA 36, p. 308.
20 Rudolf Steiner: "Der Baugedanke des Goetheanum." Lecture in Bern, June 29, 1921. In: *Das Goetheanum als Gesamtkunstwerk*, p. 21.
21 GA 268, p. 249.

22 GA 175, p. 32f.
23 Cf. GA 268, pp. 344-351.
24 Cf. GA 148 and Peter Selg: *Rudolf Steiner and the Fifth Gospel.* Great Barrington, MA: SteinerBooks 2010.
25 Christoph Lindenberg: *Rudolf Steiner. Eine Biographie.* Volume I. 1861–1914. p. 544.
26 GA 268, p. 344.
27 Cf. Ch. 3 of the present book.
28 GA 152, p. 44.
29 In: *Mitteilungen aus der anthroposophischen Arbeit in Deutschland.* Easter 1950, p. 22.
30 GA 268, p.346.
31 In: Rudolf Steiner: *Schicksalszeichen auf dem Entwicklungswege der Anthroposophischen Gesellschaft.* Dornach 1943, p. 23.
32 Cited in Peter Selg: *Christian Morgenstern. Sein Weg mit Rudolf Steiner,* p. 244.
33 Margarita Woloschin: *Die grüne Schlange. Lebenserinnerungen.* Stuttgart 2009, p. 78. In English: Margarita Woloschin: *The Green Snake: An Autobiography.* Edinburgh: Floris Books 2010.
34 Margarita Woloschin: "Erinnerungen. Aus Tagebuchaufzeichnungen." In: *Mitteilungen aus der anthroposophischen Arbeit in Deutschland,* 2; 120, 1977, p. 121.
35 Assja Turgenieff: *Erinnerungen an Rudolf Steiner und die Arbeit am ersten Goetheanum.* Stuttgart 1972, p. 55. English version may be found in: Assja Turgenieff: *Reminiscences of Rudolf Steiner and Work on the First Goetheanum.* Forest Row, U.K.: Temple Lodge 2003.
36 Ibid.
37 Cf. Peter Selg: *Die Arbeit des Einzelnen und der Geist der Gemeinschaft. Rudolf Steiner und das "Soziale Hauptgesetz."* Dornach 2007. In English, Peter Selg: *The Fundamental Social Law: Rudolf Steiner on the Work of the Individual and the Spirit of Community.* Great Barrington, MA: SteinerBooks 2011.
38 GA 261, p. 301.

39 Cf. Peter Selg: *Edith Maryon, Rudolf Steiner und die Dornacher Christus-Plastik.* Dornach 2006 (Studien zu esoterischen Schülern Rudolf Steiners, Band 3).

40 Margarita Woloschin: "Erinnerungen. Aus Tagebuchaufzeichnungen." In: *Mitteilungen aus der anthroposophischen Arbeit in Deutschland,* 2; 120, 1977, p. 121f. English version may be found in: Margarita Woloschin, Assja Turgenieff, Andrei Beyli. *Reminiscences of Rudolf Steiner.* Ghent, N.Y.: Adonis Press 1987.

41 Christian Morgenstern: *Werke und Briefe. Stuttgarter Ausgabe. Band II. Lyrik 1906–1914.* Ed. Martin Kiessig. Stuttgart 1992, p. 98.

41 Rainer Maria Rilke: *Die Gedichte.* Ed. Ernst Zinn. Frankfurt am Main. 1987, p. 214.

43 For the relationship of Rudolf Steiner's spiritual-scientific research to his artistic work, compare the methodical groundbreaking lecture in the Munich lecture of May 5 and 6, 1918, in the art gallery *Das Reich.* In: *Rudolf Steiner: Kunst und Kunsterkenntnis.* GA 271.

44 Marie Steiner: Preface. In: *Rudolf Steiner: Wege zu einem neuen Baustil.* GA 286. Dornach 1982, p. 13.

45 Natalie Turgenieff-Pozzo: *Zwölf Jahre der Arbeit am Goetheanum.* 1913–1925. Dornach 1942, p. 11f.

46 GA 286, p. 62.

47 Ibid., p. 63.

48 Assja Turgenieff: *Erinnerungen an Rudolf Steiner und die Arbeit am ersten Goetheanum,* p. 58.

49 Margarita Woloschin: "Erinnerungen. Aus Tagebuchaufzeichnungen." In: *Mitteilungen aus der anthroposophischen Arbeit in Deutschland,* 2; 120, 1977, p. 124. English version may be found in: Margarita Woloschin, Assja Turgenieff, Andrei Beyli. *Reminiscences of Rudolf Steiner.*

50 Assja Turgenieff: *Was ist mit dem Goetheanumbau geschehen?* Basel 1957, p. 26.

51 Margarita Woloschin: "Erinnerungen. Aus Tagebuchaufzeichnungen." In: *Mitteilungen aus der anthroposophischen Arbeit in Deutschland,* 2;120, 1977, p. 123. English version

may be found in: Margarita Woloschin, Assja Turgenieff, Andrei Beyli. *Reminiscences of Rudolf Steiner.*

52 Rudolf Steiner: "Der Baugedanke des Goetheanum." Lecture in Bern, June, 29, 1921. In: *Das Goetheanum als Gesamtkunstwerk,* p. 34f.

53 GA 277a, p. 108.

54 GA 36, p. 321.

55 Cf. Max Wolffhügel: "Rudolf Steiner in der Werkstatt." In: Caroline von Heydebrand (Ed.): *Rudolf Steiner in der Waldorfschule.* Stuttgart 1927, p. 96. "Another time (in the studio of the Waldorf School) he looked at an unusual sculpture for a long time, and inquired about the creator of the work. Later, Dr. Steiner spoke to that person in the school courtyard about his work and gave him gratifying encouragement, saying he would use the inspiration in Dornach."

56 Cf. Lex Bos: "Theo Faiss." In: *Mitteilungen aus der anthroposophischen Arbeit in Deutschland.* No. 161. Michaelmas 1987, p. 209f. and Peter Selg: *The Path of the Soul after Death: The Community of the Living and the Dead as Witnessed by Rudolf Steiner in His Eulogies and Farewell Addresses.* Great Barrington, MA: SteinerBooks 2011.

57 GA 261, p. 152.

58 Assja Turgenieff: *Erinnerungen an Rudolf Steiner und die Arbeit am ersten Goetheanum,* p. 55. English version may be found in: Assja Turgenieff: *Reminiscences of Rudolf Steiner and Work on the First Goetheanum.*

59 GA 286, p. 64.

60 Ibid., p. 74.

61 Rudolf Steiner: *Schicksalszeichen auf dem Entwicklungswege der Anthroposophischen Gesellschaft,* p. 28f.

62 GA 343. Dornach 1993, p. 471.

63 Rudolf Steiner: *Schicksalszeichen auf dem Entwicklungswege der Anthroposophischen Gesellschaft.* Dornach 1943, p. 37.

64 Marie Steiner (Ed.): *Die Sehnsucht nach dem Geist. Ein Zeichen der Zeit. Worte Rudolf Steiners am ersten Jahrestag der Grundsteinlegung des Goetheanum in Dornach am 20. September 1914.* Dornach 1937, p. 21.

65 Cf. concerning this statement by Rudolf Steiner: Peter Selg: *Edith Maryon, Rudolf Steiner und die Dornacher Christus-Plastik* and Peter Selg: *The Figure of Christ: Rudolf Steiner and the Spiritual Intention behind the Goetheanum's Central Work of Art.* Forest Row, U.K.: Temple Lodge 2009.

66 GA 13. Dornach 1989, p. 294.

67 Natalie Turgenieff-Pozzo: *Zwölf Jahre der Arbeit am Goetheanum. 1913–1925*, p. 16f.

68 Adelheid Petersen: "Dornach in den Jahren 1914–15." In: *Erinnerungen an Rudolf Steiner: Ed. Erika Beltle and Kurt Vierl.* Stuttgart 1979, p. 187.

69 Cf. P. Selg: *Die Arbeit des Einzelnen und der Geist der Gemeinschaft. Rudolf Steiner und das "Soziale Hauptgesetz,"* p. 21ff. See in English, Peter Selg: *The Fundamental Social Law: Rudolf Steiner on the Work of the Individual and the Spirit of Community.*

70 Viktor Stracke: "Wie es zu den 'Arbeitervorträgen' am Goetheanum kam." In: *Erinnerungen an Rudolf Steiner*. Ed. Erika Beltle and Kurt Vierl, p. 199.

71 Ibid.

72 Ibid.

73 Ibid., p. 201.

74 Assja Turgenieff: "Arbeiter und Künstler am Goetheanum." In: *Erinnerungen an Rudolf Steiner.* Ed. Erika Beltle and Kurt Vierl, p. 207.

75 GA 36, p. 332.

76 GA 260, p. 152.

77 Cited in Peter Selg: *Willem Zeylmans van Emmichoven. Anthroposophie und Anthroposophische Gesellschaft im 20. Jahrhundert.* Arlesheim 2009, p. 68.

78 GA 257, p. 13.

79 Cf. Emanuel Zeylmans van Emmichoven: *Wer war Ita Wegman. Eine Dokumentation.* Volume I. Heidelberg 1990, p. 123ff. See in English: J.E. Zeylmens van Emmichoven: *Who Was Ita Wegman. A Documentation.* Vol. 1. Tr. Dorit Winter. Spring Valley, N.Y.: Mercury Press 1995; and Peter Selg: *"Ich bleibe bei Ihnen." Rudolf Steiner und Ita Wegman.*

München, Pfingsten 1907. Dornach, 1923–25. Stuttgart 2007, p. 53ff.

80 GA 36, p. 322.

81 Manuscript of lecture in London on January 27, 1931. Ita Wegman Archive. Cf. in Peter Selg (Ed.): *Ita Wegman. Erinnerung an Rudolf Steiner.* Arlesheim 2009, p. 36.

82 GA 36, p. 326.

83 Ibid., p. 318.

84 Ibid., p. 314.

85 GA 257, p. 11.

86 Ibid., p. 10f.

87 Ibid., p. 88.

88 GA 154. Dornach 1985, p. 59.

89 Volume 2. GA 236, p. 96.

90 GA 257, p. 10f.

91 GA 226, p. 129.

92 GA 349, p. 251. Cf. in Peter Selg: *Christus und die Jünger: Vom Schicksal der inneren Gemeinschaft.* Arlesheim 2009, p. 124ff. See in English, Peter Selg: *Christ and the Disciples: The Destiny of an Inner Community.* Great Barrington, MA: SteinerBooks 2011.

93 GA 257, p. 13.

94 Ibid., p. 104.

95 Christian Morgenstern: *Werke und Briefe. Stuttgarter Ausgabe. Band II. Lyrik 1906–1914*, p. 207.

96 From the talk in Vienna preceding the lecture of April 14, 1914. (GA 153).

97 GA 260.

98 In his book *An Outline of Occult Science,* Steiner calls it "the highest ideal" of human development on earth: "the spiritualization that one attains through one's own work" (GA 13, p. 413).

99 GA 219, 12.31.1922.

100 Ibid.

101 That the origin of the "I" lies on the other side of the zodiac, Rudolf Steiner indicated in the lecture of April 18, 1920 (GA 201), where he said: "With our 'I', we are on the other side

of the starry world outside of the zodiac.... That is the essential content of our human 'I'."

102 GA 260, 12.24.1923.

103 See GA 265, 5.27.1923.

104 About the spiritual exercises of the Jesuits and their occult background see GA 131, 10.5.1911.

105 According to the presumably very short notation from the memory of a participant, Rudolf Steiner stated in this connection: "The two human streams [the Masonic and the Jesuits] maintain strict opposition between themselves. They united themselves in harmony only once: in their hate against the center stream [against Johannine Christianity]. The result of this harmonious unity of both otherwise hostile movements was the destruction of the Johannes Building (Goetheanum)" (GA 265, 5.27.1923). Rudolf Steiner had given his esoteric students the task to "recognize what comes from both directions." He added: "Fire because both were united against the middle. Hate against continuation of this middle" (ibid.). He meant the continuation of Johannine Christianity in Anthroposophy. See more details in Sergei O. Prokofieff, *May Human Beings Hear It! The Mystery of the Christmas Conference,* Supplement V: *"The Tragedy of 1 January 1924."*

106 The text literally reads: "Spiritual fire sparks, the flashes hissing at the wooden mousetrap [the Goetheanum was implied], are sufficiently available and it will require some of Steiner's intelligence to make up for it, so that one day a real fire spark doesn't cause an inglorious end to the Dornach marvel" (GA 203, 1.23.1921). Assja Turgenieff, who was at the reading of these words, remembered, "Also the opposition increased, and Dr. Steiner made us continually aware of their effectiveness. We were all shocked as he read us a passage from such a publication." Then the passage cited here was quoted. (Assja Turgenieff: "New Year's Eve 1922" in Assja Turgenieff: *Reminiscences of Rudolf Steiner and Work on the First Goetheanum*).

107 Max Kully (1878–1936), Catholic Priest in Arlesheim.

108 Rudolf Steiner pointed out in the lecture of August 6,

1920, that the Jesuits were behind Kully's agitation against Anthroposophy and the Goetheanum (GA 199).

109 In the lecture from January 17, 1914 (GA 286), Rudolf Steiner literally said: "There are everywhere [in our building] speech organs of the gods." Therefore in the Goetheanum one could experience: "Here you sit and the spirits of the world speak to you!"

110 "In the metal melting in the consuming fire we see the activity of the Seraphim, Cherubim and Thrones inside the earthly world." (GA 231, 11.18.1923).

111 Later, looking back on the first and the following eight events in the first Goetheanum, Rudolf Steiner writes: "That [a festive inauguration of the building] should take place only when it is possible for an event to be in full harmony with the original building idea" (GA 36, essay "Das Goetheanum in seinen zehn Jahren," part VI).

112 Heinz Müller, *Spuren auf dem Weg. Erinnerungen,* Stuttgart 1976.

113 Rudolf Steiner spoke about the Seraphim's cosmic enthusiasm, with which they enveloped old Saturn as it was developing, in the lecture of January 4, 1924 (GA 233a).

114 See Assja Turgenieff: "New Year's Eve 1922," in Assja Turgenieff: *Reminiscences of Rudolf Steiner and Work on the First Goetheanum.*

115 See the description of old Saturn in my lecture of April 27, 2008, at the Goetheanum: "Das Mysterium von Golgatha und 'Die Geheimwissenschaft im Umriss' von Rudolf Steiner," published in *Eurythmische Gesten. Kunst und Technik der eurythmischen Formführung,* the first complete edition of eurythmy exercises by Annemarie Dubach-Donath, ed. Lili Reinitzer, Dornach 2009.

116 Rudolf Steiner mentioned this new "esoteric impetus" continually after the Christmas Conference, for example in the lecture of August 12, 1924 (GA 260a). Speaking about it in the lecture of February 6, 1924, he says, "that the spirit whom it was attempted to call there [at the Christmas Conference] that this spirit is always there through the good will, through

the devotion, through the penetrating understanding of the membership for Anthroposophy and anthroposophical life" (ibid.). If one compares these words with those spoken at the Christmas Conference about the spirit of the Goetheanum, then the connection between both statements is obvious.

117 This involves a deed that is accomplished by the high initiate not out of his higher, but out of his true "I". For the difference between man's higher and true "I" see Sergei O. Prokofieff: *Das Rätsel des menschlichen Ich. Eine anthroposophische Betrachtung,* Dornach 2009. Part of this book appears in Sergei Prokofieff: *Anthroposophy and the Philosophy of Freedom,* Addendum 1: "About the Inner Being of the Human 'I'." Forest Row, U.K.: Temple Lodge 2009.

118 See GA 260, 12.31.1923—Here the connection with the New Year's event the previous year is understood: This step of the free person—Rudolf Steiner—out of the world of the senses into the world of the spirit through the foundation of the greatest comprehensive cosmic cult. In this sense Rudolf Steiner said one year later: "As I was standing for the last time on the podium that was erected there in harmony with the whole building, the view, the soul vision of the listeners should have been directed to the ascent from earthly regions into starry realms, which expresses the will and the wisdom, the light, of the spiritual cosmos" (GA 260, 12.31.1923).

119 "Many in the Middle Ages who taught their students, were patrons at that time, as I have described it to you" (GA 260, 12.31.1923).

120 Here is meant the two lectures that I held on April 25, 2009, in the framework of the "English Studies" in Dornach with the title "The Mystery of the Resurrection in the Light of Anthroposophy." See more details of this content in Sergei O. Prokofieff: *Das Mysterium der Auferstehung im Lichte der Anthroposophie,* chapter I, "Das Mysterium von Golgatha und die geistige Kommunion," Stuttgart 2008. See in English Sergei O. Prokofieff: *The Mystery of the Resurrection in the Light of Anthroposophy,* chapter 1, ""The Mystery of Golgotha and Spiritual Communion."

121 See GA 148, 10.2.1913.
122 See note 120.
123 See Margarita Woloschin: *The Green Snake: An Autobiography, "The Burning Bush."* Edinburgh: Floris Books 2010.
124 See Assja Turgenieff: *Reminiscences of Rudolf Steiner and Work on the First Goetheanum,* "New Year's Eve 1922."
125 See GA 259, lecture of January 1, 1923. Right after Rudolf Steiner read those words, he pointed to the gathering of the "Catholic Society" of Dornach, Arlesheim, and Reinach, "Jung-Solothurn," which took place on September 19, 1920 near the Goetheanum, in Dornach/Brugg, and which ended with the shout, "Rally together! Storm the Goetheanum!" (Ibid.). At this hate-filled gathering the above-mentioned Catholic priest Max Kully played a leading role. (See notes 107 and 108).
126 See Assja Turgenieff: *Reminiscences of Rudolf Steiner and Work on the First Goetheanum,* "New Year's Eve 1922."
127 See GA 260, 12.24.1923.
128 See GA 233a, 4.22.1924.
129 See GA 260, 12.31.1923 and "Aus dem Mitgliederkreise" (Ibid.).
130 See GA 130, 1.9.1912.
131 See more details in Sergei O. Prokofieff: *The Mystery of the Resurrection in the Light of Anthroposophy,* chapter I, "The Mystery of Golgotha and Spiritual Communion."
132 See note 120.
133 See in Sergei O. Prokofieff: *The Cycle of the Year as a Path of Initiation Leading to an Experience of the Christ Being: An Esoteric Study of the Festivals,* Part IX.I: "The Three Stages of Christ's Union with the Spheres of the Earth and Their Reflection in the Festivals of Easter, Ascension and Whitsun." London: Temple Lodge 1995.
134 See in Sergei O. Prokofieff: *Und die Erde wird zur Sonne. Einige Zusammenhänge des Golgatha-Geschehens aus anthroposophischer Sicht."* Forthcoming, Stuttgart June 2012.
135 See GA 346, 9.11.1924.

136 Rudolf Steiner speaks about matter existing in its deepest nature out of light in GA 120, 5.27.1910.

137 See in more detail about the path through the glass windows in Rudolf Steiner: *Die Goetheanum-Fenster. Sprache des Lichtes,* edited by Assja Turgenieff, Dornach 1996 (GA K12).

138 The *Manichaean motif* of the redemption of the opponents Lucifer and Ahriman in the side motifs of the rose window in the North should not remain unmentioned. See about their redemption also in Sergei O. Prokofieff: *The Occult Significance of Forgiveness,* chapter V.5, "The Redemption of the Opposing Forces." Forest Row, U.K.: Temple Lodge 2004.

139 See in Sergei O. Prokofieff: *The Mystery of the Resurrection in the Light of Anthroposophy,* chapter 2, "Easter, Ascension and Whitsun in the Light of Anthroposophy."

140 GA 260, 12.25.1923.

3. Christ's Reappearance in the Etheric in Relation to the Fifth Gospel

1 Notebook No. 335 (1923). Rudolf Steiner Archive, Dornach.

2 GA 118, 1.25.1910.

3 GA 118, 3.6.1910.

4 GA 118, 3.6.1910.

5 GA 118, 1.25.1910.

6 GA 260, 10.25.1923.

7 GA 118, 3.15.1910.

8 Mark 13: 21-23.

9 Cf. Peter Selg: *Das Ereignis der Jordantaufe. Epiphanias im Urchristentum und in der anthroposophie Rudolf Steiner,* chapter 3, "Rudolf Steiner und Epiphanias."

10 Cf. GA 133 and GA 143, lectures from May 8 and May 14, 1912.

11 GA 143, 5.8.1912.

12 GA 130, 11.4.1911.

13 GA 118, 4.18.1910.

14 Notebook No. 72, 1927. Citation from Ita Wegman: *Erinnerung an Rudolf Steiner*. Ed. Peter Selg. Arlesheim 2009, p. 21.

15 Cf. Andrei Bely: *Verwandeln des Lebens*. Basel 1975, p. 542f.

16 Citation from Marie Savitch: *Marie Steiner-von Sivers. Mitarbeiterin von Rudolf Steiner*. Dornach 1965, p. 84. See in English: Marie Savitch: *Marie Steiner-von Sivers: Fellow Worker with Rudolf Steiner.* London: Rudolf Steiner Press 1967.

17 GA 268, 9.20.1913.

18 Citation from Ita Wegman: *Erinnerung an Rudolf Steiner*, p. 35.

19 Cf. Peter Selg: *Rudolf Steiner und das Fünfte Evangelium*, p. 74f. See in English: *Rudolf Steiner and the Fifth Gospel.* Great Barrington, MA: SteinerBooks 2010.

20 GA 209, 12.25.1921.

21 "But I have a baptism to be baptized with; and how am I straightened till it be accomplished!" (Luke 12:50, KJV).

22 Cf. Peter Selg: *Christ and the Disciples*, chapters 3 and 4.

23 GA 148, 10.2.1913.

24 GA 148, 12.8.1913.

25 GA 148, 12.10.1913.

26 GA 152, 5.27.1914.

27 John 15:8.

28 "And we know: It is a difficult, an excruciating cross for you, to be among us—*because we sleep*, because we *can sleep away, overlook, and ignore* that which is nearing. We should pray and watch: but we cannot watch and we sleep away Your words; we lie in a *death sleep*. But we already know that we are sleeping; we know *in what time* we are sleeping; this knowledge is the only starting point of our awakening [...]." Citation from: *Andrei Bely. Symbolismus. Anthroposophie. Ein Weg*. Taja Gut (Ed.). Dornach 1997, p. 57. English version may be found in Margarita Woloschin, Assja Turgenieff, Andrei Belyi: *Reminiscences of Rudolf Steiner.*

29 Cf. Peter Selg: *Rudolf Steiner and the Fifth Gospel,* chapter 3, "'The evils hold sway': The Lectures Are Discontinued."

30 Cf. Peter Selg: *The Figure of Christ and the Spiritual Intention behind the Goetheanum's Central Work of Art*. Forest Row, U.K. Temple Lodge 2009.

31 GA 152, 10.14.1913.
32 GA 152, 5.2.1913.
33 GA 152, 10.14.1913.
34 Krzysytof Antończyk: *Innerer Widerstand im Konzentrationslager Auschwitz. Vortrag im Goetheanum*, 21.2.2009.
35 GA 118, 1.30.1910.
36 Cf. Peter Selg: *Geistiger Widerstand und Überwindung. Ita Wegman 1933–1935*. Dornach 2005, p. 90f.
37 Cf. Peter Selg: *Die Kultur der Selbstlosigkeit. Rudolf Steiner, Das Fünfte Evangelium und das Zeitalter der Extreme.* In English: *The Culture of Selflessness.* Forthcoming from SteinerBooks October 2012.
38 GA 268, p. 341.
39 Ibid., p. 336.
40 GA 148, 10.3.1913.
41 See GA 175, 2.6.1917.
42 See GA 245, 9.20.1913.
43 Published in *Schicksalszeichen auf dem Entwicklungswege der Anthroposophischen Gesellschaft*, Dornach 1943.
44 GA 148, 10.1-6.1913.
45 GA 147, 8.30.1913.
46 GA 148, 12.18.1913.
47 John 20:5-7.
48 GA 148, 12.18.1913.
49 See GA 116, 5.8.1910.
50 GA 148, 10.2.1913.
51 Matthew 28:20; Mark 16:15.
52 See GA 182, 10.16.1918.
53 GA 148, 10.3.1913.
54 GA 114, 9.21.1909 (Luke 3: 22).
55 GA 214, 7.30.1922.
56 This happened first in the eighth century. See GA 240, 7.19.1924.
57 About the Mystery of Golgotha as an affair of the higher hierarchies see GA 148, 12.18.1913.
58 See GA 26, 8.17.24, "Im Anbruch des Michael-Zeitalters" ("At the dawn of the Michael Age").
59 GA 182, 10.16.1918.

60 Matthew 10:16. Translation from Russian. Translation by Emil Bock reads: "Strive for the intelligence of the serpent and the simplicity of the dove." For an English rendering following Bock, see: *The New Testament, A Rendering* by Jon Madsen. Edinburgh: Floris Books 1994.

61 See GA 103, 5.26.1908.

62 See Robert de Boron, *Die Geschichte des Heiligen Gral,* Stuttgart 1964.

63 See GA 26, Jan. 25, essay, "Gnosis und Anthroposophie" ("Gnosis and Anthroposophy").

64 See GA 130, 10.1.1911.

65 See GA 130, 1.9.1912.

66 See GA 15, chapter III.

67 See GA 131, 10.10.1911.

68 See GA 130, 1.9.1912.

69 See Sergei O. Prokofieff: *The Mystery of the Resurrection in the Light of Anthroposophy,* chapter 1, "The Mystery of Golgotha and Spiritual Communion."

70 See more detail about this in Sergei O. Prokofieff: *May Human Beings Hear It! The Mystery of the Christmas Conference,* Chapter 2, "The Mystery Act of the Foundation Stone Laying on 25 December 1923."

71 See about this in Sergei O. Prokofieff: *The Mystery of the Resurrection in the Light of Anthroposophy*, chapter 1, "The Mystery of Golgotha and Spiritual Communion."

72 See detailed report about this in Sergei O. Prokofieff: *May Human Beings Hear It! The Mystery of the Christmas Conference*, Chapter 9, "The Foundation Stone Meditation. Karma and Resurrection."

73 In the lecture from 10.3.1913 (GA 148) Rudolf Steiner said in this regard that Christ on the earth "(went through) the infinite suffering of which no human thought can conceive."

74 See GA 130, 1.9.1912. —Yet Rudolf Steiner could sympathize with the fact that one person found it possible, because as a consequence of the first Goetheanum's burning, there occurred a partial separation of his etheric body from the physical body. Thus, he said to Ita Wegman: In comparison to other people

I have actually already died on earth." Then he added: "My "I" and my astral body direct the physical body and replenish the etheric" (Ita Wegman, from the concept for her lecture of February 27, 1913. Cited from *Ita Wegman. Erinnerung an Rudolf Steiner*, Ed. Peter Selg, Arlesheim 2009).

75 See GA 148, 10.2.1913.

76 About the love substance of the foundation stone of the Christmas Conference see GA 260, 12.25.1923, as well as Sergei O. Prokofieff: *May Human Beings Hear It! The Mystery of the Christmas Conference*, Chapter 2, "The Mystery Treatment of Laying the Foundation Stone on December 25, 1923."

77 GA 26, essay, "Himmelsgeschichte. Mythologische Geschichte. Erdengeschichte. Mysterium von Golgatha" (Heavenly history–Mythological history – Earth history. Mystery of Golgotha), Christmas Time 1924.

4. The Christmas Conference and the Founding of the New Mysteries

1 GA 257, p. 13.

2 Rudolf Steiner: *Schicksalszeichen auf dem Entwicklungswege der Anthroposophischen Gesellschaft*. Dornach 1943, p. 37.

3 Cf., among others, Peter Selg: *Rudolf Steiner und Christian Rosenkreutz*. Arlesheim 2010, p. 61ff. In English: *Rudolf Steiner and Christian Rosenkreutz*. Forthcoming from SteinerBooks June 2012.

4 GA 257, p. 10.

5 GA 259, p. 207.

6 GA 202, p. 256.

7 GA 204, p. 105f.

8 Benito Mussolini: *Der Geist des Faschismus—ein Quellenwerk*. Munich 1943, p. 20.

9 Mark Mazower: *Der dunkle Kontinent. Europa im 20. Jahrhundert*. Berlin 2000, p. 23.

10 Albert Schwarz: *Die Weimarer Republilk 1918–1933*. Constance 1958, p. 102.
11 Cited according to Horst Möller: *Weimar: Die unvollendete Demokratie*. Munich 1985, p. 160.
12 GA 259, p. 863.
13 GA 268, p. 289ff.
14 GA 233, p. 148.
15 George Groot: "Conversation with Rudolf Steiner." In: Peter Selg (ed.): *Anthroposophische Arzte, Lebens- und Arbeitswege im 20. Jahrhundert*. Dornach 2000, p. 263f.
16 GA 260a, p. 115.
17 GA 259, p. 75.
18 Cited according to Peter Selg: *Willem Zeylmans von Emmichoven. Anthroposophie und Anthroposophische Gesellschaft im 20. Jahrhundert*. Arlesheim 2009, p. 68.
19 GA 337a, p. 324.
20 GA 259, p. 65.
21 Ibid., p. 352.
22 GA 258, p. 171.
23 Ibid., p. 531.
24 GA 260a, p. 116.
25 GA 259, p. 495.
26 GA 258, p. 114.
27 GA 259, p. 683.
28 Cf. Peter Selg: *Rudolf Steiner und die Freie Hochschule für Geisteswissenschaft. Die Begründung der "Ersten Klasse."* Arlesheim 2009. In English: Peter Selg: *Rudolf Steiner and the School for Spiritual Science. The Foundation of the "First Class."* Forthcoming from SteinerBooks July 2012.
29 GA 300c, p. 145.
30 GA 217a, p. 113.
31 GA 259, p. 497f.
32 GA 259, p. 112.
33 GA 258, p. 141.
34 Ibid., p. 166.
35 GA 259, p. 683.
36 Ibid., p. 299.

37 Ibid., p. 484.
38 Ibid., p. 302.
39 Eugen Kolisko: "Report on the situation of the Anthroposopical Society." Stuttgart, 2.25.1923. In: Lilly Kolisko: *Eugen Kolisko. Ein Lebensbild.* Gerabronn-Crailsheim 1961, p. 76.
40 GA 259, p. 143.
41 Ibid., p. 195.
42 Cf. Peter Selg: *Willem Zeylmans van Emmichoven. Anthroposophie und Anthroposophische Gesellschaft im 20. Jahrhundert.* Arlesheim 2009, p. 68.
43 GA 263a, p. 117.
44 Mark Mazower: *Der dunkle Kontinent. Europa im 20. Jahrhundert.* Berlin 2000.
45 GA 259, p. 182.
46 GA 258, p. 171.
47 GA 257, p. 76.
48 GA 258, p. 168.
49 GA 231, p. 151.
50 GA 26, p. 14.
51 GA 224, p. 210.
52 GA 223, p. 118.
53 GA 40, p. 93.
54 Ita Wegman: Lecture draft 1935. Ita Wegman Archives, Arlesheim. Text published in: *Elisabeth Vreede. 1879–1943.* Arlesheim 2009, p. 302ff.
55 About Rudolf Steiner's spiritual experiences on the night of the fire, which centered around reflecting about the destruction of the Temple at Ephesus, compare his Dornach lectures of December 2 and December 29, 1923 (GA 232 and GA 233). Cf. also Peter Selg: *"Ich bleibe bei Ihnen." Rudolf Steiner und Ita Wegman. München, Pfingsten 1907, Dornach, 1923–1925*, pp. 53/115ff.
56 Ita Wegman's diary, 1925. First publication (facsimile and transcription) in Emanuel Zeylmans van Emmichoven: *Wer war Ita Wegman. Band I.* Heidelberg 1990, p. 319. See in English: J.E. Zeylmans van Emmichoven: *Who Was Iga*

Wegman. Vol. 1. For this text compare also Peter Selg: *"Ich bleibe bei Ihnen." Rudolf Steiner und Ita Wegman*, p. 56.

57 Cf. Emanuel Zeylmans van Emmichoven: *Die Erkraftung des Herzens. Eine Mysterienschulung der Gegenwart. Rudolf Steiners Zusammenarbeit mit Ita Wegman*. Arlesheim 2009.

58 Cited according to Peter Selg: *"Ich bleibe bei Ihnen." Rudolf Steiner und Ita Wegman*, p. 44.

59 Cf. Peter Selg: *Rudolf Steiner und die Freie Hochschule für Geisteswissenschaft. Die Begründung der "Ersten Klasse,"* Arlesheim 2009, p. 63ff. In English: Peter Selg: *Rudolf Steiner and the School for Spiritual Science. The Foundation of the "First Class."* Forthcoming from SteinerBooks July 2012.

60 Cited according to Thomas Meyer: *Ludwig Polzer-Hoditz. Ein Europäer*. Basel 1994, p. 565.

61 Cf. Emanuel Zeylmans van Emmichoven: *Die Erkraftung des Herzens. Eine Mysterienschulung der Gegenwart. Rudolf Steiner's Zusammenarbeit mit Ita Wegman*. Arlesheim 2009.

62 Ibid., p. 54ff.

63 Elisabeth Vreede: *Meine Vorstandsberufung*. Unpublished typescript. Rudolf Steiner Archive at the Goetheanum, p. 1. Cf. Peter Selg: *Elisabeth Vreede. 1879–1943*. Arlesheim 2009, p. 99.

64 Willem Zeylmans van Emmichoven: *Entwickelung und Geisteskampf*. Stuttgart 1935, p. 10f.

65 GA 262, p. 361.

66 GA 260a, p. 371.

67 GA 239, p. 74.

68 GA 84, 5.26.1924.

69 GA 84, 5.26.1924.

70 Citation according to J. E. Zeylmans van Emmichoven: *Who Was Ita Wegman. A Documentation,* Vol. 2, Spring Valley, NY: Mercury Press 1995.

71 The text of this lecture has been elaborated regarding some additional aspects of the theme.

72 Most of these applications are preserved in the archives at the Goetheanum. See Appendix: The School for Spiritual Science Admissions by Rudolf Steiner in the Last Months of His Life.

73 On February 8, 1925, the decision was made in Rudolf

Steiner's absence (he was at that time already very sick) — regarding the entry of the General Anthroposophical Society in the Commercial Registry—to combine it legally with the already registered "Verein des Goetheanum" (Goetheanum Association). Inasmuch as Rudolf Steiner signed the "Application for the Commercial Register" drawn up on this basis, there is no doubt that he was in agreement with this. (See GA 260a, pp. 564-566.) Concerning this, also see Sergei O. Prokofieff: *May Human Beings Hear It! The Mystery of the Christmas Conference*, Supplement II, "The Question of the Constitution of the Anthroposophical Society."

74 See "Additional Notes" to the "last address" GA 238, 9.28.1924.

75 In the final karma lecture from September 23, 1924, which immediately preceded the "last address," it is stated right at the end: "That is how I wanted to round off this cycle of lectures" (GA 238). This suggests that with the "last address" Rudolf Steiner wanted to begin a new cycle of karma considerations where the focus would be placed especially on the karma of Michael stream representatives, who were incarnated during the Mystery of Golgotha. For instance, he said about the individuality of Novalis, who was incarnated as John the Baptist in Palestine, this must be considered as a "shining precursor of this Michael Stream ... who shall lead all of you" (GA 238, 9.28.1924).

76 See Sergei O. Prokofieff, *May Human Beings Hear It! The Mystery of the Christmas Conference*, Supplement III, "Comments by Members of the Original Executive Council on the Christmas Conference."

77 This Executive Committee memorandum appeared at that time in the *Nachrichtenblatt*. Cited according to Marie Steiner, *Briefe und Dokumente*, Dornach 1981.

78 As to the "functions" in question, especially the following three were mentioned in this memorandum: "We accordingly request that all questions concerning the Anthroposophical Society be directed as previously to the Executive Committee; questions concerning individual sections to the respective

leaders; admission applications for the First Class of the School for Spiritual Science to the Secretary, Frau Dr. I. Wegman."

79 Marie Steiner, *Briefe und Dokumente*, p. 167-168.

80 See further excerpts from her correspondence on p. 262f.

81 Expulsion of Ita Wegman, Elisabeth Vreede, and several prominent Anthroposophists from the Anthroposophical Society.

82 See further Peter Selg: *"Ich bleibe bei Ihnen." Rudolf Steiner und Ita Wegman, München, Pfingsten 1907. Dornach 1923-1925.* Stuttgart 2007, and Peter Selg: *Rudolf Steiner und die Freie Hochschule fuer Geisteswissenschaft. Die Begruendung der "Ersten Klasse."* Arlesheim 2008.

83 See in this regard also Peter Selg: *Albert Steffen. Begegnung mit Rudolf Steiner*. Dornach 2009.

84 Cited according to Emanuel Zeylmans: *Willem Zeylmans van Emmichoven. An Inspiration for Anthroposophy.* Temple Lodge 2002.

85 Cited according to Peter Selg in his book: *Willem Zeylmans van Emmichoven. Ein Pionier der Anthroposophie und Anthroposophischen Gesellschaft im 20. Jahrhundert.* Arlesheim 2009.

86 Ita Wegman: *An die Freunde*, article from 4.26.1925, Arlesheim 1986. [Some material can be found in: *Ita Wegman: Esoteric Studies – The Michael Impulse.* Temple Lodge].

87 Ita Wegman: *An die Freunde* from 6.7.1925, Arlesheim 1986. [Some material can be found in: *Ita Wegman: Esoteric Studies – The Michael Impulse.* Temple Lodge].

88 Marie Steiner: *Briefe und Dokumente,* Dornach 1981; from the first "Verständigungsappell," 12.12.1942; italics by Marie Steiner.

89 Marie Steiner: *Briefe und Dokumente,* Dornach 1981; from the second "Verständigungsappell," 12.15.1943; italics by Marie Steiner.

90 See GA 346, 9.5-7.1924.

91 The two quotations from this lecture precede these remarks as epigraphs.

92 See more detail in Sergei O. Prokofieff, *May Human Beings Hear It! The Mystery of the Christmas Conference*, chapter 3, "The Rhythms of the Christmas Conference."

93 See GA 233.

94 At the end of the lecture opening the Christmas Conference, on the morning of December 24, 1923, Rudolf Steiner, turning himself directly to the Anthroposophists present, expressed: "I have appealed to your hearts, to your wisdom, what glows through your hearts and can be filled with enthusiasm" (GA 260, December 24, 1923).

95 Thus, in § 2 of the Christmas Conference statutes it is stated: "The basic membership of this society is formed by the personalities gathered in Dornach at the Goetheanum during Christmas 1923 as well as individuals and groups who were represented there" (GA 260, 12.24.1923).

96 For this purpose, Mr. Altermatt, the Dornach clerk to the court (who was not a member of the Anthroposophical Society), was called in for the last statute vote on December 28, 1923, because he would enter the Anthroposophical Society in the Commercial Registry.

97 See GA 233a, 1.12.1924.

98 See more detail in Rudolf Steiner's article, "Die Freie Hochschule fuer Geisteswissenschaft," April 20, 1924 (GA 260a).

99 Rudolf Steiner once stated as he was going there, that he would rather have built the first building under the earth, so that he wouldn't have to give it an external form.

100 Rudolf Steiner also pointed out that the forms of the first, as well as the second, Goetheanum bore the capability of awakening new karma vision. This provides a reference to the connection of the two buildings with Rudolf Steiner's lectures on karma and with the contents of the Michael-School. It was not without reason that Ita Wegman spoke of the second Goetheanum as a "Michael castle." (*An die Freunde*, article from May 3, 1925, Arlesheim 1986.) [Some material can be found in: *Ita Wegman: Esoteric Studies – The Michael Impulse.* Temple Lodge]. A more detailed consideration of this theme however lies outside this work.

101 See GA 233, 12.29.1923.

102 This reading in the astral light, which is today also accessible to all non-initiated people, specifically those who study spiritual

science, was provided by Rudolf Steiner from his direct reading in the cosmic astral light. The principal difference exists in that such a student does not receive the results of this reading directly out of the spiritual world—as Rudolf Steiner could—but through the mediation of modern thinking forms infused with spiritual science. The possibility of allowing one's free deeds on earth to be inspired by the results of such reading in the astral light is the same in both cases.

103 E. Lehrs: *Gelebte Erwartung*, Chapter XXI, "'Und du wirst wahrhaft...,'" Stuttgart 1979; italics by E. Lehrs.

104 See GA 104, 6.29.1908.

105 By this "Wisdom of the Outer World," also called "Wisdom of the World," Rudolf Steiner means the entire universal wisdom of previous cosmic evolution from old Saturn to Earth, that is, all that present-day initiates can research in the astral light.

106 Another time, approximately one year later in the last lecture of the cycle *The Gospel of St. Mark*, Rudolf Steiner mentioned this process of "propagating" the resurrected body, which as a result "can penetrate increasingly into human souls in the further development of humanity" (GA 139, 9.24.1912).

107 Cited according to Rudolf Steiner: *Die Sehnsucht der Seelen nach dem Geist. Ein Zeichen der Zeit*. Dornach 1938; italics by Rudolf Steiner.

108 It is noticeable that in the quotation mentioned, the path "to every human being," to the "choirs of *all* higher hierarchies," to Christ, corresponds in content to the whole composition of the Foundation Stone Meditation, which also refers to every person (the microcosmic part of the three first parts), then to a conscious relationship to the nine hierarchies (the macrocosmic part of the three first parts) and finally to Christ himself (the fourth part).

109 Three years before, Rudolf Steiner urged at the founding of the Christian-Rosenkreuz Branch in Neuchâtel and in the course of the first unveiling of the true Rosicrucian mysteries—yet without mentioning the Foundation Stone as such: "May the branch be one of the building stones for the temple, which we want to construct" (GA 130, 9.28.1911).

110 Rudolf Steiner particularly spoke about the possibility of "replication" in the spiritual world in 1909 in connection with the theme of "spiritual economy." (See the lectures in GA 109.) Also the proliferation (replication) of bread in the Gospels is connected with this process.

111 Citation according to Rudolf Steiner: *Bauformen als Kultur- und Weltempfindungsgedanken*, Dornach 1934.

112 The inner connection of the physical foundation stone of the First Goetheanum with the spiritual Foundation Stone that must be laid in the hearts of human beings, proceeds from the above-quoted lecture of September 20, 1914, which speaks about the spiritual Foundation Stone on which the "suprasensory building" can be erected, for which the visible building is only the "outer symbol." Almost in the same words this is repeated nine years later, at the end of the last lecture of the Christmas Conference, where Rudolf Steiner says, "The physical Goetheanum is only the *external symbol* for our spiritual Goetheanum" (GA 260, 1.1.1924). And immediately thereafter he points to the *spiritual Foundation Stone*, which was created at the Christmas Conference. (The detailed passage of the quotation appears later in the main text.)

113 Its appearance began at the time Steiner assumed the leadership of the German Section of the Theosophical Society.

114 See more details in Sergei O. Prokofieff: *May Human Beings Hear It! The Mystery of the Christmas Conference*, chapter 1, "Rudolf Steiner's Course of Life in the Light of the Christmas Conference." Through the burning of the Goetheanum, this founding of the new mysteries by Rudolf Steiner took place at the Christmas Conference as the spiritual culmination of his earthly task, even though under deeply tragic circumstances.

115 GA 260, 1.1.1924; "Aus dem Mitgliederkreise."

116 Rudolf Steiner pointed to the origin of this Spirit of the Goetheanum for the first time at Easter 1924 at the end of the first conference at the Goetheanum, following the Christmas Conference: "What was previously more or less an earthly concern, developed and founded as an earthly matter, was carried out with the flames into the universal expanses. Especially

because this disaster has affected us, we may say in recognizing the consequences of this disaster: Now we understand that we may not only represent an earthly concern, but a matter of the vast etheric world in which the Spirit lives. For the concern of the Goetheanum is a matter for the vast ether in which the spiritually filled wisdom of the world (Sophia) lives. It was carried there (by the flames), and we may penetrate ourselves with the Goetheanum impulses coming out of the cosmos" (GA 233a, 4.22.1924). This indicates the cosmic-etheric origin of the good Spirit of the Goetheanum.

117 This is the rhythm that was presented on Wednesday, which is under the sign of Mercury. Mercury is connected with the second half of earthly evolution, which began after the Mystery of Golgotha.

118 Rudolf Steiner connected the two names for the first time in the article "Das Michael-Christus-Erlebnis des Menschen" (The Michael-Christ experience of man), (GA 26, 2.11.1924).

119 See GA 130, 10.1.1911.—See also Sergei O. Prokofieff: *Das Erscheinen des Christus im Aetherischen. Geisteswissenschaftliche Aspekte der etherischen Wiederkunft*, Dornach 2010.In English: *The Appearance of Christ in the Etheric.* Forthcoming by Temple Lodge 2012.

120 For the Foundation Stone, at first only the macrocosmic part appears and for the meditation, the microcosmic. The reason is that the first is formed out of the macrocosm and the second was given primarily for meditative practice.

121 At the meeting with the "Circle of Thirty" in Stuttgart on February 8, 1923, Rudolf Steiner literally said: "The Anthroposophical Society is shot full of holes everywhere by Ahriman" (GA 259).

122 Regarding Michael-thoughts and Michael-will, see Rudolf Steiner's last address (GA 238, 9.28.1924), which was held just one year after the Vienna lecture quoted.

123 This lecture is published in: *Schicksalszeichen auf dem Entwicklungswege der Anthroposophischen Gesellschaft*, Dornach 1943.

124 See more details about this being in Sergei O. Prokofieff:

The Heavenly Sophia and the Being Anthroposophia. Forest Row, U.K. Temple Lodge 2006.

125 See GA 231, edition 1982, closing of the last lecture of November 18, 1923.

126 What they call to humanity is expressed in the threefold Rosicrucian words in the Foundation Stone Meditation, about the birth, death and resurrection of Christ in connection with each person.

127 About the relationship of Sophia to the world of imagination, also see Mario Betti: *The Sophia Mystery in our Time: The Birth of Imagination.* London: Temple Lodge 1996.

128 The Proverbs of Solomon 8:30.

129 Rudolf Steiner says that after the Mystery of Golgotha, Michael's cosmic intelligence gradually left the sun realm and since about the eighth century has reached the earth, whereby human beings have received the basis for independent thinking (the ability to produce their own thoughts) and, with it, to experience freedom arising, which is possible for human beings on the earth only in the area of thinking. (See GA 240, 7.19.1924). Such time estimates naturally are only approximate. Therefore, Steiner also indicates the ninth century as the time Michael's cosmic intelligence was received on earth. (See the Leading Thought "Im Anbruch des Michael—Zeitalters" (At the dawn of the Michael Age), GA 26).

130 In 1902 the German Section of the Theosophical Society, of which Rudolf Steiner became the General Secretary, was founded. At that time, this group formed the external framework for unfolding his Anthroposophy.

131 In the karma lectures of 1924, Steiner characterized the entire development of Anthroposophy in these three seven-year periods as "preparatory work" for what came into the world with the Christmas Conference, and its consequences. (See GA 240, 4.16.1924).

132 See Sergei O. Prokofieff: *The Mystery of the Resurrection in the Light of Anthroposophy,* chapter 1, "The Mystery of Golgotha and Spiritual Communion." .

133 GA 109, 2.15.1909, italics by Rudolf Steiner.

134 GA 238, 9.28.1924.

135 "Day Spirit" in the sense that Michael's second revelation is currently accessible only to the human being's full day-consciousness, which corresponds only to the "I" stage in the epoch of the consciousness soul.

136 On Rudolf Steiner's founding the whole of Anthroposophy out of this new Christ consciousness, see more details in Sergei O. Prokofieff: *Das Erscheinen des Christus im Aetherischen. Geisteswissenschaftliche Aspekte der aetherischen Wiederkunft*, chapter 7, "Das uebersinnliche Mysterium von Golgotha und die Einweihung Rudolf Steiners," Dornach 2010. In English: *The Appearance of Christ in the Etheric.* Forthcoming by Temple Lodge 2012.

137 See about this Sergei O. Prokofieff: *The Mystery of the Resurrection in the Light of Anthroposophy,* chapter 1, "The Mystery of Golgotha and Spiritual Communion." Forest Row, U.K.: Temple Lodge 2010.

138 Thus, the second and third classes of the School were not given and also many other suggestions for the area of practical life were omitted.

139 Cited according to Marie Steiner: *Briefe und Dokumente*, letter from Ehrenfried Pfeiffer to Marie Steiner from 2.29.1948; italics by E. Pfeiffer, Dornach 1981.

140 See note above, letter from 3.11.1948.

141 From Ehrenfried Pfeiffer's enclosure to his letter of 3.5.1948; italics by E. Pfeiffer. (See note 64).

142 This enclosure was presented as the "Precinct Petition" to the board and the general meeting of the Anthroposophical Society at Easter 1948.

143 In the first, "will part" of the Foundation Stone Meditation there is instead of "will" the word "life" ("And you will truly *live*," GA 260, 12.25.1923; italics by Rudolf Steiner). This is interpretation is substantiated by the fact that the will after death (or by initiation) becomes our life element in the spiritual world. (Cf. also GA 153, 4.13.1914).

144 "But the Comforter, who is the Holy Ghost, whom the Father will send in my name, he shall teach you all things,

and bring all things to your remembrance, whatsoever I have said unto you" (John 14:26). That this refers to the being of the Mystery of Golgotha ("whatsoever I have said unto you") follows from the further writings in the same chapter: "And now I have told you before it comes to pass, that, when it is come to pass, ye might believe" (John 14:29; "so that you possess soul security"—in the translation by E. Bock). Then in the next chapter confirmed once again: "But whenever the Comforter is come, Whom I will send unto you from the Father, even the Spirit of Truth ("the Spirit of Truth and Knowledge"—in the translation by E. Bock), which proceedeth from the Father, He shall testify of me" (John 15:26).

145 In one of Ita Wegman's notes from 1925, reflecting on Rudolf Steiner's sickbed, where she was able to have many esoteric conversations with him, Ita Wegman noted for herself: "Not understanding hinders; illness also through not understanding" (cited from J. E. Zeylmans van Emmichoven, *Who Was Ita Wegman. A Documentation, Vol. 1,* Mercury Press 1995). Rudolf Steiner said directly to Ita Wegman during this time: "A person's not understanding is ignorance, which lames him" (Ita Wegman, *An die Freunde*, article from October 4, 1925; Arlesheim 1986). [Some material may be found in: *Ita Wegman: Esoteric Studies – The Michael Impulse*].

Bibliography

Works by Rudolf Steiner referred to in the text and notes, listed in English when available.

All German titles are from the Rudolf Steiner Gesamtausgabe (GA), published by Rudolf Steiner Verlag, Dornach, Switzerland.

GA 4 *Intuitive Thinking as a Spiritual Path: A Philosophy of Freedom*. Tr. Michael Lipson. Great Barrington, MA: Steiner-Books 1995. Also translated as: *The Philosophy of Spiritual Activity*. Tr. W. Lindeman. Anthroposophic Press 1986, 2007; and *The Philosophy of Freedom*. Tr. M. Wilson. Rudolf Steiner Press, republished 1999. In German: *Die Philosophie der Freiheit.*

GA 11 *Cosmic Memory*. Tr. Karl E. Zimmer. Great Barrington, MA: SteinerBooks 2006. In German: *Aus der Akasha-Chronik.*

GA 13 *An Outline of Esoteric Science*. Tr. Catherine E. Creeger. Great Barrington, MA: SteinerBooks 1997. *Occult Science, An Outline*. Tr. G. and M. Adams. Rudolf Steiner Press, republished 2005. In German: *Die Geheimwissenschaft im Umriss.*

GA 14 *Four Mystery Dramas*. Tr. Ruth and Hans Pusch. Great Barrington, MA: SteinerBooks 2007.

GA 15 *The Spiritual Guidance of the Individual and Humanity: Some Results of Spiritual-Scientific Research into Human History and Development*. Tr. Samuel Desch. Great Barrington, MA: SteinerBooks 1992. In German: *Die geistige Führung des Menschen und der Menschheit.*

GA 24 *The Renewal of the Social Organism*. Tr. E. Bowen-Wedgewood and Ruth Mariott. Hudson, NY: Anthroposophic Press/SteinerBooks 1985. In German: *Aufsätze über die Dreigliederung des sozialen Organismus und zur Zeitlage 1915-1921.*

GA 26 *Anthroposophical Leading Thoughts*. Tr. George and Mary Adams. Forest Row, England: Rudolf Steiner Press 1998. In German: *Anthroposophische Leitsätze*.

GA 28 *Autobiography: Chapters in the Course of My Life*. Tr. Rita Stebbing. Great Barrington, MA: SteinerBooks 2006. *Mein Lebensgang*: 8th edition 1982.

GA 36 *Der Goetheanumgedanke inmitten der Kulturkrisis der Gegenwart* [The Goetheanum-idea in the middle of the present cultural crisis] (1921-1925): 1st edition 1961.

GA 40 *Truth-Wrought-Words*. Tr. Arvia MacKaye Ege. Spring Valley, NY: Anthroposophic Press 1979. In German: *Wahrspruchworte*.

GA 52 *Spirituelle Seelenlehre und Weltbetrachtung*. [Spiritual teachings on the soul and observations of the world]: 2nd edition 1986.

GA 54 *Die Welträtsel und die Anthroposophie* [World mysteries and anthroposophy] (1905/06): 2nd edition 1983.

GA 56 *Die Erkenntnis der Seele und des Geistes* [Knowledge of the soul and the spirit] (1907/08): 2nd edition 1985.

GA 58 *Transforming the Soul, Vol 1*. Tr. Pauline Wehrle. Forest Row, U.K.: Rudolf Steiner Press 2006. In German: *Metamorphosen des Seelenlebens*.

GA 82 *Damit der Mensch ganz Mensch werde*. [So that the human being can become whole]: 2nd edition 1994.

GA 83 *The Tension between East and West*. Tr. Dr. B.A. Rowley. Spring Valley, NY: Anthroposophic Press 1983. *Westliche und östliche Weltgegensätzlichkeit* (1922): 3rd edition 1981.

GA 84 *Was wollte das Goetheanum und was soll die Anthroposophie?* [What was the intention of the Goetheanum and Anthroposophy?]: 2nd edition 1986.

GA 89 *Awareness – Life – Form*. Tr. Anna Meuss. Lower Beech-mont, Australia 2001. In German: *Bewußtsein – Leben – Form. Grundprinzipien der geisteswissenschaftlichen Kosmologie*.

GA 95 *Founding a Science of the Spirit*. Tr. revised M. Barton. Forest Row, England: Rudolf Steiner Press 1999. In German: *Vor dem Tore der Theosophie*.

GA 96 *Original Impulses for the Science of the Spirit.* Lower Beechmont, Australia 2001. Tr. Anna Meuss. In German: *Ursprungsimpulse der Geisteswissenschaft. Christliche Esoterik im Lichte neuer Geist-Erkenntnis.*

GA 97 *The Christian Mystery.* Tr. James H. Hindes. Great Barrington, MA: Anthroposophic Press 1998. In German: *Das christliche Mysterium* (1906/07).

GA 103 *The Gospel of St. John.* Tr. Maude B. Monges. Great Barrington, MA: SteinerBooks/Anthroposophic Press 1984. In German: *Das Johannes-Evangelium.*

GA 104 *The Apocalypse of St. John.* Great Barrington, MA: SteinerBooks/Anthroposophic Press 1993. In German: *Die Apokalypse des Johannes.*

GA 105 *Universe, Earth, and Man.* Abridged from the German *Welt, Erde und Mensch.* London: Rudolf Steiner Press 1987.

GA 109 *The Principle of Spiritual Economy. In Connection with Questions of Reincarnation.* Tr. Peter Mollenhauer. Hudson, NY: Anthroposophic Press/SteinerBooks 1986. In German: *Das Prinzip der spirituellen Ökonomie im Zusammenhang mit Wiederverkorperungsfragen.*

GA 110 *The Spiritual Hierarchies and the Physical World: Zodiac, Planets, and Cosmos.* Tr. René Querido. Great Barrington, MA: SteinerBooks 2008. In German: *Geistige Hiearchien und ihre Wiederspiegelung in der physischen Welt. Tierkreis, Planeten, Kosmos.*

GA 112 *The Gospel of St. John and Its Relation to the Other Gospels.* Tr. Samuel and Loni Lockwood, revised by Maria St. Goar. Great Barrington, MA: SteinerBooks/Anthroposophic Press 1982. In German: *Das Johannes-Evangelium im verhältnis zu den drei andern Evangelien, besonders zu dem Lukas-Evangelium.*

GA 114 *The Gospel of St. Luke.* See *According to Luke.* Tr. Catherine E. Creeger. Great Barrington, MA: SteinerBooks 2001. In German: *Das Lukas-Evangelium.*

GA 116 *Der Christus-Impuls und die Entwicklung des Ich-Bewußtseins.* [The Christ impulse and the development of "I" consciousness] (1909-1910): 4th edition 1982.

GA 118 *Das Ereignis der Christus-Erscheinung in der ätherischen Welt.* See *The Reappearance of Christ in the Etheric.* Great Barrington, MA: SteinerBooks 2003.

GA 120 *Manifestations of Karma.* Tr. Heidi Hermann-Davy. Forest Row, U.K.: Rudolf Steiner Press 2000. In German: *Die Offenbarungen des Karma.*

GA 123 *According to Matthew.* Tr. Catherine E. Creeger. Great Barrington, MA: SteinerBooks 2003. *Das Matthäus-Evangelium* (1910): 7th edition 1988.

GA 127 *Die Mission der neuen Geistesoffenbarung. Das Christus-Ereignis als Mittelpunktsgeschehen der Erdenevolution* [The Mission of the new spiritual revelation: The Christ event as the central event of evolution] 1911: 2nd ed. 1989.

GA 129 *Wonders of the World: Ordeals of the Soul, Revelations of the Spirit.* London: Rudolf Steiner Press 1983. In German: *Weltenwunder, Seelenprüfungen und Geistesoffenbarungen.*

GA 130 *Esoteric Christianity and the Mission of Christian Rosenkreutz.* London: Rudolf Steiner Press 1984.

GA 131 *From Jesus to Christ.* Tr. Charles Davy. Forest Row, England: Rudolf Steiner Press 2005. In German: *Von Jesus zu Christus.*

GA 132 *Inner Experiences of Evolution.* Tr. Jann Gates. Great Barrington, MA: SteinerBooks 2009.

GA 133 *Earthly and Cosmic Man.* Blauvelt, NY: Garber Books 1986. In German: *Der irdische und der kosmische Mensch.*

GA 137 *Man in the Light of Occultism, Theosophy, and Philosophy.* Blauvelt, NY: Garber Communications 1989. In German: *Der Mensch im Lichte von Okkultismus, Theosophie, und Philosophie.*

GA 139 *The Gospel of St. Mark.* Tr. S.C. Easton. Hudson, NY: SteinerBooks/Anthroposophic Press 1986. In German: *Das Markus-Evangelium.*

GA 143 *Erfahrungen des Übersinnlichen* [Experiences of the suprasensory] (1912): 4th edition 1994.

GA 147 *Secrets of the Threshold.* Tr. Ruth Pusch. Great Barrington, MA: SteinerBooks 2007. In German: *Die Geheimnisse der Schwelle.*

GA 148 *The Fifth Gospel: From the Akashic Chronicle.* Tr. Anna Meuss. Forest Row, England: Rudolf Steiner Press 1998. In German: *Aus der Akasha-Forschung. Das Fünfte Evangelium* (1913/14): 5th edition 1992.

GA 149 *Christ and the Spiritual World and the Search for the Holy Grail.* Tr. C. Davy and D. S. Osmond. Forest Row, England: Rudolf Steiner Press 2008. In German: *Christus und die geistige Welt.*

GA 152 *Approaching the Mystery of Golgotha.* Tr. Michael Miller. Great Barrington, MA: SteinerBooks 2006. In German: *Vorstufen zum Mysterium von Golgatha.*

GA 153 *The Inner Nature of Man and Our Life between Death and Rebirth.* Tr. Anna Meuss. Forest Row, England: Rudolf Steiner Press 1994. In German: *Inneres Wesen des Menschen und Leben zwischen Tod und neuer Geburt.*

GA 154 *The Presence of the Dead on the Spiritual Path.* Tr. Christian von Arnim. Hudson, NY: Anthroposophic Press 1990. In German: *Wie erwirbt man sich Verständnis fur die geistige Welt?*

GA 155 *Christ and the Human Soul.* Tr. C. Davy and M. Cotterell. Forest Row, England: Rudolf Steiner Press 2008. In German: *Christus und die menschliche Seele.*

GA 162 *KunstundLebensfragenimLichtederGeisteswissenschaft.* [Questions of art and life in light of spiritual science]: 2nd edition 2000.

GA 175 *Building Stones for an Understanding of the Mystery of Golgotha.* Tr. A. H. Parker. London: Rudolf Steiner Press 1985. In German: *Bausteine zu einer Erkenntnis des Mysteriums von Golgatha* (1917): 2nd edition 1982.

GA 181 *Earthly Death and Cosmic Life.* Blauvelt, NY: Garber Communications 1989. In German: *Erdensterben und Weltenleben. Anthroposopische Lebensgaben.*

GA 182 *Death as Metamorphosis of Life.* Tr. Sabine Seiler. Great Barrington, MA: SteinerBooks 2008. In German: *Der Tod als Lebenswandlung.*

GA 184 *Die Polarität von Dauer und Entwickelung im*

Menschenleben (The polarity of duration and development in human life): 3rd edition 2002.

GA 189 *Die soziale Frage als Bewusstseinsfrage* [The social question as a question of consciousness] (1919): 3rd edition 1980.

GA 192 *Geisteswissenschaftliche Behandlung sozialer und pädagogischer Fragen* [Spiritual-scientific treatment of social and pedagogical questions] (1919): 2nd edition.

GA 194 *Die Sendung Michaels.* See *The Archangel Michael.* Tr. Marjorie Spock. SteinerBooks/Anthroposophic Press 1994.

GA 199 *Spiritual Science as a Foundation for Social Forms.* Tr. Maria St. Goar. Hudson, NY: Anthroposophic Press 1986. In German: *Geisteswissenschaft als Erkenntnis der Grundimpulse sozialer Gestaltung*: 2nd edition 1985.

GA 200 *The New Spirituality and the Christ Experience of the Twentieth Century.* Tr. Paul King. Hudson, NY: Anthroposophic Press/SteinerBooks 1988. In German: *Die Neue Geistigkeit und das Christur- Erlebnis des zwanzigsten Jahrhunderts.*

GA 201 *Mystery of the Universe: The Human Being, Model of Creation.* Tr. revised by Matthew Barton. Forest Row, U.K.: Rudolf Steiner Press 2001. In German: *Der Mensch in Zusammenhang mit dem Kosmos 1: Entsprechung zwischen Mikrokosmos und Makrokosmos Der Mensch—Eine Heiroglype des Weltenalls.*

GA 202 *The Bridge between Universal Spirituality and the Physical Constitutuion of Man.* Tr. D. S. Osmond. Great Barrington, MA: SteinerBooks 2007. In German: *Die Brücke zweischen der Weltgeistigkeit und dem Physischen des Menschen* (1920).

GA 203 *Die Verantwortung des menschen für die weltentwicklung* [Human beings in connection with the cosmos]: 2nd edition 1989.

GA 204 *Materialism and the Task of Anthroposophy.* Hudson, NY: Anthroposophic Press 1987. In German: *Perspektiven der Menschheitsentwickelung.*

GA 211 *The Sun Mystery and the Mystery of Death and Resurrection.* Tr. Catherine E. Creeger. Great Barrington, MA: SteinerBooks 2006. In German: *Das Sonnenmysterium und das Mysterium von Tod und Auferstehung.*

GA 212 *Menschliches Seelenleben und Geistesstreben im Zusammenhange mit Welt- und Erdentwickelung* (1922). 2. Auflage 1998. See *The Human Heart.* Spring Valley, NY: Mercury Press 1985.

GA 214 *The Mystery of the Trinity.* Tr. James H. Hindes. Hudson, NY: Anthroposophic Press 1991. In German: *Die Geheimnis der Trinität.*

GA 217a *Youth and the Etheric Heart.* Tr. Catherine E. Creeger. Great Barrington, MA: SteinerBooks 2007. In German: *Die Erkenntnis-Aufgabeder Jugend.*

GA 219 *Man and the World of the Stars.* Tr. D.S. Osmond. Great Barrington, MA: Anthroposophic Press/SteinerBooks 1963. In German: *Das Verhältnis der Sternenwelt zum Menschen und des Menschen zur Sternwelt. Die geistige Kommunion der Menschheit.*

GA 221 *Earthly Knowledge and Heavenly Wisdom.* Hudson, NY: Anthroposophic Press/SteinerBooks 1991. In German: *Erdenwissen und Himmelserkenntnis.*

GA 223 *The Cycle of the Year as a Breathing Process of the Earth.* Tr. Barbara Betteridge and Frances Dawson. Hudson, NY: Anthroposophic Press 1988. *Der Jahreskreislauf als Atmungsvorgang der Erde und die vier groß en Festeszeiten.*

GA 224 *Die menschliche Seele in ihrem Zusammenhang mit göttlich- geistigen Individualitaten.* [The human soul and its connection with divine-spiritual individualities] (1923). 3rd edition 1992.

GA 226 *Man's Being, His Destiny, and World-Evolution.* Tr. Erna McArthur. Spring Valley, NY: Anthroposophic Press 1984. In German: *Menschenwesen, Menschenschicksal und Welt-Entwicklung.*

GA 231 *At Home in the Universe.* Tr. H. Collison. Hudson, NY: Anthroposophic Press 2000. (Previously published as *Supersensible Man*). In German: *Der übersinnliche Mensch, anthroposophisch erfasst.*

GA 233 *World History and the Mysteries in the Light of Anthroposophy.* Tr. George and Mary Adams; D. Osmond. London: Rudolf Steiner Press 1997. In German: *Die Weltgeschichte in anthroposophischer Beleuchtung und als Grundlage der Erkenntnis des Menschengeistes.*

GA 233a *Mysterienstätten des Mittelalters* [Mystery sites of the middle ages]: 5th edition 1991. Partial in English: *Rosicrucianism and Modern Initiation.* London: Rudolf Steiner Press 1982.

GA 236 *Karmic Relationships Vol 2.* Tr. George Adams. Revised M. Cotterell, C. Davy, D. S. Osmond. London: Rudolf Steiner Press 1997. In German: *Esoterische Betrachtungen karmischer Zusammenhänge II.*

GA 239 *Karmic Relationships Vol. 5.* Tr. D. S. Osmond. London: Rudolf Steiner Press 1997. In German: *Esoterische Betrachtungen karmischer Zusammenhänge V.*

GA 240 *Karmic Relationships Vol. 6.* Tr. D. S. Osmond. London: Rudolf Steiner Press 1971. In German: *Esoterische Betrachtungen karmischer Zusammenhänge VI.*

GA 243 *True and False Paths in Spiritual Investigation.* Hudson, NY: Anthroposophic Press/SteinerBooks 1985. In German: *Das Initiaten-Bewusstsein. Die wahren und die falschen Wege der geistigen Forschung.*

GA 245 *Guidance in Esoteric Training: From the Esoteric School.* London: Rudolf Steiner Press 2001. In German: *Anweisungen für eine esoterische Schulung)*

GA 254 *The Occult Movement in the Nineteenth Century.* London: Rudolf Steiner Press 1973. In German: *Die okkulte Bewegung im 19. Jahrhundert und ihre Beziehung zur Weltkultur.*

GA 257 *Awakening to Community.* Tr. Marjorie Spock. Spring Valley, NY: Anthroposophic Press 1974. In German: *Anthroposophische Gemeinschaftsbildung.*

GA 258 *The Anthroposophic Movement.* Tr. Christian von Arnim. London: Rudolf Steiner Press 1993. In German: *Die Geschichte und die Bedingungen der anthroposophischen*

Bewegung im Verhältnis zur Anthroposophischen Gesellschaft. Eine Angregung zur Selbstbesinnung.

GA 259 *Das Schicksalsjahr 1923 in der Geschichte der Anthroposophischen Gesellschaft* [The Year of Destiny 1923]: (1923) 1st edition 1991.

GA 260 *The Christmas Conference for the Foundation of the General Anthroposophcal Society 1923/1924.* Hudson, NY: Anthroposophical Press/SteinerBooks 1990.In German: *Die Weihnachtstagung zur Begründung der Allgemeinen Anthroposophischen Gesellschaft.* 1923/24.

GA 260a *The Foundation Stone/The Life, Nature and Cultivation of Anthroposophy.* London: Rudolf Steiner Press 1996. See also: *The Constitution of the School of Spiritual Science.* In German: *Die Konstitution der Allgemeinen Anthroposophischen Gesellschaft* (1924/25).

GA 261 *Our Dead. Addresses, Words of Remembrance, and Meditative Verses (1906-1924).* Tr. Sabine Seiler and Christopher Bamford. Great Barrington, MA: SteinerBooks 2011. In German: *Unsere Toten.*

GA 262 *Correspondence and Documents. 1901-1925.* Tr. Christian/Ingrid von Arnim. Spring Valley, NY: Anthroposophic Press 1988. In German: *Rudolf Steiner/Marie Steiner-von Sivers: Briefwechsel und Dokumente (1901-1925).*

GA 263/1 *Rudolf Steiner/Edith Maryon: Briefwechsel 1912-1924* [Rudolf Steiner/Edith Maryon: correspondence 1912-1924]: 1st edition 1990.

GA 264 *From the History and Contents of the First Section of the Esoteric School 1904-1914.* Tr. John Wood. Great Barrington, MA: SteinerBooks 2010. In German: *Zur Geschichte und aus den Inhalten der ersten Abteilung der Esoterischen Schule 1904-1914.*

GA 265 *Freemasonry and Ritual Work. The Misraim Servic: Texts and Documents from the Cognitive-Ritual Section of the Esoteric School 1904-1914.* Tr. John Wood. Great Barrington, MA: SteinerBooks 2007. In German: *Zur Geschichte und aus den Inhalten der erkenntniskultischen Abteilung der Esoterischen Schule von 1904-1914.*

GA 266/1 *Esoteric lessons (1904-1909) Volume I.* Tr. James H. Hindes. Great Barrington, MA: SteinerBooks 2007. In German: *Aus den Inhalten der esoterischen Stunde.* Band I (1904-1909).

GA 266/3 *Esoteric Lessons 1913-1923. Vol. 3.* Tr. Marsha Post. Great Barrington, MA: SteinerBooks 2011. In German: *Aus den Inhalten der esoterischen stunden. Band III.*

GA 268 *Mantrische Sprüche. Seelenübungen Band II* [Soul exercises. Vol. 2]: (1903-1925). 1st edition 1999.

GA 271 *Kunst und Kunsterkenntnis* [Art and knowledge of art]: 3rd edition 1985.

GA 277a *Die Entstehung und Entwickelung der Eurythmie* [The origin and development of eurythmy]: 3rd edition 1998.

GA 284 *Rosicrucianism Renewed. The Unity of Art, Science, and Religion. The Theosophical Congress of Whitsun 1907.* Tr. Marsha Post. Great Barrington, MA: SteinerBooks 2007. In German: *Bilder okkulter Siegel und Säulen.*

GA 286 *Architecture as a Synthesis of the Arts.* London: Rudolf Steiner Press 1999. In German: *Wege zu einem neuen Baustil.*

GA 300c *Faculty Meetings with Rudolf Steiner.* Tr. Robert Lathe and Nancy Parsons Whittaker. In 2 volumes, 1919-1924. Hudson, NY: Anthroposophic Press 1998. *Konferenzen mit Lehrern der Freien Waldorfschule 1923-1924.*

GA 337a *Soziale Ideen—Soziale Wirklichkeit—Soziale Praxis. Fage- und Studienabende des Bundes für Dreigliederung de sozialen Organismus in Stuttgart* [Social ideas, social reality, social practice. vol. 1]: (1919-1920) 1st edition 1999.

GA 343 *Vorträge und Kurse über christlich-religiöses Wirken II* [Lectures and courses on christian religious work, Vol. 2] (1921): 1st edition 1993.

GA 346 *The Book of Revelation and the Work of the Priest.* Tr. J. Collis. Forest Row, U.K.: Rudolf Steiner Press 2001.

GA 349 *From Limestone to Lucifer.* Tr. A. R. Meuss. London: Rudolf Steiner Press 1999. In German: *Vom Wesen des Menschen und der Erde. Über das Wesen des Christenmus.*

GA K12 *Die Goetheanum-Fenster. Sprache des Lichtes* [The Goetheanum glass windows]: 2nd edition 1996.

Books in English Translation by
Sergei O. Prokofieff

THE APPEARANCE OF CHRIST IN THE ETHERIC
Spiritual-Scientific Aspects of the Second Coming

ANTHROPOSOPHY AND THE PHILOSOPHY OF FREEDOM:
Anthroposophy and Its Method of Cognition

THE CASE OF VALENTIN TOMBERG. Anthroposophy or Jesuitism?

THE CREATIVE POWER OF ANTHROPOSOPHICAL CHRISTOLOGY

THE CYCLE OF THE SEASONS AND THE SEVEN LIBERAL ARTS

THE CYCLE OF THE YEAR AS A PATH OF INITIATION:
Leading to an Experience of the Christ Being

THE EAST IN THE LIGHT OF THE WEST: Two Eastern Streams of the 20th Century in the Light of Christian Esotericism

THE ENCOUNTER WITH EVIL: And Its Overcoming through Spiritual Science

THE ESOTERIC SIGNIFICANCE OF SPIRITUAL WORK IN ANTHROPOSOPHICAL GROUPS: And the Future of the Anthroposophical Society

ETERNAL INDIVIDUALITY: Towards a Karmic Biography of Novalis

THE FOUNDATION STONE MEDITATION: A Key to the Christian Mysteries

THE GOETHEANUM CUPOLA MOTIFS OF RUDOLF STEINER (Foreword)

THE GUARDIAN OF THE THRESHOLD AND THE PHILOSOPHY OF FREEDOM: On the Relationship of The Philosophy of Freedom to The Fifth Gospel

THE HEAVENLY SOPHIA AND THE BEING ANTHROPOSOPHIA

HYMNS TO THE NIGHT / SPIRITUAL SONGS OF NOVALIS (Foreword)

THE INDIVIDUALITY OF COLOUR: Contributions to a Methodical Schooling in Colour Experience (Foreword)

MAY HUMAN BEINGS HEAR IT! The Mystery of the Christmas Conference

THE MYSTERY OF JOHN THE BAPTIST AND JOHN THE EVANGELIST AT THE TURNING POINT OF TIME: An Esoteric Study

THE MYSTERY OF THE RESURRECTION IN THE LIGHT OF ANTHROPOSOPHY

THE OCCULT SIGNIFICANCE OF FORGIVENESS

PROPHECY OF THE RUSSIAN EPIC: How the Holy Mountains Released the Mighty Russian Heroes from their Rocky Caves

RELATING TO RUDOLF STEINER: AND THE MYSTERY OF THE LAYING OF THE FOUNDATION STONE

RUDOLF STEINER AND THE FOUNDING OF THE NEW MYSTERIES

RUDOLF STEINER'S RESEARCH INTO KARMA: And the Mission of the Anthroposophical Society

RUDOLF STEINER'S SCULPTURAL GROUP
A Revelation of the Spiritual Purpose of Humanity
and the Earth (2012)

THE SPIRITUAL ORIGINS OF EASTERN EUROPE: And the Future Mysteries of the Holy Grail

THE TWELVE HOLY NIGHTS AND THE SPIRITUAL HIERARCHIES

VALENTIN TOMBERG AND ANTHROPOSOPHY: A Problematic Relationship

WHAT IS ANTHROPOSOPHY?

THE WHITSUN IMPULSE AND CHRIST'S ACTIVITY IN SOCIAL LIFE

WHY DOES ONE BECOME A MEMBER OF THE ANTHROPOSOPHICAL SOCIETY? (2012)

WHY DOES ONE BECOME A MEMBER OF THE FIRST CLASS? (2012)

Books in English Translation by

Peter Selg

On Rudolf Steiner:

RUDOLF STEINER AS A SPIRITUAL TEACHER: From Recollections of Those Who Knew Him

RUDOLF STEINER AND CHRISTIAN ROSENKREUTZ (2012)

On Christology:

THE CREATIVE POWER OF ANTHROPOSOPHICAL CHRISTOLOGY

CHRIST AND THE DISCIPLES: The Destiny of an Inner Community

THE FIGURE OF CHRIST: Rudolf Steiner and the Spiritual Intention behind the Goetheanum's Central Work of Art

RUDOLF STEINER AND THE FIFTH GOSPEL: Insights into a New Understanding of the Christ Mystery

SEEING CHRIST IN SICKNESS AND HEALING

On General Anthroposophy:

THE PATH OF THE SOUL AFTER DEATH: The Community of the Living and the Dead as Witnessed by Rudolf Steiner in his Eulogies and Farewell Addresses

THE MYSTERY OF THE HEART: The Sacramental Physiology of the Heart in Aristotle, Thomas Aquinas, and Rudolf Steiner (2012)

THE FUNDAMENTAL SOCIAL LAW: Rudolf Steiner on the Work of the Individual and the Spirit of Community

THE AGRICULTURE COURSE, KOBERWITZ, WHITSUN 1924: Rudolf Steiner and the Beginnings of Biodynamics

RUDOLF STEINER'S INTENTIONS FOR THE ANTHROPOSOPHICAL SOCIETY: The Executive Council, the School of Spiritual Science, and the Sections

Rudolf Steiner and the School for Spiritual Science The Foundation of the First Class (2012)

The Culture of Selflessness: Rudolf Steiner, the Fifth Gospel, and the Time of Extremes (2012)

On Anthroposophical Medicine:

I Am for Going Ahead: Ita Wegman's Work for the Social Ideals of Anthroposophy

Ita Wegman and Karl König: Letters and Documents

Karl König's Path to Anthroposophy

Karl König: My Task: Autobiography and Biographies (Ed.)

The Child with Special Needs: Letters and Essays on Curative Education (Ed.)

On Child Development and Waldorf Education:

Unbornness: Human Pre-existence and the Journey toward Birth

The Therapeutic Eye: How Rudolf Steiner Observed Children

The Essence of Waldorf Education

I Am Different from You: How Children Experience Themselves and the World in the Middle of Childhood

A Grand Metamorphosis: Contributions to the Spiritual-Scientific Anthropology and Education of Adolescents

Ita Wegman Institute

for Basic Research into Anthroposophy

Pfeffinger Weg 1 A CH-4144 Arlesheim, Switzerland

www.wegmaninstitut.ch
e-mail: sekretariat@wegmaninstitut.ch

The Ita Wegman Institute for Basic Research into Anthroposophy is a non-profit research and teaching organization. It undertakes basic research into the lifework of Dr. Rudolf Steiner (1861–1925) and the application of Anthroposophy in specific areas of life, especially medicine, education, and curative education. The Institute also contains and cares for the literary estates of Ita Wegman, Madeleine van Deventer, Hilma Walter, Willem Zeylmans van Emmichoven, Karl Schubert, and others. Work carried out by the Institute is supported by a number of foundations and organizations and an international group of friends and supporters. The Director of the Institute is Prof. Dr. Peter Selg.

www.ingramcontent.com/pod-product-compliance
Lightning Source LLC
Chambersburg PA
CBHW030102170426
43198CB00009B/457
* 9 7 8 0 8 8 0 1 0 7 3 3 4 *